Bloody Biscay

Bloody Biscay

The story of the Luftwaffe's only long-range
maritime fighter unit,
V *Gruppe/Kampfgeschwader* 40,
and its adversaries, 1942-1944

Chris Goss

Crécy Publishing Limited

Bloody Biscay

First published in hardback in 1997 by Crécy Publishing
Revised paperback edition published 2001 by Crécy Publishing
This reformatted paperback edition first published 2013

Chris Goss is hereby identified as author of this work in accordance
with Section 77 of the Copyright, Designs and Patents Act 1988

A CIP record for this book is available from the British Library

Print managed in the UK by Jellyfish

ISBN 9780859 791755

Crécy Publishing Limited
1a Ringway Trading Estate, Shadowmoss Road, Manchester M22 5LH
www.crecy.co.uk

CONTENTS

Introduction

As a young boy, my parents used to take my brother and myself camping along France's Atlantic coast. My father, at this time, told us that during the last war Nazi Germany's submarine fleet was based close to where we camped. Only once did I glimpse what remained of the massive concrete and steel U-boat pens but, even as a young child, it made such an impression on me then that, even as I write, I can visualise what I saw some 30 years ago.

As I grew older, my interests in submarines diminished while my interest in the air battles of the Second World War grew. However, probably because of those childhood camping holidays in France, I became increasingly interested in the missions flown by the *Luftwaffe* over the Bay of Biscay – normally in support of the *Kriegsmarine*'s U-boats. I could find very little on the subject as nothing definitive had been written and only a few stories had emerged. One story that tended to be remembered was the shooting down, by Junkers Ju 88s, of an unarmed airliner as among its passengers was the British actor Leslie Howard. Today Leslie Howard's fame has diminished but, because of his part in such classic films as *First of the Few* and *Gone With The Wind*, he was as well known and popular in the 1940s as Ralph Fiennes is now. His death was deeply felt by a country that needed such film stars to help boost morale in a bloody war which had, until then, lasted nearly four years.

With my interest growing, I was lucky to contact a German pilot who had flown Ju 88s over the Bay of Biscay from 1942 to 1944. His logbook and operational missions log were a fascinating insight into an almost daily battle with Allied aircraft over an ocean where, if you were shot down, the chances of survival were slim. His substantial photograph album proved this. Pasted in it were photos of long dead comrades and burning Allied aircraft whose only grave was a pall of oily smoke and scraps of wreckage. He recalled, sadly, that overwhelming Allied airpower had resulted in the decimation of his unit over the battlefields of northern France in June and July 1944. As a result only a handful of survivors, like himself; could remember what his unit had endured for the two years of its existence.

Bloody Biscay is the story of this unit, initially designated V *Gruppe/Kampfgeschwader* 40, which was destined to be the *Luftwaffe*'s only long-range maritime fighter unit. Its two-year existence is illustrated by those German and Allied aircrew who flew over the Bay of Biscay and through the photographs that have survived over 50 years. Hopefully it will enlighten the reader as to what happened during two years of bitter and bloody air battles over a largely forgotten theatre of the war and will be a tribute to the hundreds or men, German and Allied, who died.

Christopher Goss

Acknowledgements

The two hardest things about writing a book are getting started and producing an acknowledgement to all who have helped in the end result. Having done the former, I now hope that the latter includes all that have helped in one way or another. However, first and foremost, special thanks must go to Bernd Rauchbach, my German co-researcher. Without your diligence, patience, hard work, time and energy, this book would never have been written and much of the credit must go to you – thank you again. I must also thank Graham Day of the Air Historical Branch for his help in answering my numerous (too numerous) questions and to Mark Postlethwaite for both the striking painting that adorns the cover of the original book, his enthusiasm for the book and also for proof-reading the manuscript. As well as these three, the following helped in one way or another – I hope that I have remembered all of you:

UNITED KINGDOM

Participants:
Sqn Ldr Tony Binks, DFC (235 Sqn), Howard Bradshaw (53 Sqn), Wg Cdr G. H. Briggs, DFC (295 Sqn), Eddie Cheek (224 Sqn), Sqn Ldr Bob Cherry (547 Sqn), Sqn Ldr Freddie Cooper (39 Sqn), Charles Corder (248 Sqn), John Grant, DFM (295 Sqn), Denis Helps (51 Sqn), George Kelsey (151 Sqn), Gp Capt Bill Kent (264 Sqn), Sqn Ldr Fred Lacy (248 Sqn), Len Newens (248 Sqn), Sir Arthur Korman (295 Sqn), John Prout (Glider Pilot Regt), Wg Cdr H. Randall (235 & 248 Sqns), Harry Reed (264 Sqn), Wg Cdr Joe Singleton, DFC (25 Sqn), Tom Scott, DFC (248 Sqn)

Contributors:
Chaz Bowyer, David Carroll, Barry Elsdon, John Foreman, Roger Freeman, Eric Harrison (228 Sqn Association), The Imperial War Museum, Mr R. King, Jock Manson (53 Sqn Association), Alan Miles, The Polish Air Force Association, Royal Air Forces Association, Ben Rosevink, Brian Sadler, Andy Thomas, Mrs Elaine Thornton, John Vasco.

GERMANY

Participants (all are from V/KG 40/ZG 1 unless otherwise indicated):
Robert Baumann, Aegidius Berzborn, Hans-Georg Ernst, Karl Geyr (I/KG 6), Herbert Hintze, Heinz Hommel, Rolf Johermeken, Leo Kasprowiak and *Flottillenadmiral* Paul Kriebel (5/196), Hans Namhoff, Manfred Riegel (Z/KG 30), Karl-Fritz Schroeder and Bruno Stolle (8/JG 2).

Contributors:
Winfried Bock, Horst Bredow (U-Boot Archiv), Frau Busekow (WASt, Berlin), Manfried Griehl, Frau Eva-Maria Gutermann, Frau Kuechl (BA, Koblenz), Michael Meyer, Ingo Mueller, Soenke Neitzel, Guenther Ott, Peter Petrick, Frau G. Rauch, Hans Ring, Frau Scholl (BA/MA Freiburg), Frau Petra Schuetz (DSM, Bremerhaven), Frau Zimmermann (BA Aachen).

OTHER COUNTRIES

Participants:
John Barnes (53 Sqn, Canada), Pete Dubourg (VB-105, USA), Larry Grauerholz (96th BG, USA), Joe Guthrie (VB-103, USA), Bruce Higginbotham (VB-103, USA), Franciszek Jankowiak (307 Sqn, Canada), George Koshiol (VB-110, USA), the late Karl Manowarda (II/KG 2, Austria), Sqn Ldr George Melville Jackson (248 Sqn, Spain), William Middleton (VB-103, USA), Sqn Ldr Charles Schofield (248 Sqn, Canada), Wg Cdr John Smyth (157 Sqn, Australia), Lt Cdr Ralph Spears, USN (VP-63, USA), Harry Sullivan (51 Sqn, Canada), Capt Bill Tanner (VP-63, USA), Howard Vandewater (235 Sqn, Canada), Mr W. G. Woodcock (235 Sqn, USA).

Contributors:
Bernard Cavalcante and staff (Operational Archives Branch, USN Naval Historical Centre, USA), Lt Col Buck Cummings, USMC Ret'd (USA), Patrick de Gmeline (France), Mrs J. Handasyde (Australia), Claude Helias (France), Jim Kitchens (USA), Eric Mombeek (Belgium), Jaroslav Popelka (Czech Republic), Juan Carlos Salgado (Spain).

Finally, as always, I must thank my family for their help. To my parents for the inspiration (remember all those holidays spent on the Bay of Biscay coast?), and to my patient wife Sally and daughters Katherine, Megan and Alexandra – thanks all of you for allowing me to disappear into my study for hours on end and for allowing me to get on with it!

Glossary & Abbreviations

Ac	Aircraft
ACHGD	Aircraft Charge Hand General Duties
ACM	Aviation Chief, Metalsmith
ACMM	Aviation Chief Machinists Mate
ACOM	Aviation Chief Ordnance Mate
ACRM	Aviation Chief Radioman
Adj.	Adjutant
AFC	Air Force Cross
AG	Air gunner
AMM	Aviation Machinists Mate
AOM	Aviation Ordnanceman
AP	Aviation Pilot
ARM	Aviation Radioman
Arm	Armourer
ASG	Anti-Submarine Group
Aufklärungsgruppe	Reconnaissance Wing (usually abbreviated to 3(F)/123 = 3 Squadron (Long Range) Reconnaissance Wing 123)
AV-M	Air Vice-Marshal
B	Bomb aimer
Bordfunker (BF)	Radio operator
Beobachter (BO or B)	Observer
BG	Bomb Group
Bomb	Bombardier
Bordfliegelgruppe	Shipborne (lit) Flying Wing
Bordmechaniker (BM)	Flight engineer
Bordschütz (BS)	Air gunner
BS	Bombardment Squadron
BV	Blohm und Voss
CO	Commanding Officer
Col	Colonel
Condor	FW200 (also known as Kurier or Kondor)
Cpl	Corporal
Deutsche Kreuz in Gold	German Cross in Gold (award for bravery)
Ditch	Force land in the sea
DFC	Distinguished Flying Cross

DFM	Distinguished Flying Medal
DSO	Distinguished Service Order
E	Evaded capture
E or Eng.	Flight engineer (see also FE)
Ehrenpokal	Goblet of Honour (awarded for outstanding achievements in the air war
Einzelmeldung	Detailed report such as detailing the air activities of *Luftwaffe 3* on a daily basis
Eiserne Kreuz	Iron Cross
Ens.	Ensign
ERCO	Turret on PB4Y-1 made by Emerson Company
Experten	Ace
FAGr	*Fernaufklärungsgruppe* (Long Range Reconnaissance Wing)
FAW	Fleet Air Wing
FE	Flight engineer
Feindflug	Operational flight
Feldwebel (*Fw*)	Flight Sergeant (FS)
Fern	Long range
FG	Fighter Group
Fg Off	Flying Officer
Fit	Fitter
Fliegerführer	Air Commander for the Atlantic region
Flt	Flight
Flt Lt	Flight Lieutenant
Flugzeugführer (*F*)	Pilot
FM	Flight mechanic Flight
FMEAG	Flight Mechanic Engines Air Gunner
F/O	Flight Officer
Freie Jagd	Fighter sweep
Frontflugspange	Mission Clasp (awarded for operational flights)
F/S	Flight Sergeant
Führer	Leader
FW	*Focke Wulf*
FIIA	Fitter IIA
G	Gunner
Gefreiter (*Gefr*)	Leading aircraftman
Geschwader (*Gesch*)	Group (three *Gruppen*), commanded by a *Kommodore* (*Gesch Komm*)

Gp	Group
Gp Capt.	Group Captain
Gruppe (Gr), Gruppen	Wing (three *Staffeln*), commanded by a *Kommandeur (Gr Kdr)*
Hauptmann (Hptm)	Flight Lieutenant (Flt Lt)/Captain (Capt.)
I	Injured
Ia	Operations officer
inj	Injured
Jagdgeschwader	Fighter Group
jg	Junior grade
JU	Junkers
Kampfgeschwader (KG)	Bomber Group
Kette	Three-aircraft tactical formation
Kriegsmarine	German Navy
Küstenfliegergruppe (Kü.Fl.Gr)	Coastal Reconnaissance Wing
LAC	Leading Aircraftman
Lehrgeschwader (LG)	Operational training group
Leutnant (Lt)	Pilot Officer (Plt Off)/2nd Lieutenant (2/Lt)
Leutnant zur See (LtzS)	Sub Lieutenant
LMM	Leading Machinists Mate
Luftflotte	Air Fleet
M	Missing
Major (Maj.)	Squadron Leader (Sqn Ldr)
MC	Military Cross
Met	Meteorological
N	Navigator
Nachtjagdgeschwader	Night Fighter Group
nm	nautical miles
NO	*Nachrichtenoffizier* (responsible for communications)
O	Observer
OA	Priority signal sent by an Allied aircraft, which indicated that they were under attack or about to be attacked
Oberfeldwebel (Ofw)	Warrant Officer (WO)/Master Sergeant (MSgt)
Obergefreiter (Ogefr)	Senior Aircraftman
Oberleutnant (Oblt)	Flying Officer (Fg Off)/1st Lieutenant (1/Lt)

Oberleutnant zur See (ObltzS)	Lieutenant
Oberstleutnant (Obstlt)	Wing Commander (Wg Cdr)/Lieutenant Colonel (Lt Col)
OTU	Operational Training Unit
P	Pilot
PB4Y	USN designation for the B-24-Liberator
PBY-5	USN designation for the Catalina
Plt Off	Pilot Officer
PlQ	*Planquadrat.* The Bay of Biscay was, in the main, Grid Square *PlQ* 14W, which was between 40 deg and 49 deg N, 0 deg and 10 deg W. This was subdivided into 90 grids, each of which were subdivided into 8 grids, each of which was then divided into 9 grids, and finally each of which was subdivided into 4.
2/P	2nd pilot
POW	Prisoner of War
Rad Op	Radar operator
Reichsluftfahrministerium (RLM)	German Air Ministry
RG	Rear gunner
Ritterkreuz	Knights' Cross (award for bravery)
Rotte	Two-aircraft tactical formation
Rottenflieger	Wingman
Rottenführer	*Rotte* Leader
S	Seaman
Seeaufklärungsgruppe (SAGr)	Coastal Reconnaissance Wing
Schwarm	Four aircraft tactical formation, commanded by a *Schwarm Führer*
Schwer Jagd	Heavy fighter
Seenotstaffel	Air Sea Rescue Sqn
Sqn	Squadron
Sqn Ldr	Squadron leader
sm	Sea miles
Sonderführer (Sd Fhr)	Rank usually given to war reporters
Sonderkommando	Special Detachment

Sperrebrecher	Anti-boom ship or boom defence vessel. Would precede U-boats or convoys in order to explode mines or to draw off enemy submarines
S/Sgt	Staff Sergeant
Stab	Staff or Headquarters (formation in which a *Grüppenkommandeur* or *Geschwader Kommodore* usually flew)
Stabsfeldwebel	Senior Warrant Officer
Staffel (*St Kap*)	Squadron, commanded by a *Staffel Kapitän*
TO	*Techniker offizier* (Technical officer)
T/Sgt	Technical Sergeant
Uninj	Uninjured
Unteroffizier (Uffz)	Sergeant (Sgt)
USAAF	United States Army Air Force
USN	United States Navy
W	Wounded
WAG	Wireless Operator Air Gunner
Werk Nummer (*Wk Nr*)	Serial number
Wg Cdr	Wing Commander
W/O	Warrant Officer
WOM	Wireless Operator Mechanic or Warrant Officer Machinists Mate (USN term)
WOp	Wireless Operator
Zerstörergeschwader (*ZG*)	Heavy fighter group
+	Killed

Prologue

The Junkers Ju 88 was designed as a *Schnellbomber* (literally high-speed bomber) and following early trials it was obvious that it met this specification admirably. However it soon became obvious that its excellent performance and long range would suit the aircraft in the role of a heavy fighter or, as the *Luftwaffe* preferred to call it, *Zerstörer*. It was not until the middle of 1939 that serious thought was given towards fitting a battery of forward-firing guns in the nose of the Ju 88 and the prototype first flew early in 1940. Satisfied with the trials, the *RLM* authorised the limited production of a Junkers Ju 88 *Zerstörer*, which was designated the Junkers Ju 88 C.

The first unit to receive the Ju 88 C was *Kampfgeschwader* 30, a bomber unit that was based at the airfield of Westerland on the island of Sylt off the north German coast. A *Zerstörerstaffel* (Z/KG 30) was formed at the airfield of Perleberg on 21 February 1940 under the command of 29-year-old *Oberleutnant* Herbert Bönsch. Training on the new aircraft as well as formulating tactics continued for nearly a month and a half before it was felt that Z/KG 30 could become operational. Although the *Staffel* had been moved to the airfield of Westerland, it would appear that Z/KG 30 did not take an active part in the invasion of Scandinavia on 9 April 1940, but it did move forward to the Norwegian airfield of Stavanger-Sola two days later. Their task was to defend Norway's western coast from attacks by the RAF and to protect the vulnerable Ju 52 transport planes.

Z/KG 30 did not have to wait long for its first taste of combat when on 12 April 1940, in company with the Messerschmitt Bf 110s of I/ZG 76, a *Kette* of Ju 88 C-2s intercepted a mixed force of RAF bombers attacking shipping off Stavanger. This was the largest RAF bombing operation of the war so far and they lost nine bombers to German fighters and flak. Z/KG 30's *Ofw* Martin Jeschke and *Uffz* Peter Lauffs each claimed a Wellington of 149 Squadron, but *Uffz* Erwin Maus and his crew were killed when their *Zerstörer* was damaged by crossfire and crashed on landing.

Further kills for the *Staffel* were recorded on 13 April 1940 (*Uffz* Lauffs claimed a Lockheed Hudson east of Stavanger), 17 April 1940 (*Ofw* Jeschke claimed a Bristol Blenheim west of Stavanger), and finally three kills on 16 May 1940 (*Oblt* Bönsch claimed a Blackburn Roc and *Uffz* Lauffs claimed two Blackburn Skuas south-east of

Narvik). By this stage, Z/KG 30 was mainly involved in escorting the Ju 88 bombers of KG 30 attacking Narvik and ground attack missions in the Narvik area and had moved to the airfield at Trondheim-Vaernes at the end of April. Ground attack successes were recorded on 25 April 1940 when *Lt* Manfred Riegel destroyed three Gloster Gladiators of 263 Squadron on the lake airfield of Lesjaskog, with his *Bordfunker*, *Ogefr* Heinz Richard, destroying a further one. Five days later, Lt Wilhelm Pack, Ofw Kurt Herrmann and Uffz Albrecht Wiessmann each destroyed a Norwegian Fokker C-V on the

The official document, signed by the *Staffel Kapitän*, crediting *Lt* Rigel with the destruction of three Gladiators on 25 April 1940.

Sketched by an unknown artist in 263 Squadron, this sketch shows Lake Lesjaskog after Z/KG 30 had paid a visit.

ground at Setnesmoen. Such ground attack missions were not without incident as, during one of the last missions of the Norwegian Campaign, one of the *Staffel*'s *Zerstörers* was shot down by flak and crash-landed at Bjornfjell on 7 June 1940 without any injuries to the crew.

On 16 June 1940 Z/KG 30 was transferred to Germany as the *Luftwaffe* had become concerned that its night defences against RAF air attacks were woefully inadequate and intended converting Z/KG 30 from day fighter missions to night fighters. On 30 June 1940 Z/KG 30 was disbanded and, still under the leadership of *Oblt* Bönsch, reformed as 4/NJG 1.

The Ju 88 C-2 had been popular with its crews and, with its range of 1,800 miles, had proven to be ideally suited to coastal patrols. It also proved that it was capable of engaging in air combat enemy coastal aircraft and shooting them down, facts borne out by its pilots:

Hptm Manfred Riegel, in a photograph taken in 1943. *Riegel*

Leutnant **Manfred Riegel**

The *Zerstörer* version of the Ju 88 answered the expectations in a remarkable way. Its range was sufficient, the plane could operate in every weather condition and was also equal to enemy fighters of that time. I can remember a dogfight with a Hurricane near Narvik – the Hurricane was not able to outmanoeuvre the Ju 88 and soon disappeared after it had been fired on. However, it was not advisable to attack warships because their defensive armament was too heavy and they opened fire as soon as a plane came near. Here too the Ju 88's handling was important.

I found the Ju 88 C-2 completely satisfactory. As soon as you sat down in the pilot's seat, you felt at home. The offensive and defensive armament, the intercom with my crew and the radio communication with the ground gave confidence. Furthermore, its characteristics, especially when flying on instruments, were outstanding.

However, there was no sign of the *Luftwaffe* developing or expanding this role for the Ju 88 C as the *Luftwaffe*'s efforts were soon to be devoted to the Battle of Britain, an increasing night fighter war, and air campaigns in other theatres of operation. Nevertheless, almost two years to the day later, the Ju 88 C began to re-emerge as a long-range maritime fighter.

Chapter One

'Someone must have been watching over me'
July-December 1942

Following the surrender of France in June 1940, the German armed forces soon saw the military potential of France's Atlantic coast. From their bases at Brest, Lorient, La Pallice, Sainte Nazaire and Bordeaux, U-boats soon began to inflict heavy losses against the vital supply convoys from Canada and the United States and, between June and October 1940, had already sunk in the region of 1,400,000 tons of shipping.

A Do 217 E-4 of *Stab* I/KG 2 'attacks' a U-boat in the Bay of Biscay, 19 June 1942.

Utilising the former French Air Force bases at Lorient (also known as Kerlin-Bastard), Vannes and Bordeaux-Mérignac also meant the *Luftwaffe* could play its part in the U-boat war. On 15 March 1941 the *Luftwaffe* formed *Fliegerführer Atlantik (Fl.Fü. Atlantik),* which was subordinate to *Luftflotte 3,* to coordinate and control in the region of seventy bomber, ten reconnaissance and fifty sea and floatplanes whose hunting ground was the Western Approaches, the Atlantic and the UK's south-western coast. Because of the maritime nature of most of these missions, it was normal to find aircraft engaged in such tasks having a mixed *Luftwaffe/Kriegsmarine* crew, as one such observer remembers:

Leutnant zur See Paul Kriebel

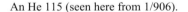

From late summer 1940 to October 1942, I was based in France. Initially, I was with 1 *Staffel/Küstenfliegergruppe* 106 (1/106) based at Hourtin in south-west France [with Heinkel He 115 floatplanes – Author], which came under the command of *Küstenfliegergruppe* 406 (*Kü.Fl.Gr.* 406) based at Brest.

From Hourtin, we flew armed reconnaissance missions, anti-submarine missions and escort sorties in the Bay of Biscay up to 16 degrees west. At one stage, we flew by night from Brest to attack British shipping in the Bristol Channel.

An He 115 (seen here from 1/906).

Arado Ar 196 As of 5/196 at Hourtin. *via Meyer*

In the summer of 1941, 1/106 received Junkers Ju 88s, but because I suffered from night blindness I was posted to 5 *Staffel/Bordfliegergruppe* 196 (5/196), under the leadership of *Hptm* Werner Techam and also flew from Hourtin on anti-submarine and escort missions with the Arado Ar 196. In order to protect our U-boats, 5/196 was moved to Brest at the end of April 1942. From then until September 1942, 5/196 shot down twelve British anti-submarine aircraft of the Sunderland, Vickers Wellington and Armstrong [Whitworth] Whitley types.

Initially, the lack of a credible escort or effective defences made the Allied convoys easy pickings for the Focke Wulf FW 200 Condors of I *Gruppe/Kampfgeschwader* 40 (I/KG 40). From the airfield of Bordeaux-Mérignac, these four-engined aircraft were very effective against the early Allied convoys. So effective were they that they were instrumental in the formulation of *Fl.Fü. Atlantik*'s initial operational doctrine. Concentrating on Allied shipping sailing from Gibraltar, the South Atlantic and North America, the primary tasks of the assigned aircraft were:

1. Reconnaissance reports to *Fl.Fü. Atlantik* concerning the location of shipping so that they could be attacked by U-boats. This task was ideally suited to KG 40's Condors, which were able to shadow convoys, reporting and fixing positions as well as attacking shipping when the opportunities arose.

2. Attacks on targets around the UK coastline by shorter-range *Luftwaffe* aircraft.

However, with Germany fighting in North Africa and Russia, the forces available to *Fl.Fü. Atlantik* were systematically depleted whilst its shorter-range bombers, the Ju 88s and Dornier Do 217s, were used in attacks on mainland Britain. It appeared that the importance of the missions over the Atlantic was very much secondary to the other *Luftwaffe* tasks. For example, by March 1942 only seven Heinkel He 115s of *Kü.Fl.Gr* 406 and 2/906, fifteen Ar 196s of 5/196, a mix of fifteen Ju 88s, Bf 110s and Bf 109s of 3 *(Fern)/Aufklärungsgruppe* 123 (3(F)/123), seven He 111s of 9/KG 40, and thirty-two Ju 88s of *Kü.Fl.Gr* 106 were assigned to *Fl.Fü. Atlantik;* even the FW 200s of I/KG 40 had been detached to Norway. Two months later, even though the FW 200s had returned, the remaining numbers of aircraft had been halved, not through operational losses but by operational requirements elsewhere.

A Short Sunderland of 461 Squadron. *via Cummins*

A Vickers Wellington of 311 Squadron at RAF Dale in late 1942. *via Thomas*

An Armstrong Whitworth Whitley of 502 Squadron at RAF Chivenor, March 1941. *via Thomas*

By now the Battle of the Atlantic was being fought more towards the mid-Atlantic. The Allies realised that the U-boats had to transit through the Bay of Biscay to either get to their hunting grounds or return, sometimes damaged, to their French bases. Destruction of these U-boats was left to the aircraft of the RAF's Number 19 Group flying from airfields in the south-western UK. Using such aircraft as the Short Sunderland and Armstrong Whitworth Whitley, these aircraft did have numerous successes, while at the same time suffering relatively few losses. The only German aircraft to counter the RAF was the lightly armed Ar 196. With its offensive armament of two 20mm cannon and one 7.92mm machine gun and high manoeuvrability, it did have limited success against Whitleys and to a lesser extent the heavily armed Sunderlands. However, when matched against the heavily armed Bristol Beaufighters of Coastal Command, the result was very one-sided, as the following report shows:

A FW 200 C of KG 40. *via Hall*

A Condor's victim – a freighter set on fire by a FW 200 C of I/KG 40. *Hintze*

235 Squadron Diary Entry, 5 August 1942

Two Beaufighters, coded LA-X and LA-S, took off from St
Eval with Plt Off Neal/Plt Off Cameron-Rose and Sgt
Woodcock/Sgt Ginger on search for Arados. Two Ar 196s
were sighted at 6 miles distance from patrol line flying at 2-
4,000 feet. LA-X & LA-S were flying in line formation, LA-
X leading. Plt Off Neal made a beam attack and in 2 minutes
one Ar 196 went straight into the sea.[1] Meanwhile, the other
Ar 196 was attacked by Sgt Woodcock but was lost to view in
the haze but was picked up again and more than twenty
attacks were delivered during which lumps were shot off it.
900 rounds of cannon and 1,200 rounds of .303 were
expended and only when ammo was exhausted was the Arado
allowed to go limping home with its rear gun pointed upwards
as if the rear gunner had no further interest. Plt Off Neal dived
onto the Arado in an endeavour to harangue it into the sea.

It was obvious to *Fl.Fü. Atlantik* that some form of long-range fighter
cover was needed. No solution immediately sprang to mind, but early
in 1942 the latest version of the Ju 88 *Zerstörer,* the C-6 variant, was
coming off the production line. With increased offensive and

Finnish tanker *Josefina Thorda* under attack by a Condor of I/KG 40 on 19 May 1941. *Hintze*

defensive armament, someone in the *RLM* must have remembered the operations of Z/KG 30 two years previously and four Ju 88 *Zerstörer* aircraft appeared at Bordeaux on or about 10 June 1942; the tempo of the air war over the Bay of Biscay was about to increase dramatically.

Beaufighters of 235 Squadron.

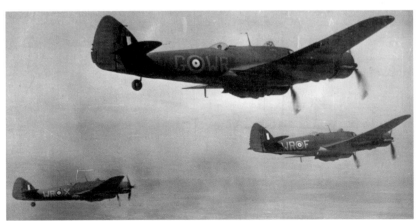

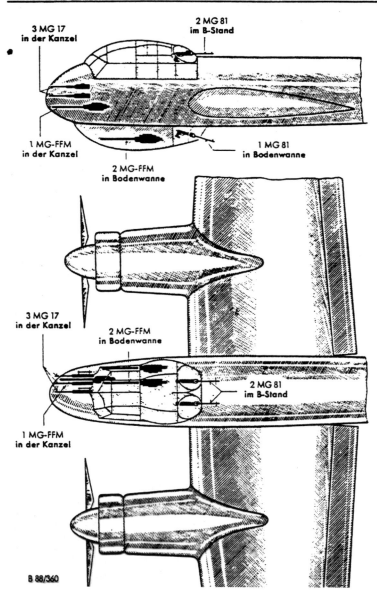

The offensive and defensive armament of the Ju 88 C-6.

It is not known for certain the initial unit designation of the new *Zerstörer Staffel*. Some records say that the first two missions were flown on 24 and 28 June 1942 when five Junkers Ju 88 *Zerstörers*, which were part of *Maj.* Gerd Roth's *Kü.Fl.Gr.* 106, took off on an escort for *U-753* and *U-105* respectively. Other records have the new unit as being *Zerstörerstaffel/Kü.Fl.Gr.* 106, others say *Zerstörer Kommando/KG 6,* III/KG 40, and finally IV/KG 40. It is known that the initial operational training was undertaken by IV/KG 6 at Brétigny, and at the end of August 1942 *Kü.Fl.Gr* 106 was reformed as II/KG 6 and that there is evidence that some of the first Ju 88 C-6s carried the KG 6 code '3E'. Irrespective of this, on 22 July 1942 the unit was redesignated IV/KG 40, and some time in August 1942, 13 and 14 *Staffeln* of V/KG 40; 15 *Staffel* was formed on or around 12 September 1942.

The Ju 88 C-6 was a vast improvement on the earlier Ju 88 C-2. The uprated Junkers Jumo 211 J-1 or J-2 engines gave the C-6 a maximum speed (at average weight) of about 310mph and a range, without auxiliary tanks, of about 1,829 miles. Its armament was impressive – three 7.92mm MG 17 machine guns and one 20mm MG-FFM cannon in the nose, and a further two MG-FFMs in the gondola; later versions had the MG-FFMs replaced by the MG 151/20 cannon. For defensive armament, two rear-facing 7.92mm MG 81 machine guns were located in the rear of the canopy and a further rear-facing MG 81 in the gondola if no forward-facing cannon

A Ju 88 C-6 of 13/KG 40. *Kasprowiak*

The sting in the nose and gondola – the Ju 88 C-6 of *Uffz* Hommel of 13/KG 40.
Hommel

were fitted in the gondola. It was certainly a match for all of the RAF anti-submarine aircraft currently operating over the Bay of Biscay.

It is believed that the first kill for the new unit came on 15 July 1942 when *Fw* Henny Passier shot down a Wellington of 311 Squadron, resulting in the deaths of its Czech crew. The first documented kill was five days later:

Luftflotte West, Report No 36 dated 11 September 1942

20 July 1942. Two Wellingtons shot down by *Lt* Stöffler. Junkers Ju 88 coded 'KD', 1210hrs. We climbed at once and started our attack. In the first and second attacks, we used all of our guns. Hits were seen on the fuselage, wing and starboard engine. Pieces of the wing flew off, the enemy caught fire, the undercarriage was lowered and the plane hit the water. Then a second Wellington appeared flying from north to south. It immediately turned west so we climbed and attacked. All our weapons were firing. During the first attack, we encountered heavy defensive fire and our plane was hit several times. The enemy then caught fire but by this time, *Lt* Stöffler and the observer *Ofw* Möller were out of action. The Ju 88 was in danger of crashing so the *Bordfunker Ofw* Werner climbed into the cockpit and managed to gain height. Turning in a wide turn to starboard just using the ailerons, land came into sight. With the starboard engine on fire, *Ofw* Werner managed to ditch and throw off the canopy roof. Two hours later he was picked up by a trawler.

Although *Lt* Stöffler was credited with two Wellingtons, only one was shot down; the other managed to fly on slightly damaged. Both were from 15 OTU and were being delivered to the Middle East. Plt Off Alan Houston and his crew in the first Wellington were never seen again, whilst F/S Smallwood must have thanked his lucky stars, not knowing he was the first RAF pilot to escape from one of the new *Zerstörers* as well as his aircraft being the first RAF aircraft to shoot one down. Although the combat was not witnessed, the crew of the Spanish fishing boat *San Antonio de Padua* were some 20 nautical miles off the Sisargas Islands on Spain's northern coast when they saw a plane gliding towards the sea very fast. It crashed and soon disappeared from view. When the fishing boat reached the area of the crash, the crew found a small dinghy containing an injured *Ofw* Werner who, for the past two and a half hours, had tried to keep hold of the bodies of his other two crew members. As the fishermen tried to pull the body of *Lt* Stöffler aboard, it slipped away beneath the waves but they did manage to recover the body of *Ofw* Möller and the injured *Ofw* Werner. The Spanish fishermen also recovered some debris from the crashed plane and handed it over to the Spanish Air Force.

Even after landing in Spain, the indefatigable *Ofw* Werner managed to give false information to the Spanish authorities, probably realising that any information would make its way to the British Consulate. He stated that they had been flying a reconnaissance mission and the plane had suffered an engine failure 100km off Cape Finisterre and they had tried to head for Spain. No mention of the combat or the fact that the aircraft was a *Zerstörer* was made and the fact that a document for a Junkers Ju 88 A-4 was found indicated to all that there was nothing unusual about the plane or its mission. Amazingly, *Ofw* Werner was never given any award for his efforts, something that occurred regularly throughout V/KG 40's existence.

Nevertheless, the *Luftwaffe* must have made an effort to give the *Zerstörer* crews more combat experience by attaching a number of combat-experienced night fighter pilots to each of the *Staffeln*. Two of these pilots also had experience of nocturnal intruder missions over England in 1941. *Fw* Vincenz Giessuebel had started the war as a bomber pilot with 2/KG 2 and had been shot down and taken prisoner on 15 May 1940. After France's capitulation, he returned to fly with 2/NJG 2, flying intruder missions over the UK. It was near the airfield at Marham that on 24 April 1941 he had shot down a twin-engined aircraft – his first kill. He then stayed with 2/NJG 2 when it moved to the Mediterranean before being posted to IV/KG 40 as a combat instructor in the early summer of 1942. The other combat instructor was *Hptm* Heinz-Horst Hissbach. Originally a bomber pilot with I/KG 28, he had joined 3/NJG 2 in June 1941, but his first kill was not until 25-26 July 1942. He joined 14/KG 40 on 6 August 1942 and both he and his comrade from 2/NJG 2 made an immediate impression as they were each involved in V/KG 40's next two kills. V/KG 40 was starting to be effective.

With an increase in the tempo of the U-boat war, Bomber Command began to transfer and detach a number of its squadrons to Coastal Command in April and May 1942 as well as detaching crews from 10 OTU for combat experience. One of those detached was the Whitley-equipped 51 Squadron:

Crews of 51 Squadron pose in front of a nocturnally camouflaged Whitley. *Helps*

Sergeant Dennis Helps

The Squadron moved down from Dishforth to Chivenor on 6 May 1942 with its all black Whitleys. On arrival, they were repainted white for daylight sweeps and then, two days later, when it was thought we would go on the 1,000 Bomber Raids, back to black. This arrangement was cancelled and we were yet again repainted white. Ye Gods! How did we win the war!

I carried out fourteen anti-submarine sorties with Dickie Matthews's crew [F/S R. G. D. Matthews] until the first Sunday in September 1942 when I got weekend leave to go to a girlfriend's 21st birthday party in London. My crew took another WOp/AG and all were lost in the Bay.[2]

On 21 October 1942 the remnants of 51 Squadron flew from Chivenor to Snaith for re-equipment with Halifaxes. This golden summer of 1942 with hardly a cloud in the sky over the Bay of Biscay was a bad time for casualties and I shall never forget the constant anxiety. I lost a good many friends but someone must have been watching over me.

During September 1942, RAF losses increased dramatically. Eight anti-submarine aircraft were lost to the new German unit, all but two of them being claimed by 13 *Staffel*. Furthermore, closer to the Brittany coast, 8/JG 2, under the leadership of *Oblt* Bruno Stolle, had also been tasked to play its part against the RAF's anti-submarine aircraft:

Oberleutnant Bruno Stolle

Fl.Fü. Atlantik asked III/JG 2 if it could undertake fighter escort for 5/196. I thought it would be impossible to fly close escort for the slower Ar 196 and suggested meeting them at a point out to sea. *Gen Lt* Ulrich Kessler [Commanding Officer of *Fl.Fü. Atlantik*] thought that this was impossible and had his doubts about the use of fighters. I knew of these doubts and using my knowledge as a blind flying instructor with I(*Schwere Jagd*)/LG 1 decided to do something about it. Fitting our FW 190s with long-range tanks, we started to fly missions from August 1942 to July/August 1943 using three aircraft; we still flew escort sorties as well as fighter sweeps in opposition to the British anti-submarine aircraft.

Oblt Bruno Stolle, 8/JG 2. *Stolle*

My first kill on such a mission was on 18 August 1942. Flying in a *Kette*, I spotted an aircraft on the horizon which turned out to be a Wellington. I attacked from beneath and behind. The Wellington crashed in flames.[3]

The air war had truly begun to escalate. On 20 July 1942 the Bristol Beaufighters of 235 Squadron had moved from Docking in Norfolk to Chivenor in Cornwall and began flying fighter sweeps in support of the anti-submarine aircraft. Apart from some successes against the Ar 196s, it was not until 8 September 1942 that they first met V/KG 40:

235 Squadron Diary Entry, 8 September 1942

Joy, Oh Joy, Oh Boy, Oh Boy! If you want it, you've got to buy it 'cos we ain't givin' anything away!

Sqn Ldr Thompson and Plt Off Ward in 'T for Tommy', and Plt Off Neal and Plt Off Cameron Rose in 'W', set course and first sighted a large column of water, which appeared as if jettisoned bombs had exploded. Tommy altered course to investigate and sighted a Ju 88 4 miles north. Whoopee! 'W' and 'T' positioned for attack (hold tight Jerry, here it comes!). Whilst carrying out this attack, an RAF dinghy was observed containing four crew, one of whom was apparently injured. 'W' dropped a smoke float. Our first indication of joy from these fearless

Oblt Stolle straps in for another mission – on his left knee is a map of Brittany. *Stolle*

airmen was a W/T message: 'Am over two dinghies; four live aircrew; one Ju 88 shot down.'

The four men in the dinghy were the surviving crew members of a Hudson of 500 Squadron, which had been shot down by *Lt* Wolfgang Graf von Hönsbröch of 13/KG 40. The German pilot had radioed back to say that he had shot down a Handley Page Hampden and it was he and his crew who were shot down and killed by 235 Squadron. Also, at the same time, 235 Squadron met *Oblt* Stolle for the first time. The diary continues:

> With deep regret, we record here the loss of F/S 'Pete' Lothian and F/S Graham in Beaufighter T5220/LA-M, whilst doing a fine job of work over the Bay. The loss of this crew was deeply felt by the Squadron. We hope that they were picked up by a nearby tunnyman.

The Bay of Biscay was a large, featureless expanse of water. Many occasions, crews were seen in the water but were never rescued. This was the case for both the Beaufighter and Ju 88 crews. However, crew members from one of two 51 Squadron Whitleys shot down on 30 September 1942 were luckier.

Flying Officer Harold Sullivan

On 30 September 1942, when we arrived at the datum point, we were buzzed by three Beaufighters that had been sent out to protect us. They gave us quite a scare because they looked so much like a Ju 88. I should say that we always flew to a datum point roughly 100 miles west of Brest and then fanned out south and south-east to cover the Bay, then returned by the same route to the datum point before flying home. Our flying time was 8 to 9 hours.

Meanwhile, we had narrowly avoided shooting at one of the Beaufighters because our front gunner had spotted the roundel. We saw one of our Whitleys (the only one in sight) drop its bomb load and head for home. When we had recovered from our scare and as we had not dropped our bombs and depth charges, we continued our 'op'. We flew south until we saw the mountain tops of Spain. However, when we returned to the datum point, we were attacked by three Ju 88s.

In their first attack, they mortally wounded our tail gunner and damaged our main defensive weapon – the rear turret. Our front gunner got in a good burst with the Vickers Gas Operated as I saw the tracers hitting one of the enemy planes. Then the gun broke down. I sent the front gunner to check on the rear turret and he soon reported that the rear gunner, although badly wounded, had managed to crawl out of the turret. He also reported that the rear turret was out of action. He then stood with his head in the 'dome' and directed me and we managed to avoid two or three attacks by the (now) two enemy planes. Finally, they both made a concerted attack, hitting us with both cannon and machine gun fire, badly wounding the second pilot and navigator and setting fire to some flares in the fuselage. The front gunner threw these down the flare chute, burning his hands in the process.

By this time, one engine was gone and the other soon began to vibrate very noisily, having probably lost its coolant.

The windscreen was smeared with a oily substance (either front turret hydraulic fluid or engine coolant) and by looking out of the side window I managed to ditch the plane, using the last gasp of the noisy engine to get the nose up.

Old 'S for Sugar' stayed afloat long enough for us to get the dinghy out and for five of our six crew to board it. Our rear gunner had expired by that time.

About 5 hours later, at last dusk, we were picked up by a small French fishing boat operating out of the fishing village of Les Sables D'Olonne; the captain's name was *Monsieur* Chérier. Of the five of us who were picked up, Sgts Bushell and Shaw died soon after. The rest of us survived to be prisoners of war – Sgt Tice had only burns to his hands, Sgt Robinson had a piece of shell splinter in his eye (and lost the sight of that eye). I had two minor wounds from shell splinters.

October 1942 was a successful month for the *Zerstörers* of V/KG 40. Despite losing the *Staffel Kapitän* of 13/KG 40 in a combat with a Whitley of 77 Squadron and four other Ju 88s, in the main to 235 Squadron, during the month of September, in October 1942 they shot down six RAF aircraft (including one of their protagonists from 235 Squadron) for only one combat loss. This loss was caused by Beaufighters of 248 Squadron, which had been moved into No 19 Group to support 235 Squadron. Both of these RAF squadrons were to remain operating over the Bay of Biscay for much of the next two years and were to become a constant thorn in the side of V/KG 40. Nevertheless, on 16 October the RAF fighters could do little to prevent two more losses:

Luftflotte West, **Report No 43 dated 30 October 1942**

16 October 1942. The shooting down of a Wellington and a Whitley by three Ju 88s. Three Ju 88s over the Bay of Biscay. A spot grows out of the endlessness. A Whitley which was soon surrounded. *Lt* Necesany attacks first. The British do not alter course; instead they shoot from the front and rear turrets. Then some parts of his rudder fly away and he reacts, flying slightly evasive turns. Finally, during the fifth and sixth attacks, which were carried out simultaneously, the plane's starboard engine began to burn and flames were seen. *Lt* Necesany had shot the Whitley to pieces. A short time after it had crashed into the sea, five depth charges exploded, sending fountains of water some 70 metres into the air. 200 metres away, two more depth charges exploded. Nothing more than a film of oil on the water was left of the Whitley.

The Ju 88s reformed and circled the spot again. Suddenly, they sighted a Wellington. After chasing the plane for some 15 minutes, both opponents opened fire. The English pilot was flying with great skill.[4] Although flying evasive turns, he was always heading for England. He also flew in such a way that his machine guns were effective. Then he dropped his depth charges to gain more speed. After his attack, *Lt* Meister flew very low over the Wellington and got into the rear gunner's range of fire. One engine was shot to pieces, coolant began to leak as well as fuel. The two other Ju 88s forced the enemy away. *Lt* Meister's Ju 88 fell behind and tried to gain height. Flying a new attack, *Uffz* Steurich's cone of fire was well aimed and the British pilot collapsed over his control column. The Wellington's nose went down and the plane crashed into the water. A yellow dinghy was observed. The Ju 88s took their damaged comrade between them and finally they arrived at their base.

November 1942 was a much quieter month, with just two combat losses being suffered on the very first day at the hands of 235

Squadron. Unfortunately, both 235 and 248 Squadrons lost four Beaufighters to 8/JG 2 during this month and a further nine the month after. Perhaps a mixture of weather and caution by the RAF fighters gave V/KG 40 a respite. At this time, the German propaganda machine got to hear of V/KG 40 and a report made it into the German press of the second and last kill during that month:

Lt Kurt Necesany.

Kriegsberichter Hans Kestner

The first air combat victory over the Atlantic for a young crew, 30 November 1942. I am at the *Staffel* Command Post. A *Rotte* of Ju 88s is flying a mission over the Atlantic. Just 5 minutes ago the Ju 88 *Anton Zeppelin* [F8+AZ] reported 'We attack!' *Anton Zeppelin* with *Lt* Thies, one of our youngest pilots. The *Staffel Kapitän* is a little bit worried. Now, at this moment, a fierce air

Lt Dieter Meister.

A Ju 88 C-6 of V/KG 40, dumping fuel, returns on one engine. *Gmelin*

battle takes place over the waves of the Atlantic. This combat will only see one victor and the *Staffel* knows how hard it is for the young comrade. 'Everyone can fly but when contact is made with the enemy, it will soon prove if you are a real man!' he used to say to his young crews. Now it is the time for *Lt* Thies and his crew in the Ju 88. For the second time, the *Staffel Kapitän* asks the wireless station, 'Any news from *Anton Zeppelin*?' The *Gefreiter* answers, 'Nothing – waiting!'

Suddenly, the telephone rings. Ten hands reach for the receiver. Calmly, the *Staffel Kapitän* takes the phone. Radio message from *Anton Zeppelin*. 'At 1405hrs, Whitley shot down in *PlQ* XY.' Anything else? Yes: 'Are continuing the mission.' All? Thank you.

The *Staffel Kapitän's* face relaxes. 'He has made it, our youngest!' is all he says and he draws another mark on the *Staffel* kill table.

Two hours later, the *Rotte* roars over the airfield at low level. A smart formation – now the leading plane waggles its wings and both planes climb and land after a wide turn.

Beaming with joy, *Lt* Thies jumps out of his plane and reports:

'We were flying in *Rotten* formation over the water at an altitude of 10 metres. At 1400hrs my *Rottenflieger* reported a plane astern. I turned and sighted the plane at a distance of 1,000 metres flying 800 metres higher under a layer of clouds. We both climbed and now flying at the same altitude recognised a Whitley about 400 metres away. I immediately attacked from the side (90 degrees) and opened fire when the Whitley flew through my sights. We watched hits in the cockpit and port engine. I then saw that the engine was burning and shortly after the Whitley dived at an angle of 45 degrees and crashed into the water. My *Rottenflieger* had no time for an attack. There were no survivors observed.'

This was the condensed combat report. Clear-headed and distinct in its style, this report does not reveal the tension and difficulty of the fight far out over the Atlantic.

Despite this dramatic article, full of journalistic licence, it did not elevate the importance of what V/KG 40 was doing in the eyes of the *Luftwaffe* or the German people as a whole.

Two Ju 88 C-6s of V/KG 40 return to Bordeaux-Mérignac. *Gutermann*

A Rotte from V/KG 40 returns to base. *Gutermann*

Even though there were few combats and operational losses in November 1942, accidents were common. By now V/KG 40 had its own *Gruppen Kommandeur* following the formation of 15 *Staffel*. *Hptm* Gerhard Korthals was a very successful bomber, as opposed to a *Zerstörer*, pilot. He had started the war as the *2 Staffel Kapitän* of the specialist unit *Kampfgruppe* 100 before being posted as *Staffel Kapitän* 8/KG 51. He was awarded the *Deutsche Kreuz in Gold* in July 1942 and the *Ritterkreuz* on 21 October 1942. Two weeks later he was killed in a freak accident:

Leutnant **Herbert Hintze**

Hptm Korthals was an outstanding bomber pilot with more than 300 missions and the *Ritterkreuz*. Unfortunately he crashed during a tactical briefing flight/training with his Ju 88 C-6 because a mechanic had lost his cutlery during a check of the oil in one wing. His knives and forks got stuck in one of the ailerons!

The *Gruppen Kommandeur* and his crew were all killed when control was lost and the plane crashed at Lorient. His place was temporarily taken by *Hptm* Alfred Hemm on 13 November. *Hptm* Hemm was much older than his unfortunate predecessor and had some combat experience as a FW 200 pilot. His suitability as

Gruppen Kommandeur must have been in doubt, as command of the *Gruppe* was then given to *Hptm* Helmut Dargel. *Hptm* Dargel's leadership of the *Gruppe* did not last long as he was killed in action just before the end of the year; it is believed that leadership of the *Gruppe* in the air was then given to *Hptm* Georg Esch. *Hptm* Hemm continued to be temporary *Gruppen Kommandeur* until it

Oblt Gerd Korthals, seen here when with 2/KGr 100 in Norway in 1940.

Hptm Alfred Hemm, *Gr Kdr* V/KG 40. On the left is *Oblt* Kurt Necesany. *Gutermann*

became permanent on 1 March 1943. Although he did fly occasionally, he was not popular with the pilots of the Gruppe.

As the year drew to a close, the first American aircraft began to appear in the Bay of Biscay. Because of the heavy demands placed on Coastal Command in connection with the large movement of shipping towards North Africa following Operation 'Torch'[5], on 8 November eight B-24s were sent from the 330th BS/93rd BG to undertake anti-submarine patrols. They flew from their base at Alconbury to the airfield at Holmsley South on the edge of the New Forest in Hampshire on 25 October 1942 and remained on this special assignment for exactly a month.

The 330th BS spent the first two days getting orientated and lectured by RAF officers on duties and methods pertaining to anti-submarine patrols and attacks. On the third and fourth days, missions were flown but one crew got lost and crashed into a hill at Porlock in Somerset with the loss of all but one of the crew.[6] As a result, a further week of training and lectures was held before restarting the patrols. When the 330th BS finally returned to Alconbury, they had flown sixty-two sorties without any combat losses. Only one submarine and five enemy ships were sighted. V/KG 40 did encounter the American B-24s a number of times and the Americans claimed to have shot down three in a running battle between Maj. R. D. Potts Jr, the Commanding Officer of the 330th BS, on 21 November 1942. The American gunners

A B-24 D of the 93rd BG seen after a mishap at RAF Lympne in 1943.

misidentified their assailants as Me 210s and one German pilot, *Uffz* Heinz Hommel, made a note of the inconclusive combat in his logbook; no German aircraft were lost.

At the same time as the 330th BS was operating over the Bay of Biscay, six B-24s of the 409th BS/93rd BG were detached to St Eval from 22 to 24 November to look for a B-17 of the 341st BS/93rd BG that had crashed in the Bay of Biscay following an accidental fire on 17 November 1942. This plane had been carrying Brigadier General Asa Duncan and was on its way to North Africa. Despite thirteen sorties being flown, no trace of the B-17 was found, but there were a number of inconclusive combats with the Luftwaffe. Finally, the 1st Anti-Submarine Squadron of what was to become the 480th ASG arrived at St Eval on 10 November 1942, but for the remainder of the year it had little impact on the Bay of Biscay air war.

With the build-up in North Africa continuing and the Allied air traffic crossing the Bay increasing daily, it was only a matter of time before V/KG 40 intercepted one of the formations. To keep clear of 8/JG 2, the American fighters and bombers flew much further out to sea, so intercepting them would be a matter of luck. On 23 December 1942, after a very quiet month for the *Zerstörers*, luck was with the Germans.

On this day, Lt Col William Covington led a flight of 51 P-38 Lightnings of the 82nd FG to Gibraltar. For navigation, an A-20B, more commonly known as the Douglas Boston, of the 47th BG flown by Capt Don Martz would lead them. About 2 hours out from St Eval the massive formation was bounced by four aircraft from 14/KG 40. In the confusion that followed, *Ofw* Georg Heuer shot down the A-20B, something that was not seen by any of the P-38 pilots who were concerned with their own predicament. The loss of Capt Martz and his crew was not fully realised until 29 May 1943, and official notification of the deaths of him and his crew was not made until November 1943!

Meanwhile, an unnamed pilot from 14 *Staffel* shot down the P-38 flown by Lt Earl Green of the 95th FS. Lt Green survived and managed to evade to Spain. Lt Broadhead of the 96th FS was forced back to St Eval while Capt Buddy Strozier, also of the 96th FS, force-landed in Portugal. Finally, Lt T. S. Miller of the 97th FS crash-landed in Spain. Although the P-38 pilots claimed to have shot down a Ju 88, none were lost in combat, although two crash-landed in France, low on fuel. A further loss was experienced when a 15 *Staffel* Ju 88 tried to join in the battle:

Leutnant **Robert Baumann**

During take-off for my second mission from Lorient, my plane swung off the runway and because of the soft ground my take-off run was longer than usual. Nevertheless, I did manage to take off but hit a bank of earth at the end of the runway. The undercarriage was torn off as well as both engines. Nobody expected any survivors when they arrived at the wreckage and it was a miracle that the 3,600 litres of aviation fuel did not ignite. Although all of us were injured, at the sick bay I talked to my crew who both appeared quite well. Later I was told that my *Beobachter*, *Ogefr* Walter Boldt, had died of a brain haemorrhage [3 January 1943 – author].

Due to bad weather, only one more day saw V/KG 40 in action in 1942. It is believed that an unknown pilot shot down a B-17 returning from an attack on the U-boat pens at Lorient on 30 December. However, 2 hours earlier 17 P-39 Airacobras of an unidentified unit and led by a B-25, all of which had been using the B-17 attack as a diversion, had again been bounced by V/KG 40. Again, *Ofw* Georg

Lt Robert Baumann (centre), flanked by *Fw* Werner Herrmann (left) and *Gefr* Boldt. *Baumann*

Heuer shot down one of the American fighters, whose pilot was seen to bale out. However, the *Gruppen Kommandeur*, *Hptm* Dargel, was last seen in combat with another P-39 350km south-west of Lorient; he and his crew were never seen again.

A P-39 D Airacobra is seen at Kaldanas, Iceland, on its way to North Africa in August 1942. *via Thomas*

The first six months of operating Junkers Ju 88 C-6s over the Bay of Biscay had proven to be a success. Even though the victories outweighed the losses, the deaths of two *Gruppen Kommandeur* and two *Staffel Kapitän*, two of whom were killed in avoidable accidents, were setbacks that the *Gruppe* could well do without. All of them had vast experience in combat flying, albeit not as fighter pilots, and to lose a pilot of the calibre and experience of *Hptm* Gerhard Korthals must have been a severe blow. With the U-boat war still as important as ever to both the Allies and the Germans, 1943 was to see a further escalation in the air war and a lot more lives lost in comparison to 1942.

Chapter Two

Crescendo
January-April 1943

The seasonally bad weather continued during January 1943 with few contacts made by either side. It was *Oblt* Bruno Stolle's 8/JG 2 that had the most luck, shooting down a 10 OTU Whitley and a B-24D of the 1st Squadron of the recently operational 480th ASG on 6 January, both of which had strayed too close to the French coast. The deaths of Capt Lawrence Lolley and his nine crew were the first operational loss for the 480th ASG and the first for a unit of the USAAF directly involved the air war over the Bay of Biscay; many more would follow before the end of the year.

It should be stressed at this point that the majority of *Luftwaffe* kills for the last few months of 1942 had been achieved by *Oblt* Stolle's *Staffel*. In just two months they had accounted for 13 Beaufighters from the two Beaufighter Squadrons – 235 and 248 – with *Oblt* Stolle claiming six himself. It would appear that the Coastal Command Beaufighter crews must have become very aware of the potency of the FW 190s and the dangers of straying too close to the French coast, as successes by 8/JG 2 against Beaufighters were never again repeated.[1]

The funeral pyre of one of V/KG 40's losses on 29 January 1943.

The Beaufighters of 248 Squadron head for home after their victories on 29 January 1943.

V/KG 40's first combat for the year took place on 3 January when two crew members of a Ju 88 were wounded by return fire from a B-17 attacking Lorient, but for much of remainder of the month a series of uneventful searches for enemy U-boats, *Freie Jagds* and reconnaissances resulted in the words *Keine Feindberührung* ('no enemy contact') being written in log books. The first conclusive contact with the RAF came on 29 January when four Beaufighters of 248 Squadron led by Flt Lt Aubrey Inniss shot down two of V/KG 40's fighters in a very one-sided combat without suffering any loss themselves:

Coastal Command Intelligence, Summary No 187

No 248 Sqn Beaufighters coded WR-B, WR-L, WR-D and WR-K, captains Flt Lt Inniss, Sgt McLeod, Fg Off Payne and Sgt Catrane, sighted, whilst flying at 50 feet, two Ju 88s 2 miles astern, also at sea level. Formation immediately changed course, aircraft WR-D and WR-K attacking one enemy aircraft and WR-B and WR-L the other. In the first case, WR-D attacked first and enemy aircraft's starboard engine caught fire; aircraft WR-K then made two attacks, WR-D making final attack as enemy aircraft was fluttering along the wave tops on one engine.

The port engine then caught fire and enemy aircraft dived into the sea in flames. Meanwhile, WR-B and WR-L were attacking the second enemy aircraft. WR-B made first attack and sustained some damage from return fire. WR-L then attacked, registering hits and dense clouds of white smoke were emitting from enemy aircraft's port engine. WR-B then delivered a final attack and enemy aircraft's starboard engine caught fire and enemy aircraft was seen to crash into the sea, burning furiously, and then appeared to disintegrate into burning patches.

The day after, the combat was much more spectacular. Again, it was 248 Squadron that was involved, except this time they were outnumbered:

Coastal Command Intelligence, Summary No 187

F/S Duncan in aircraft WR-F sighted four Ju 88s 3 miles distant at 1131 hours on 30 January 1943 Bay of Biscay. Aircraft WR-F, followed by WR-M and WR-G, closed to within 300 yards of the nearest enemy aircraft and WR-F delivered an attack from astern; hits were seen to register on port engine of enemy aircraft, which was observed to be on fire; return fire was experienced from enemy aircraft but no hits were registered. WR-F then broke away to starboard and a few seconds later the enemy aircraft was seen to crash in the sea and break up. WR-F then commenced to climb and another unidentified aircraft was observed pursuing a second which was on fire; suddenly the pursuing aircraft was seen to explode and both machines dived into the sea; the identity of both of these aircraft is unknown. During this engagement, a Beaufighter was seen circling in the vicinity. WR-F continued to climb until reaching 5,000 feet when the aircraft following was identified as a Ju 88. Enemy aircraft commenced firing when half a mile astern but no damage was sustained. WR-F then entered cloud and enemy aircraft was not seen again. WR-M and WR-G failed to return.

248 Squadron had bounced a *Schwarm* from 14/KG 40, which was being led by the *Staffel Kapitän*, *Hptm* Hans-William Reicke. The bounce cost *Ofw* Georg Heuer and his crew their lives, but what happened next is unclear. The surviving German pilots saw their *Staffel Kapitän* collide with one of the Beaufighters and both aircraft

plunged into the sea, something that was observed by F/S Duncan. The circling Beaufighter also observed by F/S Duncan was then shot down by *Uffz* Heicke. This, again, was a severe loss for V/KG 40 as yet again another Executive Officer had been lost. Furthermore, the 31-year-old *Hptm* Reicke was a very experienced pilot, having flown FW 200s with I/KG 40 and Ju 88s with *Kü.Fl.Gr* 606, and was a very popular *Staffel Kapitän*.

Hptm Reicke's 14/KG 40 at Lorient in the summer of 1942. Left to right, they are *Lt* Flothmann, *Lt* Hintze, *Lt* Olbrecht, *Hptm* Reicke, *Lt* Thies and *Lt* Messerschmidt. In the front is 'Brandy', the 14 Staffel's dog. *Hintze*

If the *Beaufighter-Trauma*, as the Luftwaffe crews now called it, was bad enough, plans were afoot by the RAF's Fighter Command to involve the far more potent de Havilland Mosquito in the air war over the Bay. In December 1942 the night fighters of 264 Squadron were detached in ones and twos to Cornwall to fly *Instep* patrols or *Rangers* over the Bay as a counter to increasing *Luftwaffe* air activity. The official difference between the two types of mission was that *Insteps*

Enter the De Havilland Mosquito.

were 'operations in the western approaches and Bay of Biscay against German fighters molesting Coastal Command aircraft', while *Rangers* were 'Squadron (or Wing or Group) freelance intrusions specifically to draw up German fighters'. As the detachments to Cornish airfields tended to be in Section and up to flight strengths, *Insteps* were the preferred tactic, as one pilot remembers:

Flying Officer Bill Kent

Insteps we flew in fours, at wave-top height and more or less line abreast spaced anything up to half a mile apart. This way we were not wasting effort keeping formation and could devote time to scanning the horizons. We sometimes did cross-overs but anything less than about 90-degree turns we just trailed until we caught up. Most sorties therefore had only one cross-over turn, as we turned to come home. Short-range sorties, normal Mosquito tankage, were usually three and a half hours with the turn around at about 45 degrees North, and with belly tanks on we often made landfall at the Spanish coast. A problem was that with R/T, only the leader's nav knew what courses he was actually steering (as opposed to what had been pre-planned at briefings). The other three navs had to use what we as crews reckoned the course was from averaging out the general compass heading. On short legs it was difficult. If the leader found the Scillies right on the nose and on time, fine, but if he didn't, there was very little chance of the others' navigation being more accurate! There were a few incidents in which some visiting detachments from other squadrons got fairly lost and made landfalls in France, and losing the odd Mossie. I remember a simple scheme was introduced to defeat the Germans who were happy to give us heading for base if a Mossie team leader called. He was supposed to ask for his name to be read back before accepting the homing.

Despite the potential of the Mosquito, because of reduced air activity due to the weather it would be a few months before the first *Instep*-related kill was achieved.

February 1943 was again a relatively quiet month for all involved. On the 5th *Oblt* Hermann Horstmann from 13/KG 40 shot down another Airacobra attempting to reach North Africa via Gibraltar. Five 346th FS/350th FG Airacobras, again being 'navigated' by a lone USAAF bomber, had taken off from Cornwall and soon met very thick cloud; not long after, the small formation became totally lost. Lt Clyde Wilson, in an attempt to orientate himself by finding land, turned 90 degrees and found the coastline 10 miles north of Bordeaux. Climbing back up, he followed the coast to Spain where, out of fuel, he landed at a Spanish Air Force airfield. Lt Charles Kirchner decided to head back for England but, overshooting, landed safely in Northern Ireland. Sadly, Lt Henry Nelson was caught by *Oblt* Horstmann, who promptly shot down the hapless American pilot, whose body was never found. Twenty-four-year-old Hermann Horstmann had only been with the *Gruppe* since 20 January and he could not have asked for a better start to his career with 13/KG 40. Although he had no previous experience as a fighter pilot, he had proven during training to be a talented pilot. He had flown with a number of reconnaissance units before ending up on the staff of a *Zerstörer* school. Despite his age and relative inexperience, he was destined to be one of V/KG 40's *Experten*.

Oblt Hermann Horstmann.

The next combat took place four days later. Because of the potency of their fighter adversaries, the *Staffeln* now were forced to fly in a minimum of *Schwarm* size. During the afternoon of 9 February, at least two *Schwarm* from 15/KG 40 were engaged in a sea search and *Freie Jagd*, and just before 1500 hours the four Ju 88s from one of the *Schwarm* spotted three Beaufighters from 248 Squadron being led by Sqn Ldr David Cartridge, a pilot who was destined to be one of Coastal Command's top aces. The two formations manoeuvred to get the best position and then tore into each other. In a very confused dogfight, *Lt* Dieter Meister, another pilot who would become one of V/KG 40's *Experten*, claimed to have shot down two Beaufighters. The reality was very different:

Coastal Command Intelligence, Summary No 189

[Four Beaufighters of 248 Squadron] while flying almost due north at 50 feet sighted four Ju 88s at sea level, 4 miles up sun on port quarter... Our aircraft made climbing turns to port and continued into attack from starboard at 1,000 feet; the Ju 88s turned to port to meet the attack, forming a wide circle. When about to make an attack on one of the enemy aircraft, Beaufighter WR-G [Sqn Ldr Cartridge] was attacked on the port quarter by a second enemy aircraft. In turning to meet his opponent, [the Beaufighter] was favourably placed to attack third enemy aircraft and fired a long burst of cannon and machine gun fire closing in to 50 yards. Enemy aircraft turned steeply to port, went into a spiral dive and disappeared into the sea. Two hits were registered on WR-G between the starboard mainplane and fuselage during this attack. Meantime, WR-F [Flt Lt Melville-Jackson] attacked one of the Ju 88s as it was manoeuvring to attack WR-G. WR-F fired a short burst of cannon, closing to 50 yards. Enemy aircraft's port inner tank immediately exploded and burst into flames. The Ju 88 went into a gentle dive, hit the sea and burned on the water until swamped. WR-F was hit during this encounter. WR-H [Plt Off White], after following the other Beaufighters and finding itself surrounded, dived to attack one enemy aircraft which was lower than the rest, firing a short burst of machine gun fire. A second Ju 88 was attacked from below without result. On turning from this attack, WR-H was set upon by two Ju 88s approaching head-on in line astern. Rear enemy aircraft broke away to starboard, leading enemy aircraft and WR-H opened fire simultaneously. Machine gun fire blew off enemy aircraft's port engine and was seem to glide towards the sea, alight and finally sank after floating for 4 minutes. The fourth Ju 88 apparently made its escape.

The RAF fighters claimed three of the German fighters without loss, but in fact only the aircraft of *Oblt* Franz Isslinger and *Ofw* Heinrich Dettmer were lost; as usual, there were no survivors. Concern about meeting RAF twin-engined fighters must have been high at this stage. The *raison d'être* for the Ju 88 C-6 was to intercept RAF anti-submarine aircraft and not to get into combat with enemy long-range fighters; so far in 1943, anti-submarine aircraft had been a rare commodity. The German crews were now instructed to avoid the Beaufighter unless they were in equal numbers, and as for the Mosquito, which they had not encountered as yet, they were to avoid combat at all costs. Nevertheless, even when they outnumbered Beaufighters, as in the last two combats, the cost to the Germans was always high. Therefore, it was stressed to the crews that only odds of two-to-one offered reasonable chances of success, and in such cases the dead-astern attack was recommended. However, because of the Beaufighter's higher speed, most attacks had to be delivered from either the bow or dead ahead, and as a result the German aircraft would both be seen and be within the range of the Beaufighter's potent armament.

Oblt Franz Isslinger (centre) and his crew, lost on 9 February 1943. *Baumann*

It was to be another month before the next kill was achieved, when *Lt* Meister shot down a 10 OTU Whitley on 10 March. Twelve days later, the first *Instep* kills occurred when 264 Squadron Mosquitoes shot down two 14 *Staffel* fighters. The following day, the first RAF Flying Fortress (from 59 Squadron) was shot down by *Oblt* Hermann Horstmann, while about an hour later a Ferry Command Liberator of 511 Squadron, which was flying back to the UK from Gibraltar and was carrying amongst its passengers the Air Officer Commanding Gibraltar, AV-M Robert Whitham, CB, OBE, MC, was shot down by 15/KG 40. During the latter combat, *Lt* Friedrich Apel misjudged his attack on the relatively defenceless Liberator and dived into the sea.

24 March saw no let-up in this sudden flurry of activity. *Oblt* Hermann Horstmann shot down his third confirmed victim, a Halifax of 58 Squadron, whose gunners killed two crew members of one of the attacking Ju 88s, which, severely damaged, force-landed at the Spanish airfield of La Albericia. Horstmann was not to know that after being on his *Staffel* for just two months, today would see

Another victim over the Bay on 10 March 1943 – *Oblt* Ernst Stichel's Ju 88 D-1 of *Wekusta 51* falls victim to 248 Squadron.

Lt Ernst Rabolt's FW 200 C-4 of III/KG 40 is shot down by 248 Squadron on 12 March 1943.

Above: Fg Off Richard Weatherhead (front centre) and his crew from 59 Squadron, victims of *Oblt* Horstmann on 23 March 1943.

Right: Sgt Albert Miles, co-pilot of the 58 Squadron Halifax lost on 24 March 1943. *Miles*

him being given command of it, for while on another mission searching for *U-665*, and for reasons that are not clear, *Hptm* Georg Esch, the *Staffel Kapitän* of 13/KG 40, crashed in the sea north of the Spanish coast. All three crew were seen to get into a dinghy and a frantic rescue attempt began. In an attempt to get the *Staffel Kapitän* rescued, it was reported that *Lt* Dieter Meister flew to the Spanish mainland and a crew member baled out, the aim being this man could direct the Spanish to the dinghy. However, this desperate plan failed and the bodies of Georg Esch and his crew were later washed ashore and buried at La Coruna.

Again, the loss of another experienced Executive Officer, especially in yet another freak accident, was a bitter pill to swallow. The only experienced officer left was the *Staffel Kapitän* of 15/KG 40, 32-year-old *Hptm* Hans Morr. By the time he arrived to command 15 *Staffel* he had flown 54 operational sorties with I and III/KG 40 and was the only holder of the Gold *Frontflugspange* in the *Gruppe*. Nevertheless, he was still not an experienced fighter pilot.

Hptm Georg Esch (right), *Staffel Kapitän* of 13/KG 40, killed on 24 March 1943. *Hommel*

One of V/KG 40's Ju 88 C-6s is seen at La Albericia, on either 24 March or 1 July 1943. *Arróez/Azola, via Salgados*

Hptm Hans Morr returns from his 100th operational flight. *Baumann*

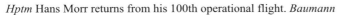

Command of the *Gruppe* was now formally given to the inexperienced *Hptm* Alfred Hemm, while command of the 13 *Staffel* was given to Hermann Horstmann. Command of the 14th *Staffel* had already been given to 22-year-old *Oblt* Kurt Necesany following the death of *Hptm* Reicke. Both Horstmann and Necesany had arrived at V/KG 40 straight from training, but of all of the *Gruppe* Executives only these two had any kills – Horstmann had three and Necesany three, plus a further two shared.

April 1943 would show an improvement in the weather and an increase in inconclusive sorties, with only one kill made and no combat losses. However, May 1943 saw a change in U-boat tactics and, if the German crews thought that April was busy, May would see their work load increase immensely. Sadly for the *Gruppe,* their inexperience in air combat training would now start to show and they would start to see their losses creep up as the RAF rose to the challenge.

Chapter Three

Carnage
May-July 1943

Surviving logbooks from the German crews of V/KG 40 show a marked increase in operational sorties from 1 May 1943 onwards. These tasks were predominantly in direct support of the U-boats, with the German fighters performing close escort for the submarines and sweeps ahead of the submarines both going into and coming back from the Atlantic. We now know that this was in direct response to the sudden escalation of the Battle of the Atlantic, which for the RAF officially started on 31 May 1943.

A Ju 88 C-6 of V/KG 40 meets up with a blockade breaker. *Ernst*

An interesting note was that at the start of the month the British Press announced the sinking of six German 'blockade runners' during the first three months of 1943. These ships had sailed, via the Cape of Good Hope, to Japan, where they had picked up cargoes of India rubber, crude oil and greases, various metals and ores, quinine and other items vital for the German war effort. Between August 1942 and October 1943, nineteen blockade runners had departed from the Japanese ports of Yokohama and Kobe and, if they were lucky enough to get to the North Atlantic, it was left to V/KG 40 and the *Kriegsmarine* to escort and defend these ships and their crews as they entered the Bay of Biscay.

For those first few trips of 1943, the British Press had indeed been correct – the *Höhenfriedberg* had been sunk in the Bay of Biscay by the Royal Navy on 26 February, a fate also shared by the blockade breakers *Rhakotis* and *Irene*. The *Karin* had just made it into the South Atlantic before becoming a victim of the United States Navy, while the *Regensberg* had only made it to Singapore before being torpedoed. The sixth loss was the unfortunate *Doggerbank*, which was a victim of a German U-boat. It can be seen that although V/KG 40 was on hand to defend these ships and their crews, at least for the first half of 1943, they had little chance to assist, and even if they did, such as the case of the *Pietro Orseolo*, V/KG 40 were unable to prevent this 'blockade runner' being torpedoed by the American submarine *Skad*. This ship managed to reach Bordeaux on 2 April, nearly 24 hours after being torpedoed, and the majority of its cargo was salvaged.

The first conclusive combat and kill of the month was on the 13th when *Fw* Vincenz Giessuebel, who was still flying with the 13 *Staffel* and presumably was no longer acting in the role of combat

The *Pietro Orseolo. DSM, Bremerhaven*

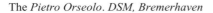

A 224 Squadron Liberator. *Cheek*

instructor, shot down a 224 Squadron Liberator, then, two days later, shot down the first Sunderland to be claimed by the *Gruppe* for eight months; from then on, the *Gruppe* inflicted a heavy toll against Sunderlands, despite their reputation of being heavily armed, as well as many other RAF aircraft.

An RAF Liberator under attack by V/KG 40. *Hommel*

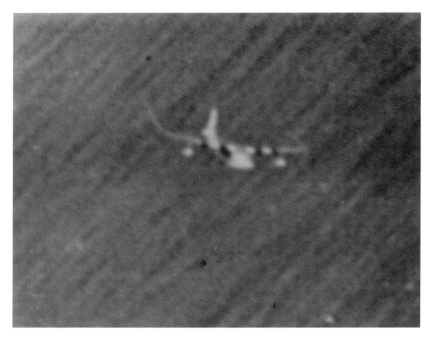

A Sunderland desperately tries to get away from V/KG 40. *Hommel*

The crew of *Lt* Bellstedt's victim on 17 May 1943 managed to make it to Spain and back to England. *Gutermann*

In response to the sudden flurry in German air activity, Beaufighters of 235 Squadron were moved back to Cornwall to assist both 248 Squadron and the *Instep* Mosquitoes. The following accounts give some idea as to how busy the skies above the Bay were now becoming; it also gives a feel for what happened during and immediately after a dogfight:

Squadron Leader Tony Binks

On 20 May 1943 Plt Off Howard Vandewater and myself were sent on a fighter-cum-reconnaissance patrol in the Bay of Biscay in a pair of Beaufighters, which I was to lead. At our briefing before take-off, we were told to be on the look-out for three Mosquitoes that were due to leave the area at about the same time that we were due on patrol.

We duly entered the patrol area, flying low over the water, and almost immediately I sighted two aircraft, also flying low over the water, going in the opposite direction. Thinking they were the Mosquitoes returning from their patrol, my navigator fired a Very cartridge with the colour of the day, but we received no acknowledgement. I then turned my head and was horrified to see one of the aircraft flying into an attacking position on Vandewater's tail – at the same time I recognised it as being a Ju 88.

I immediately executed a 180 degrees turn and flew straight at the enemy aircraft. As it came within range, I fired my cannon and machine guns and immediately observed pieces flying off it. I then had to take evasive action to avoid being hit by the debris. We then saw the Ju 88 hit the water and burst into flames and, as all other activity had ceased, we returned to base.

Pilot Officer Howard Vandewater

Mac [F/S McLachlan] and I noticed two aircraft proceeding north on our starboard, about 300 yards away. I asked Mac what they were as we did not expect to rendezvous for about 15 minutes. He wasn't sure so I suggested he keep an eye open.

About 30 seconds later, Mac said they were forming on our tail and looked like Ju 88s. I alerted Binky on VHF, 'Bandits at 6 o'clock!' He climbed, peeled off to port and shot one down. I chased one and, upon firing, he appeared to shake and smoke came from his engines as he headed for home. As I was more concerned about Binky, I turned away in search of his aircraft, opened up on VHF, heard nothing in return and started searching for him.

After about 5 to 10 minutes with no success, we proceeded back to base and much to our delight Binky was shooting up the airdrome. It was a successful trip as we both got back and was followed by a few beers in the evening!

It was now unusual for V/KG 40 to operate in less than *Schwarm* strength, and in this case had caused the deaths of 13/KG 40's *Lt* Hans Vieback and his crew. The fact that Vieback was from 13/KG 40 might explain why the mission had been flown with two aircraft, as on 7 May a number of crews from 13 *Staffel* had flown to Amsterdam-Schiphol airfield and started flying missions over the North Sea. The reason for this is not clear and log books only record attacks on British motor torpedo boats and fishing boats. The only notable mission of the whole detachment occurred on 14 May when the German aircrew flew to visual range of Lowestoft on England's eastern coast. This was one of the rare occasions that V/KG 40 flew to within sight of mainland Britain. It was with a conspicuous lack of success that the detached crews from 13 *Staffel* returned to Lorient on 28 May, and the following day started flying again over the Bay.

The increase in flying activity began to push the various *Staffeln* closer to the 500 combat sorties total, and it is possible that competition to be the first to achieve their *Staffel's* '*500 Feindflug*' could have, at this time, dictated some of the missions flown. However, this honour first fell to 14 *Staffel*, and its *Staffel Kapitän, Oblt* Kurt Necesany, was the pilot who flew the 500th mission on 21 May 1943. It must have been quite an event as photos show a garlanded Necesany and the rest of his *Staffel* at the start of what must have been a big party. 13 *Staffel's* 500th occurred on 1 June, the day that V/KG 40 will always be remembered as causing the death of one of Britain's most able film actors.

On 29 May it was announced that U-boat tactics in the Bay of Biscay would change with effect from 3 June 1943. From then on, U-boats would transit the Bay of Biscay, normally in groups of two or three, and if attacked by enemy aircraft were to 'fight it out' on the surface. This change in tactics was probably supported by the combat between a Sunderland of 228 Squadron and *U-441* on 24 May 1943,

Oblt Kurt Necesany returns after the 500th operational sortie on 21 May 1943. *Hintze*

This page and opposite: More views of the 21 May 1943 celebrations. *Hintze*

which saw the first U-boat equipped for an anti-aircraft battle shooting down the attacking aircraft, even if the U-boat was badly damaged during the combat. In preparation for this change, on 1 June the *Gruppe* intensified its missions; it was unfortunate that on this day a number of Allied aircraft, both military and civil, happened to be in the Bay.

The Allied losses began early. The Wellingtons of 420 Squadron had recently been temporarily detached from Bomber Command to the Middle East and, from 19 May onwards, had begun ferrying its aircraft to North Africa. In order to be clear of the Bay of Biscay before V/KG 40 was on the prowl, most aircraft had taken off from Portreath in Cornwall in darkness, and this was what three 420 Squadron Wellingtons had done, the first lifting off into the darkness at 0421 hours on 1 June, the other two at short intervals afterwards, heading for Ras El Mar. Unfortunately for them, at least five Ju 88s of 13/KG 40, flown by *Oblt* Hermann Horstmann, *Oblt* Arthur Schröder, *Lt* Knud Gmelin, *Lt* Friedrich Maeder and *Uffz* Heinz Hommel, had taken off from Lorient at 0656 hours on a reconnaissance and *Freie Jagd*. Just over an hour into their sortie, they came across the first of the three Wellingtons, flown by Sgt Alexander Sodero. After a short combat, *Oblt* Horstmann was credited with shooting down the Wellington at 0805 hours; 15 minutes later, they attacked a second flown by Fg Off Gordon McCulloch:

Unteroffizier Heinz Hommel

On 1 June 1943 I was flying as *Rottenflieger* to my *Staffel Kapitän*, *Oblt* Horstmann. After sighting the Wellington, my *Rottenführer* climbed over the enemy plane and attacked from the front and above. I had to break off my first attack because of the enemy plane's evasive actions and I had got into its rear turret's field of fire and got a lot of machine gun fire. During this first action, my plane was hit by one bullet in the port wing. A short time after that I was able to get into a favourable position and attacked head-on from above, watching the cannon and machine gun hits in the enemy plane's starboard wing. From a distance of 100 metres, I saw a tongue of fire coming out from the starboard wing, which became even larger. Soon the whole wing was ablaze and then broke off. The plane went into a spin and exploded on hitting the water. I saw the rear gunner baling out but his parachute was also burning. No survivors were seen, only wreckage.

As 13 *Staffel* returned triumphantly from their 500th operational mission, they were replaced by eight Ju 88s from 14 *Staffel*, which

had taken off from Bordeaux at 1000 hours to look for and, if successful, escort back two U-boats. The names of only four of the eight pilots are known – *Oblt* Herbert Hintze (who was the *Staffel Führer* on this particular mission), *Lt* Max Wittmer-Eigenbrot, *Oblt* Albrecht Bellstedt and *Ofw* Hans Rakow. Because of poor weather conditions, the search for the U-boats was called off

Uffz Heinz Hommel (second from left) with his crew and mechanics on 23 December 1942. *Hommel*

Uffz Hommel's Ju 88 C-6. *Hommel*

and the German fighters continued on a general search for nothing in particular. What happened next is recorded in the *Luftflotte 3 Einzelmeldung*, which confirms that at 1245 hours a DC-3 was spotted in *PlQ* 24W/1785 heading north. Five minutes later 14/KG 40 attacked.

At 0735 hours GMT, Flight 777-A took off from Lisbon for Whitchurch airfield near Bristol. The aircraft was a KLM (Royal Dutch Airlines) Douglas DC-3 coded G-AGBB and named *Ibis*, captained by Captain Q. Tepas. He had a crew of three, all of whom were Dutch, and a passenger complement of eight males, three females, one child and one infant. There was no indication of any freight being carried and the total baggage weight was 264lb.

The KLM DC-3s had been flying regular flights to Portugal from Whitchurch since September 1940 and only on two occasions had the *Luftwaffe* been encountered; in both instances the unarmed airliners had returned with varying degrees of damage. Nevertheless, by the end of the second year of operations more than 4,000 passengers had been carried, and by June 1943 they were flying four return flights per week to Lisbon. It must therefore be assumed that the Germans were fully aware of this regular flight, especially as Lisbon Airport must have had its fair share of spies.

On the morning of 1 June 1943 Sqn Ldr Wally Lashbrook, who, as the pilot of a Halifax bomber from 102 Squadron, had been shot down over Belgium in April 1943 and had successfully evaded as far as Lisbon, tried to hitch a lift on Flight 777-A. He arrived too late, and in any case was told that the aircraft was full. He knew full well that one of the passengers was the famous British actor Leslie Howard, who was returning from a working tour of Spain and Portugal – it was common knowledge to many at the Airport. In fact, Leslie Howard had caused a slight delay to the aircraft's departure as, apparently, he had to retrieve a package from Customs. Nevertheless, Whitchurch received a departure message for the flight and a regular exchange of signals continued until 1054 hours GMT, when Whitchurch received the chilling message that the DC-3 was being followed and immediately afterwards that it was being fired upon in approximate position 46.54N, 09.37W; that was the last that was ever heard from Flight 777-A:

Oberleutnant **Herbert Hintze**

The DC-3 was flying on a reciprocal course towards us. I first saw her as a grey silhouette from a range of 2-3,000 metres.

Bellstedt radioed, 'Indians at 11 o'clock, attack, attack!' – markings were not visible but, considering the silhouette and construction, it was an enemy aircraft.

Bellstedt and Wittmer, who had been flying as the Lookout *Rotte* above the rest of us, attacked from above; the rest of us intended attacking from below. By the time we got within range of the aircraft, Bellstedt had attacked and set fire to the

Oblt Herbert Hintze. *Hintze*

port engine and wing, and as we closed up I saw that the aircraft was a DC-3 and had civil markings. I immediately ordered cease fire. I saw what appeared to be three parachutes emerge from the aircraft, which didn't open as they were burning and the plane went into a flat turn and ditched, floating for a short while before sinking. There were no signs of survivors.

On our return we were told that we had shot down a civilian aircraft with VIPs on board. I can still remember quite clearly that we were all rather angry, particularly because no one had told us, before, that there was a scheduled flight between Lisbon and the UK. If we had, it would have been an easy thing for us to escort the DC-3 to Bordeaux. In the debrief that followed, we were told that the DC-3 was carrying a double of Winston Churchill, a General and various high-ranking officials. They were not named, as wasn't Leslie Howard. From our [V/KG 40's] point of view, it would have been useful and certainly sensational to capture a high-ranking opponent. However, as we did not know [who was aboard], we shot the DC-3 down.

To give extra range, the V/KG 40 Ju 88s sometimes carried long-range tanks. *Ernst*

Leslie Howard seen during the making of *First of the Few. Mrs P. Howard-Williams*

Conjecture remains to this day as to whether the *Luftwaffe* had deliberately sanctioned the shooting down of the DC-3. Rumours of Churchill and other high-ranking officials on the aircraft were rife, but the German intelligence network certainly would have been able to confirm or deny them. Furthermore, there was no one passenger who immediately stands out as being vital to the war effort. For instance, Tyrell Shervington was the director of Shell Oil (Lisbon), Wilfred Israel was compiling data on concentration camps, Alfred Chenhalls was a chartered accountant who worked within the film industry, and K. Stonehouse is reputed to have been the Director of Reuters in Washington. It is true to say that 14/KG 40 were operating further west than normal that day, but there is nothing to prove that they were deliberately aiming to shoot down the unarmed DC-3. On the contrary, official contemporary German records give credence to Herbert Hintze's account that they were carrying out normal operations in support of U-boats, and that the intensity of the day's operations were as a direct result of the impending change in U-boat tactics. Nevertheless, the death of Leslie Howard, who had recently finished playing the designer of the Supermarine Spitfire in the film *First of the Few*, was a considerable blow to British morale.

The days that followed saw a series of combats and skirmishes in which the RAF always came off worse. The most costly loss in terms

Leslie Howard shares a moment during filming with Flt Lt Robbie Robson and Sqn Ldr Peter Howard-Williams. *Mrs P. Howard-Williams*

of the experience of the RAF aircrew killed during the following two weeks was when on 3 June a Hudson of 117 Squadron was shot down by *Lt* Heinz Olbrecht from 14/KG 40. The loss in itself was bad enough, but it was who the Hudson was carrying that caused the greatest upset. Returning to North Africa from Britain were seven passengers, all above the rank of Squadron Leader. The most senior passenger lost was Gp Capt Robert Yaxley, DSO, MC, DFC, while two other passengers were seasoned and experienced fighter pilots, both of whom had fought in the Battle of Britain. Wg Cdr Howard 'Billy' Burton, DSO, DFC, had recently finished his tour as Wing Leader of 239 (Kittyhawk) Wing and was returning to North Africa to a new job following a spell of leave, while Sqn Ldr Osgood Hanbury, DSO, DFC, had, like 'Billy' Burton, just finished his tour but as the CO of 260 Squadron and was also returning to North Africa after leave. Between the two of them, they had shot down 18 enemy aircraft, probably destroyed three and damaged a further seven. For the relatively inexperienced German pilot it must have been an easy kill, but he would never know how devastating his kill had been purely because of who the transport aircraft was carrying.

Wg Cdr 'Billy' Burton, DSO, DFC. *via Pitchfork*

11 June saw the second *Instep* kill over the Bay of Biscay. Flt Lt Joe Singleton of 25 Squadron had been detached, with three other crews, to 264 Squadron at Predannack in Cornwall. On what was to be his last *Instep* before rejoining his squadron at Church Fenton in Yorkshire, he had taken off at 1430hrs that day leading a formation of six aircraft on *Instep* Patrol 147.

The formation flew in two vics in loose line astern but was forced to reform when one of the Mosquitoes returned with engine trouble. At about 1617hrs Fg Off James Wootton sighted five aircraft that were identified as Ju 88s, flying in loose echelon to starboard and at a height of 5-6,000 feet. The RAF aircraft were in a dangerous position, flying at just 50 feet, so Joe Singleton ordered the formation to close and climb to get into the sun:

Flight Lieutenant Joe Singleton

The Section was then obviously seen by the enemy aircraft because they altered course and immediately commenced a climbing orbit to port in loose line astern. Three of the enemy aircraft were successively seen to fire a three-star red cartridge but the Section continued to climb to manoeuvre into the sun with the enemy down sun and, at the same time, the enemy aircraft were attempting to outfly the Section to gain the same advantage. When the enemy aircraft were about 2,000 feet above, I ordered the Section, which was then at 5,500 feet, to break and go into the attack. Shortly afterwards, I experienced fire simultaneously from three or four of the enemy aircraft – the fire was seen to come from the dorsal turret in all cases, the tracer passing well above. I then selected the rearmost enemy aircraft in the formation, which was nearest to me, and doing a climbing turn to port inside the enemy aircraft opened fire when about 200 feet below him with a full deflection shot of 70 degrees, giving a short burst of less than 1 second with cannon only (as my machine guns had failed to fire). The enemy aircraft's port engine emitted considerable volumes of thick black smoke and he peeled off to starboard in a dive. I followed on his tail and gave another short 1-second burst from dead astern and slightly above and sheets of flame were seen outboard of the enemy's port engine. Return machine gun fire was experienced from the dorsal position of the enemy aircraft but the Mosquito was not hit. The enemy aircraft then pulled out of the dive and I followed, gained on him and closing in to within 25 yards, gave another three-second burst from dead astern whilst closing right in and flames inboard of the port engine, followed by black smoke emitted from the enemy aircraft's starboard [engine] were observed. My windscreen thereupon became covered with oil from the enemy aircraft, which made sighting difficult, and I was compelled to peel off suddenly to starboard to avoid colliding with the enemy aircraft, which simultaneously was seen to go into a steep dive. I again turned into the attack, followed and overtook the enemy aircraft and, from slightly above at a range of 500 feet, gave a burst of approximately 1 second from the starboard quarter at an angle of 45 degrees. Bits of cowling from the starboard engine and pieces of his mainplane flew off as a result of the attack and immediately afterwards, as I passed above and from behind the enemy aircraft, two of the enemy aircraft's crew were seen to bale out. One was observed to make his exit through the top hatch and was struck a glancing blow by the port mainplane and the enemy aircraft then turned over and in a vertical dive entered the sea.

This kill was to be the second of seven confirmed kills by Joe Singleton during the war, his victim being 15/KG 40's *Fw* Fritz Hiebsch. Joe's camera gun film has many times been credited to other pilots and the Ju 88 has even been misidentified. However, the original film is still kept by him and graphically shows the death of the V/KG 40 Ju 88 and, sadly, its crew.

The Mosquitoes were a potent weapon but were by no means invincible. To counter the Allied air threat, *Hptm* Bruno Stolle's 8/JG 2 had regularly been reinforced by other *Staffeln* from JG 2 and, towards the end of May 1943, a *Schwarm* of Focke Wulf FW 190s. These FW

Camera gun stills from Flt Lt Joe Singleton's combat on 11 June 1943 show the death of a 15/KG 40 Ju 88. *Singleton*

190s were assigned to 5/196, which still continued to fly the Arado 196, the *Schwarm* being commanded by former Arado pilot *Oblt* Heinz Wurm. Based at Brest, the *Schwarm* was known as *Jagdkommando Brest* before being designated *1/Seeaufklärungsgruppe* 128 (1/128). Nevertheless, it was never a full *Staffel* as such with twelve aircraft but did, together with JG 2, pose a threat:

Flying Officer Bill Kent

On 13 June 1943 I was on a dawn sweep. I do not remember who led, but I vaguely remember a face, a Pilot Officer who had never inspired me with leadership qualities. I was on the extreme left and the sky to the front and left was bright, to the right was still more or less dark. This was tactically advantageous; we would be able to see anyone coming out from Ushant whereas they would have great difficulty in seeing us. At the closest point to Ushant on a southerly course I spotted three dots at about 10 o'clock just above the horizon miles away but, having no apparent movement, they would be on a crash vector. I broke silence and called the leader and within seconds I confirmed they were FW 190s. There was a mumbled 'What are they?' from the leader. I confirmed again and by now they saw us at about 2 miles and turned to meet us. They flew directly at me head-on. I called again and broke hard port to avoid being caught by them. They had turned hard and were coming round onto my tail so we got into furious orbiting. The other Mossies sailed straight on without a word.

For about 20 minutes I kept very low and every time they swept in to attack I turned, on the verge of stalling, which they would not follow. One pass, one of them got careless or cocky and curved lazily across my front, though well out of range. But he was surprised, I think, when I broke off from defensive turns and, with both engines flat out, lined up my sights and let fly, and both my nav and I saw strikes. There was also a temporary puff of black smoke but I am sure that it was only a burst of full throttle and not due to serious damage. The others now bore into me again and I had to pull hard turns to keep out of trouble. All the time, whenever I could, I had been heading west and, when a sheet of cloud appeared, I took the first opportunity of zooming up into it and just made it with one FW in hot pursuit and the other two in formation standing off. I returned to base alone. My ground crew were agog seeing I was back early and that I had been firing the cannon, but did get disappointed when in answer to their question 'What did you get?' I said 'I got away!'

The German fighters that Bill Kent had 'bumped' into were probably from 8/JG 2 and had been alerted by the abortive attack on the Meaugon Viaduct near Sainte Brieuc in northern Brittany by 12 Lockheed Venturas of 464 Squadron, during which the Germans shot down one bomber and an escorting Spitfire as well as damaging one bomber and one fighter. At 1259hrs another four Mosquitoes had taken off on another *Instep*; unfortunately for them, as they were relaxing on the final run in towards friendly territory they were bounced by 8/JG 2. *Ofw* Fritz

May shot down two Mosquitoes, *Fw* Alois Schnöll got a third. Coincidentally, both German pilots had shot down aircraft in the early-morning encounter. Two crews from 25 Squadron and one from 410 Squadron were killed, the fourth aircraft returning safely.

The next day, somewhat sobered by the previous day's losses, Bill Kent was part of another four-aircraft *Instep*:

Flying Officer Bill Kent

We were well down the Bay and I was out on the starboard, the leader to the left, then another, and on the extreme port W/O Peter Hendra. I was scanning left across the four and looking to the east and saw it all. Hendra's Mossie was perhaps at 50 feet when he suddenly pulled up into a climb. My first reaction was that he must have seen something and was about to set off to look. I was amazed to see the climb continue to the vertical with no R/T call, then the Mossie slowed, stalled and spun about one turn before crashing into the sea. Before he hit, I pulled hard left and was on my way across, calling the leader. I circled the spot and was joined by the other two. The tail and part of the fuselage broke off just aft of the mainplane where the rear door weakened the structure. It bobbed to the surface along with the wing dinghy. This inflated as we watched but there was no sign of the crew. During the 10 minutes of circling and watching, lots more pieces of wooden structure floated up and began to disperse. There was no hope and nothing we could do so we noted the approximate spot and carried on. It was most odd.

No German claim can be matched to this for certain, but *Lt* Friedrich Maeder did claim a Whitley about this time. Though aircraft misidentification was common, to mistake a Whitley for a Mosquito is unlikely. However, it would appear that W/O Hendra could have been the victim of an audacious 'bounce', so the possibility exists that V/KG 40 had, at last, got the better of a Mosquito. Nevertheless, the effectiveness of the Mosquitoes remained, and for the remainder of June 1943 *Insteps* claimed a FW 200 of 7/KG 40 on the 13th and a Blohm und Voss BV 138 of 1/*Seeaufklärungsgruppe* 129 on the 19th, while a nocturnal attack by 264 Squadron on the 21st accounted for two BV 222s and two BV 138s at the seaplane base at Biscarosse, the former type of flying boat only recently appearing over the Bay of Biscay.

A BV 222 at Biscarosse in 1943. *via Metges*

A BV 138, also at Biscarosse in 1943. *via Metges*

For the remainder of the month, combats between V/KG 40 and the RAF lessened. Only two more Ju 88s were lost – one, flown by *Lt* Willi Gutermann from 14/KG 40, was shot down on 19 June by Mosquitoes of 151 Squadron on yet another *Instep*, and it is possible that a further Ju 88, from 13/KG 40, was also lost.[1] Willi Gutermann and his crew all survived the ditching and, two days later, were picked up by a fishing boat just off the Spanish coast. He and his crew were repatriated but, due to their wounds, did not start flying again until mid-September 1943.

The incidence of combats increased again on 1 July. A Liberator of 53 Squadron fought an inconclusive running battle with 14/KG 40 in the early afternoon of 1 July, and although Fg Off Merrifield

claimed to have possibly shot down one and forced another to land in Spain, what he had heard was the radio traffic from another formation from V/KG 40 when one of their number had to force-land in Spain with a severe oil leak in the port engine that was not due to combat. Although it cannot be said for certain, it is known that *Oblt* Hermann Horstmann had to land his Ju 88 in Spain at about this time and both he and his crew were later repatriated.

Six days later *Lt* Dieter Meister claimed a Ferry Training Unit Beaufighter on the way to North Africa, then the next day six fighters from 15/KG 40 claimed to have shot down another 53 Squadron Liberator in yet another running battle. Again, the Liberator, captained by Australian Fg Off John Handasyde, managed to fend off

Lt Willi Gutermann. *Gutermann*

its attackers and return to base, very badly damaged and carrying wounded crew. The Liberator's crew did put up a good fight – four German crew members from three of the attacking aircraft were wounded. It is also of note that during this combat *Hptm* Horst Grahl, who was to become the *Gruppen Kommandeur* of V/KG 40 later in the year, is first mentioned. Thirty-two-year-old Horst Grahl was originally a Stuka pilot and was posted to IV/KG 40 at the start of March 1943; he probably came to V/KG 40 at the *Gruppen Ia*. Nevertheless, he remains a bit of an enigma and, like his predecessor, *Maj* Hemm, few photos of him exist.

Fg Off John Handasyde, DFC. *Handasyde*

At about 1610hrs on 12 July the only operational loss for V/KG 40 during that month occurred. During a combat with a Whitley of 10 OTU, which was shot down by *Oblt* Hans Schuster, the Ju 88 C-6 flown by *Uffz* Georg Frassek was itself shot down and the crew took to

Fg Off John Handasyde (far left) and crew. *Handasyde*

Hptm Horst Grahl (second from left) with *Oblt* Albrecht Bellstedt (first from left), *Obstlt* Erich von Selle, *Kdre* ZG1 (second from right) and an unidentified visitor to V/KG 40. *Gutermann*

their dinghy. All three were later picked up by the RN – 25-year-old Frassek and his *Beobachter*, 21-year-old *Ogefr* Heinz Dock, were both unhurt, while the 22-year-old *Bordfunker*, *Uffz* Helmuth Heinze, was slightly wounded. For the Allies, the capture of the first crew from V/KG 40 was exciting and, although all three Germans were initially very security conscious, they were glad to be out of the war and over the next few months Wg Cdr S. D. Felkin and his team managed to piece together a very comprehensive analysis of V/KG 40, which included its history, projected expansion, aircraft used, armament, aircraft range and armament, strength and losses, activities, tactics and *Gruppe* personalities. The report they raised was very comprehensive and gave a fascinating insight into what was hitherto a mystery German unit. For example, the fact that the *Gruppe* was based at Bordeaux but also operated out of Lorient (and occasionally Cognac) resulted in an air attack on Lorient in September 1943 in an attempt to prevent the airfield's use by V/KG 40 and to destroy the aircraft of whichever *Staffel* was based there at the time.

Uffz Georg Frassek (centre) and his crew – the first POWs. *Baumann*

Nevertheless, the capture of this crew had no immediate effect on V/KG 40's operations, and during the month they notched up nine confirmed kills, including, on 21 July, a 295 Squadron Halifax that was returning from North Africa following glider-towing operations in support of the invasion of Sicily. Although the Germans did not know it, the month that followed would be the busiest and bloodiest in the unit's short life, even if the vast majority of blood that was spilt would not be theirs. Furthermore, August 1943 would see the arrival over the Bay of Biscay of another foe who, to date, had rarely been seen over the waters of the Bay; for this adversary, a mere 15 hours after the start of the August 1943 would see it experiencing its first deaths.

F/S Sidney McCormick, navigator of the 295 Squadron Halifax lost on 21 July 1943. *Mrs E. R. Thornton*

Chapter Four

Enter the Americans
July-September 1943

Apart from the brief involvement of the B-24 Liberators of the 93rd BG in November 1942, the first American units to be directly involved in the Atlantic were the B-24Ds of the 1st and 2nd Anti-Submarine Squadrons, the first elements of which arrived at St Eval in Cornwall on 10 November 1942. Subsequently reorganised into the 480th ASG, the unit had limited anti-submarines successes, despite being aided by their advanced ASV-10 radar. Brushes with V/KG 40 towards the end of 1942 and the early months of 1943 were rare and the only combat losses were to 8/JG 2 on 6 January and 26 February 1943. Nevertheless, following the February 1943 U-boat offensive, American senior officers decided to move the two anti-submarine squadrons to Port Lyautey in Morocco in March 1943, and for the moment it appeared that the American involvement had ended.

Following the departure of the American aircraft for North Africa, British senior officers pressed for continued American support in their battles with the U-boats, particularly as the Germans now had *Metox* radar receivers on their U-boats, which gave advance warning of approaching Allied aircraft. Nevertheless, improvements to ASV radars allowed the RAF to fight back, but it

This B-24D, from the 379th BG, is similar to those flown by the 479th and 480th ASGs.

was still felt that the RAF had insufficient assets to control the Atlantic; following personal requests by the British, at the end of June 1943 the first elements of the 479th ASG began to arrive in the UK. By 7 July 1943 the 4th and 19th Squadrons were established at St Eval, and on 13 July the first operational mission over the Bay was flown by the 479th ASG Commander, Col Howard Moore.

It was not long before the Americans were blooded. During an attack on *U-558* on 20 July, the B-24D of 1/Lt H. E. Dyment of the 19th Squadron was shot down, with the loss of all the crew, while the B-24D of 1/Lt C. F. Gallmeier was damaged and one of the crew wounded. Six days later, the 479th ASG met V/KG 40 for the first time:

19th Anti-Submarine Squadron Diary

Lt Lind, Lt Leal and Lt Grider on patrol missions. Lt Grider and crew were jumped by nine Ju 88s. They were at 5,000 feet between two layers of cloud when a group of five Ju 88s were sighted 1 mile to starboard. Lt Grider immediately turned due west and commenced to dive for cloud cover. Before reaching clouds, four more enemy aircraft were sighted. These aircraft were seen several times while passing in and out of clouds but, though fired upon, no damage was suffered. The crew returned to base with a much greater respect for the Ju 88 and plenty of praise for Lt Grider.

The only German pilot who is known to have been involved in this skirmish was *Uffz* Heinz Hommel of 13 *Staffel*. Lt Silas Grider was lucky this time; he was not to be so lucky the next time he met V/KG 40. However, the first loss to V/KG 40 was not to be a USAAF aircraft, but one from the USN.

Despite the 479th ASG being involved in the Battle of the Atlantic for less than a month, towards the end of July 1943 the USN, in preparation for taking over from the USAAF, sent PBY-5 Catalina flying boats, which began operating out of Pembroke Dock in South Wales on 25 July 1943. Designated VP-63, the unit was known as the *Madcats* in that its aircraft were equipped with the new magnetic airborne detectors (MAD) as an aid to hunting U-boats. The detector in the tail of the plane sent out magnetic impulses, which, when they hit metal objects within 250-300 feet of the detector, gave an indication in the cockpit. On 1 July 1943 one of VP-63's aircraft became the first American anti-submarine victim of V/KG 40.

A Catalina in RAF service.

VP-63 pilot Lt Bill Tanner had been involved in the Second World War from the early hours of 7 December 1941. On that day, while flying with VP-14 out of Honolulu in Hawaii, he had spotted a Japanese midget submarine off Pearl Harbor prior to the attack on the American Fleet by Japanese aircraft. For his actions that day, he had been awarded the DFC. However, he also has just as great a reason to remember 1 August 1943 very clearly:

Lt Bill Tanner

We had operated out of Pembroke Dock for a week or so when I embarked on my second or third patrol through the Bay of Biscay. The aircraft I was flying, 63-P-10 named 'Aunt Minnie'[1], was on the return leg, approximately 400 miles from Land's End, when the lookouts in the aft gun compartment sighted a flight of several Ju 88s closing fast from the south-east.

Our defence in the slow PBY, when attacked by fighter aircraft, was evasion if possible. Unfortunately, cloud cover was sparse and the attack was quick. The attackers came sequentially from each side and I countered with steep turns, as low to the water as possible, towards the nearest attacker to increase the speed of closure and shorten the effective firing time. On the second or third attack, during a sharp turn to starboard, we received several hits, killing the Bow Gunner Rittel immediately in front of me, Scott the radio man, immediately to my rear, and wounding me in my left arm and side. The same attack also crippled the airplane. We lost aileron control and rudder control, and one engine burst into flames. Fortunately, my manoeuvring had placed me just two or three hundred feet above the sea and our track was very nearly directly into a very strong sea and wind (30-40 knots). I was able to pull back the yoke (elevators) which were still operative and crash-land with very little forward movement and impact.

The co-pilot, Bob Bedell, who was not injured, and I were able to clear the cockpit through the pilot's windows. Patterson was thrown clear of the waist hatch but received a nasty gash on his forehead. A seven-man life raft was also thrown clear and landed in the water near Patterson. Bedell was able to inflate the raft and helped Patterson and me into it. The plane drifted off, totally ablaze, and sank within a few minutes. There was no evidence of any other survivors. Because of the strong wind and sea, we were unable to do anything as darkness approached.

The following morning we saw several destroyer-type vessels patrolling. They turned out to be RN frigates searching for me. Fortunately, we were sighted, rescued and subsequently returned to Portsmouth. Bedell returned to the Squadron. Patterson and I were returned to the USA for hospitalisation and reassigned. Unfortunately, Bob Bedell, who later became a Patrol Plane Commander, was killed flying out of North Africa later in the war.

Lt Cdr Bill Tanner. *Tanner*

A VP-63 PBY-5 tries to get away. *Hommel*

After 50 years, Bill Tanner's account has become less dramatic in its telling. According to the Action Report narrated after his rescue, the combat was a very prolonged and violent affair. Furthermore, following the crash he did not know that other members of VP-63 had been out looking for him, and for one pilot this search must have been very difficult for personal reasons:

Lt Ralph Spears

1 August 1943 was a Sunday and I had swapped flights with Bill Tanner. His crew took 'Aunt Minnie' and I was scheduled for his flight on Monday the 2nd. When we got word of the attack, I was called early and took off before daylight to search for our plane that was supposedly shot down. The RAF had received an 'OA' signal, which was our code to send when under attack, 'OA Position' when an attack had happened. I flew to the area and found a deflated rubber raft, no occupants. I climbed to about 6,000 feet and spotted a ship, later identified as HMS *Bideford*. Flew to it, set recognition for the day, got friendly response. They were under way to

southern England with Bill Tanner, Bob Bedell and Patterson. They gave me a brief description of their condition. I continued my patrol at 6,000 feet. Some 4 hours later we spotted three large ships cruising on a north-westerly course. We sent a recognition signal which was answered by a gun blast. We saw the three German destroyers and the *Bideford* from our altitude and realised that they [the German ships] would intercept in an hour. We flew immediately to the *Bideford*, dropping down to 500 feet, reported the possible intercept. They changed course due west. Base directed us to shadow the German ships, which we did until our fuel required us to return. At least the *Bideford* made it to England.

German pilots who were know to have participated in shooting down the Catalina were *Lt* Knud Gmelin and *Uffz* Heinz Hommel of 13 *Staffel*, and *Lt* Friedrich Maeder and *Lt* Lothar Wolff of 15 *Staffel*. Cautiously, the Germans carried out a series of devastating coordinated attacks from either side, each attack resulting in the death or injury of an American crew member. The *coup de grace* was a head-on attack, which resulted in the death of the bow gunner and the wounding of the pilot.

Below and overleaf: German destroyers in action in the Bay of Biscay.

The seaplane crashes into the water. *Hommel*

The wreckage of the VP-63 seaplane slips beneath the surface. *Gmelin*

In the Action Report, Ens Bob Bedell reported that he had seen hits on two, probably three, enemy aircraft by the starboard gun and it was believed that one had been forced to land in the sea as a result of damage sustained during the attack. *Lt* Knud Gmelin's Ju 88 had indeed been damaged, and just over an hour after the attack, after having attempted to fly back to France, he was forced to ditch. He and his crew successfully boarded their dinghy and 3 hours later were rescued by a Breguet Bizerte seaplane of 1 *Seenotstaffel* flown by *Oblt* Voss, who flew them to Brest. After a medical check-up and a night's rest, they were picked late the next afternoon by *Lt* Lothar Wolff in V/KG 40's Messerschmitt Bf 108 and flown back to Lorient where they were greeted as heroes, having been the first crew from 13 *Staffel* to successfully survive a ditching, and having shot down the *Gruppe's* first (and, as it would subsequently be, only) Catalina, which also was Knud Gmelin's first kill, albeit shared. In a unique series of photos, Gmelin and his crew are seen taxiing in, being greeted by their *Staffel Kapitän* and, after receiving a bouquet of flowers, starting on the champagne. For this occasion, the *Staffel* had even obtained the services of a military band, and the German pilots had launched what must have been a veritable barrage of signal flares. Such celebrations would soon become rare occasions for V/KG 40.

For the 479th ASG, missions over the Bay continued unchanged by the fate that had befallen the USN crew, and on 8 August it was their turn to be on the receiving end of V/KG 40's guns. Unlike the 479th ASG's first encounter, Capt Rueben Thomas Jr and his crew of nine from the 4th Squadron had been attacked by eight Ju 88s, which carried out a total of 27 attacks before, finally, the B-24D plunged into the waters of the Bay; credit for the kill was given to *Hptm* Horst Grahl.

Lt Knud Gmelin.

A Breguet Bizerte of 1 *Seenotstaffel*. *Metges*

Oblt Voss (front centre) and his crew pose with *Lt* Gmelin (front right) and his crew – *Uffz* Hans Becker and *Uffz* Gerhard Zimmermann (back row, fourth and fifth from left) – after the successful rescue of Gmelin on 1 August 1943. *Gmelin*

This page and opposite: At Lorient on 2 August 1943 *Oblt* Hermann Horstmann welcomes back *Lt* Gmelin and his crew after their rescue the previous day.

By now the air battles over the Bay were increasing in frequency, but in virtually every case it was the RAF that was on the receiving end. Nevertheless, the Americans still occasionally met the *Luftwaffe* – for instance, on 15 August 1943 Lt Perdue from the 19th Squadron reported that, to his horror, he had run into fifteen FW 200s but had managed to get away undamaged. Three days later, two B-24Ds flown by Lts Leal and Moore of the 19th Squadron had taken off on

A 479th ASG B-24D under attack. *Gmelin*

yet another patrol. Leal encountered four of V/KG 40's Ju 88s, which badly damaged the American bomber, forcing it to limp back to St Eval on three engines. However, at 1715hrs Lt Charles Moore, who was on a check ride with Lt Silas Grider, reported that he was being attacked by enemy aircraft. Contact was lost with the aircraft at 1742hrs and it was thought that the *Luftwaffe*, in this case *Hptm* Hans Morr, *Staffel Kapitän* of 15/KG 40, had claimed another American victim. For the aircraft itself and four of the crew, this was the case; for six of the crew it was a different matter. The following graphic account was part of their combined stories:

Entry from 479th ASG Operations Diary

At 1,000 feet Lt Grider gave the order to prepare for ditching. The aircraft was still under attack and harassed until she hit the water. Unfortunately, only the tail gunner of all the men in the rear heard the ditching order or the alarm bell signal that followed. He immediately left his turret and came forward to the waist, shouting out to the waist and tunnel gunners that ditching was imminent as he passed them. Putting the third life raft against the radar turret, he sat down with his back to the raft and awaited the impact, continuing to shout to the gunners to take their stations. They appeared not to hear.

Meanwhile, in the pilot's section the engineer clambered down from his turret. As he came forward, he noticed a black-headed man who was evidently the bombardier, leaning over the radar table with his head resting on his arm. Beside the radar position, there gaped a jagged four-inch hole that showed where a 20mm shell had exploded. He then opened the top hatch and then, standing, leaned against the armour-plate back of the pilot's seat. With one hand he grasped the life raft compartment release handle. The radio operator leaned over his table, head on arm, with the free hand holding down the key.

As the plane levelled off, the airspeed read 130mph. Pilot and co-pilot fought to keep control as the speed slowed down. Skimming the tops of the swell, the speed could have perhaps been reduced further before touching down but Lt Grider was afraid, with the poor control, of stalling and making an uncontrolled landing. So, with the plane crabbing about 10 degrees to port in level attitude, he ordered Lt Moore to 'let her go in!'

The tail of the aircraft dragged the water. There was no distinguishable bounce or second impact. The nose dropped immediately and a wall of water swept the nose, cockpit and bomb bay. In the rear, the water filled the waist from floor to ceiling. Lt Grider felt the rush of water against his waist and lost consciousness the next instant.

In the water-filled cockpit, Lt Moore sat for a moment and then reached down to unfasten his safety belt. Hands above his head, he groped, felt jagged edges and then clambered upwards. After long seconds of pawing at the water, he broke surface, gulped in air and released one cartridge of his life vest.

The engineer knocked about for seconds in the watery chamber above the flight deck. Finally, just as he was 'beginning to hear the funniest music', he saw a patch of light through the green water. He clambered towards it, shot up and up and finally came to the surface.

The radio operator doesn't remember what happened. When the plane touched, something hit him in the shins – he thinks it was his radio kit which had been on the floor. The next thing, he was on the surface.

In the rear, Sgt Bischoff, against the raft, and Sgt Rosenberg, sliding to the floor at the moment of impact, had equally little idea of what was happening. They got up to the surface – that's all they remember.

Last man to emerge was Lt Grider. When he came to, he was swallowing salt water. He struggled to get loose, then remembered to unfasten his safety belt. After more moments of struggling and swallowing water, he finally reached the surface.

The other members of the crew never came up. Whether Lt Yelton was caught by gunfire and killed in the nose before ditching, whether he remained firing to the last, perhaps having lost his headset, or whether he was caught crawling down the runway from nose to bomb bay when the plane hit the water, no one knows. Lt Levine, it is believed, was probably hit by the 20mm, which tore a hole at the side of the radar position, and was either dead or mortally wounded when the plane touched. Both Sgt La Plant and Sgt Daniels, it is assumed, were hurled forward against the rear bomb bay bulkhead and were dead from either crushed skulls or broken necks before the plane had settled.

When Lt Moore came to the surface, he found that the plane had broken in two about 4 feet aft of the trailing edge of the wing. The nose section, inclined into the water at a 70-degree angle, was floating with the life raft compartments just out of water. It floated for about two minutes more. The tail section sank as he watched.

The crew, under the watchful eyes of the victorious Ju 88s, managed to get into two dinghies in ones and twos and took stock of the situation. Lt Grider had one eye bruised shut and deep scalp cuts, and seemed dazed. Sgt Rosenberg was complaining that his back was hurting badly and that his shoulder was dislocated, while Sgt Bischoff had bad cuts to his scalp, a smashed nose, was in severe pain and was acting irrationally. The other three survivors were more or less unhurt. From a survival viewpoint, all the rations had been lost, and knives and first aid kits were missing from the rafts – in their place were 'Not In Stock' slips. There were several cans of water, plus a water keg found floating in the debris, and a Very pistol and flares.

The first night the survivors were dazed and weary – no one made any effort to eat. In fact, most of them were vomiting, wet, cold and shivering, and attempts to sleep were pointless. Dawn revealed a grey and cheerless sky, which turned to showers and the wind rose. The sea grew rougher, which, shortly after daybreak, capsized both dinghies. The airmen struggled back out of the sea only to find that a number of items had been lost. To make matters worse, Sgt Bischoff, who was by now delirious, had drunk all the water in one of the dinghies.

The second night was miserable for all – rain, cold and each dinghy capsized again. However, the next morning they all spotted two aircraft in the distance, which gave them hope as by now they were thirsty and hungry – the only food remaining was sea-salt-caked chocolate. However, that evening the overcast cleared, the wind subsided, and temperatures and spirits rose. Two planes were spotted but, despite three flares and putting a fluorescent marker in the water, they flew off unaware of the two dinghies. Spirits rose even higher when, just before the sun set, Lt Moore managed to shoot a seagull, which all then ate, blood and all.

The next morning a further five planes were seen, but they did not spot the American airmen. Hampered by poor weather on the previous days, now the sun came out with a vengeance and sunburn was the order of the day. On board the dinghies things were getting worse. Sgt Bischoff's delirium was worsening and Sgt Peeples was starting to suffer from lapses of memory, while Lt Grider was, by now, very weak. The situation looked more and more hopeless as plane after plane passed without seeing them. That night, Lt Moore, who had now taken command in light of Lt Grider's worsening condition, started making plans for yet another night and day waiting for rescue – they were by now doubting whether they would ever be rescued:

Entry from 479th ASG Operations Diary

Sunday morning was clear. A plane passed not long after dawn, then a B-24 piloted by Lt Funk of the 4th Squadron finally sighted the dinghies. Lt Moore had fortunately just finished baling out some sea water which had spilled into the bottom of the dinghy. Smoke markers were dropped and Lt Funk started circling. The men's conditions bounced high; it was about 1130 hours.

Two hours later, Lt Funk left but not before a homed Halifax had taken up the watch. Later, a Wellington relieved the Halifax. Then a Sunderland came up, looked the situation over, buzzed the rafts but couldn't land for the heavy swells. But he did drop a first aid packet, and from the packet's contents the men rescued some iodine swabs. The Sunderland finally had to leave the dinghies alone, but 2 hours later two Liberators appeared and started circling. It was almost dusk. Just as it started to grow dark, the men in the rafts could see the outlines of a large surface vessel silhouetted against the horizon. The Liberators disappeared. Then in the gathering dark one Liberator returned, but even though it tried using its landing lights it couldn't pick up the dinghies.

An extra ration of water was issued that night, but even so the men were pretty discouraged. Their powers of resistance were about gone. It was cold and they were still wet. All night long they caught glimpses of the frigate searching up and down. Lt Moore fired his .45 several times in the silence but there was no response. Using their searchlight cautiously for fear of enemy action, the searchers probed back and forth among the swells. Once the stabbing ray of the searchlight started to catch the rafts in its flow, but the small craft dropped behind a wave just as the searchlight passed over.

The men in the dinghies saw the frigate only 2 miles away when dawn broke. A plane appeared and passed 8 miles away. A short time later, Lt James Grigsby of the 19th Squadron found them. He turned away to the frigate and soon was back with her puffing up behind. Forty-five minutes after Grigsby's sighting, the frigate drew up to the rafts. As it approached, the men, who had weathered five days in their open cockleshells, could wait no longer. Cheering hoarsely, they dug at the water with hands and shoes in a needless effort to hurry their rafts to the fast boat bearing down on them.

The survivors were swiftly taken on board HMS *Nene* and, despite the threat of attack by the *Luftwaffe* and U-boats, the Americans were put ashore at Plymouth on 28 August 1943.

The 479th ASG continued to fly missions over the Bay of Biscay, but it had already been decided that the USN would take the lead in anti-submarine warfare and that the assistance of the USAAF Anti-Submarine Command was no longer necessary or desirable. The 479th ASG Diarist wrote, 'In other words, we were going out of business.' The 479th ASG, which had by now been swelled by the 6th and 22nd Squadrons, began to disband gradually, the majority of its aircraft being transferred to the 482nd BG based at Alconbury in Huntingdonshire. The last loss for the unit was on 8 September 1943 when a B-24D of the 4th Squadron flown by Lt Finneburgh was unfortunate to be caught by V/KG 40; the honour for its destruction went to *Lt* Lothar Wolff of 13/KG 40:

Flight Officer J. E. Schneider

At approximately 1601 hours, I sighted eight Ju 88s flying on a parallel course, 500 feet above our own aircraft – three planes on starboard side with one trailing to rear and four flying in echelon on the port side, approximately 3,000 yards away. Enemy aircraft pulled ahead and the three on the starboard side made the first attack, coming in on the right side of the nose. We turned towards the attacking planes as the first enemy aircraft opened fire at approximately 1,000 yards, approaching at better than 200mph. The enemy aircraft passed over us and only the first plane was observed firing. This attack shot out the radio and the Number One engine. We then turned on a 270 degrees course to the left, out-manoeuvring the enemy aircraft on the port side as they were too far ahead to attack. We went into a gradual dive, increasing speed to 230mph. Approximately 10 minutes later enemy aircraft attacked again, single planes alternating from starboard and port, pulling ahead, then peeling off into port and starboard nose attacks. The first three or four attacks were ineffective, enemy aircraft not approaching closer that 600 yards. The next one from the port side, however, came right in to 200 yards, shooting away the rudder control and trim tube and the top half of the top turret, inflicting a severe gash in the chin of the top turret gunner. This gunner remained at his guns, shooting up the enemy aircraft, which was observed by the gunner and the navigator to catch on fire and go down in flames.[2] Following this, another enemy aircraft came in from the starboard nose and was caught in crossfire from the top turret and the right waist guns. It was first feared that this plane would crash into us but at 50 yards it pulled up, passed over the plane, rolling into a dive and the rear gunner reported over the intercom that it had crashed into the sea at full speed. We were now at 1,500 feet and being continuously attacked from port and starboard nose by single planes; however, none of these attacks came into effective range. At approximately 1628 hours, one enemy aircraft came from the starboard waist, opening fire at 1,000 yards and pressing his attack to within 100 yards. Top turret was unserviceable at this moment but as the enemy aircraft broke away forward of us flying on a parallel course on the starboard side, the nose gunner caught him at 100 yards. Both the radio operator and myself saw tracers entering the cockpit and left wing and watched the enemy aircraft until it crashed into the sea. Machine gun and cannon fire from this plane was very accurate, ripping large holes in the starboard inboard and outboard gasoline tanks, and one cannon shell entered the pilot's cockpit through the starboard window, exploding on the instrument panel in front of the pilot. Pilot was seriously injured in the face, chest and left hand. I then took over controls and the radio operator applied first aid to the pilot. Due to the loss of gasoline from punctured tanks, the plane was practically out of fuel and engines Number Three and Four were feathered, leaving one engine in operation. I instituted ditching procedure and started gliding down to landing when, at 1,000 feet, one enemy aircraft attacked from starboard nose, closing to

500 yards before peeling off to the rear. Fire from this plane ripped up the fuselage and shot away the dinghy housed on the left side of the radio compartment. At 1647 hours, the plane hit the water at approximately 92mph.

In what was to be the last conclusive combat for the 479th ASG, seven out of the crew of ten managed to get out – Lt Finneburgh and two others went down with the B-24. Sadly, by the time the survivors were rescued by HMS *Red Pole* during the afternoon of 11 September, the radio operator, Sgt Sutton, had died from injuries sustained in the ditching.

The last encounter with Ju 88s was on 17 October when the B-24D of Capt Estes from the 22nd Squadron was slightly damaged; on 1 November 1943 the order for the 479th ASG to discontinue anti-submarine operations became effective. The final word comes from the 479th ASG Diarist:

> With all the thousands and hundreds of thousands of man-hours devoted before and after Pearl Harbor to the speciality of anti-submarine warfare by units of the USAAF, it was with regret and some misgivings that we saw this training and experience were of no further need in sub warfare and that the personnel involved were to go into other fields.

The American war against the U-boat and V/KG 40 was now given entirely to the USN's Fleet Air Wing 7, which, in addition to the PB5Ys of VP-63, operated the PB4Y-1, the USN designation for the B-24 Liberator. The first unit, VB-103, began operating from St Eval on 30 August 1943 and lost its first plane, flown by Lt Keith Wickstrom, to either *Oblt* Kurt Necesany, *Staffel Kapitän* of 14/KG 40, or *Lt* Knud Gmelin of 13/KG 40, on 2 September; two days later, V/KG 40 struck again.

Aviation Chief Radioman Joe Guthrie

We had an uneventful day until we got near to the Spanish coast. Our mission was to fly across the Bay of Biscay to the Spanish coast and then return to Land's End. I had just informed the pilot that I had land on radar 62 miles away – this was the coastline of Spain. We were flying at 6,000 feet – maybe 7,000 – we had climbed a bit and were still heading south. The weather was good with scattered cloud.

A VB-103 PB4Y-1 with the ERCO front turret. *via Cummings*

We sighted the German fighters who were on an easterly course 4,000 feet above us. We didn't think that they had seen us since they passed beyond us, but then turned back. That's when the attack began – it was immediate. They dived from above and came directly at us.

I couldn't see out and things happened fast. I turned to Terry Tennant [radio operator] and told him to get a message out immediately and he got out a message that we were under attack by enemy aircraft. I think that everyone was pretty calm because we had all the guns manned and were ready. I remember Bob Hoffman [top turret gunner] yelling that they were diving towards us. Bob was firing pretty heavily from the top turret as they came in.

The crew in the cockpit said the instrument panel and the navigator had been hit. He was in the nose dome and had been hit in the neck by shrapnel – I suspect from 20mm. At that time, they passed the word that we had damage in the Number Two engine and we would probably have to ditch. I headed back to the after station to get the radar up. I also fed some ammo cans up to Bob in case they came back.

The sea was pretty calm and Alexander [Lt James Alexander – the pilot] made a terrific landing and we didn't bounce. You wanted to avoid that because the fuselage would split up. We stayed down and it was smooth but the next thing

A VB-103 PB4Y-1 approaches the Cornish Coast – this aircraft was lost in action attacking a U-boat on 12 November 1943. *via Cummings*

I remember was I was outside the aircraft in the water because the after section broke off anyway and I got out that way. We were all prepared before we hit, in our ditching stations and bracing to prevent injury as well as we could. From the time of the attack until we ditched was about 10 minutes altogether, maybe not even that long.

I don't remember the water being cold – it was actually pretty warm and the first thing I told myself was to get the life rafts out. We had two up on the wing compartments that you could normally release from inside the plane. Bob Hoffmann got onto the wing and tried to get the rafts out of their compartments but he couldn't open the doors on it. The aircraft was on fire and it got too hot for him and he had to dive off so we had no rafts. The aircraft was burning good in the area of the Number Two engine. About this time we spotted a spare raft from the after section of the aircraft that had floated out. I told Bob when we got to it, 'Let's just hope that this thing doesn't have holes in it!'

We were in the raft overnight until late in the afternoon of the next day when some Spanish fishermen picked us up since they had seen the light from our raft in the dark. It had rained during the night and we caught some water from that. We didn't have any supplies to speak of and no water, but I don't remember being thirsty. Three of the crew were hurt pretty badly – the rest of us had scratches and bruises but nothing bad. It was a small fishing boat of 20-25 feet that picked us up and took us back to Corcubion; the Spanish treated us great.

The USN aircraft had been attacked by six aircraft from 13/KG 40, which inflicted very heavy punishment on the Liberator, destroying the cockpit instruments and setting three engines and the port main petrol tank on fire. Nevertheless, it was thought that the rear gunner had shot down one of the attackers and German records state that *Lt* Gerhard Blankenberg and his crew had been shot down and killed during an attack on a Liberator in roughly the same area as the VB-103 Liberator had ditched. However, no claim for the Liberator's destruction was filed as the American pilot managed to evade his assailants and, as it would appear, ditch unseen by the Germans. They had ditched fairly close to the Spanish coast but, contrary to what Jim Guthrie recalls, they were not picked up until 0715 hours on 6 September, after having spent two nights at sea, and were brought ashore an hour later. All were successfully repatriated via Madrid and Gibraltar over the next few weeks.

The USN had been bloodied in a very short time and, having gained experience the hard way, was destined to remain operating over the Bay until the end of the war. They had very quickly become victims of V/KG 40 and, as the U-boat war progressed, the two sides would meet again on a number of occasions, with mixed fortunes.

From now on, the USN was integrated into 19 Group's order of battle and both the RAF and USN would continue to lock horns with the German fighters. However, during the USAAF and USN's introduction to V/KG 40 and the Bay, the RAF was continuing to fight its battles against the common enemy, but the tide was beginning to turn for both Allied and German aircrew.

Lt Gerhard Blankenberg, the pilot who was shot down while shooting down Lt James Alexander and his crew from VB-103 on 4 September 1943.

Chapter Five

Turning of the Tide
August-December 1943

The lack of success of the new U-boat tactic of fighting it out on the surface saw it being rescinded on or about 2 August 1943, and there were no U-boat sailings from French Atlantic ports until the end of the month. Nevertheless, German submarines had to return from their patrols, but now did so individually and submerged. Furthermore, the *Luftwaffe* had, after being subjected to considerable pressure, promised the *Kriegsmarine* more and better assistance. The end result of the change in U-boat tactics saw no relaxation of Allied air operations, while the increased operations flown by V/KG 40 resulted in a sharp rise in kills.

The first RAF loss of the month was a Handley Page Hampden of 1404 (Meteorological) Flight, which was shot down early in the morning of 2 August by a number of crews from V *Gruppe*. It would appear that its destruction was credited to *Lt* Lothar Wolff of 15 *Staffel* and *Lt* Max Wittmer of 14 *Staffel*. The days that followed then saw a series of conclusive and inconclusive combats involving a wide range of aircraft types and nationalities. The most intriguing loss occurred on the 11th of the month. Coastal Command had requested the services of 192 Squadron, the RAF's electronic countermeasures squadron, and a Mosquito, flown by Fg Off Edward Salter and W/O Ronald Besant, DFM, took off for an investigation over the Bay at 1635 hours When, a few hours later, they were reported overdue, the worst was expected, especially as the aircraft carried the only 'Goldmark' receiver in the country. The Mosquito had been unlucky to be discovered by *Lt* Gerhard Blankenberg of 15/KG 40 and photographs taken by the other participating German aircrew show a Mosquito desperately trying to get away but to no avail – the final photograph of the sequence shows the burning wreckage of the wooden aircraft on the surface of the Bay.

A number of Sunderland crews were lucky to survive a series of running combats with V/KG 40 during the month of August, invariably returning with aircraft suffering varying degrees of damage and crew casualties. One of the unluckiest must have been Flt Lt

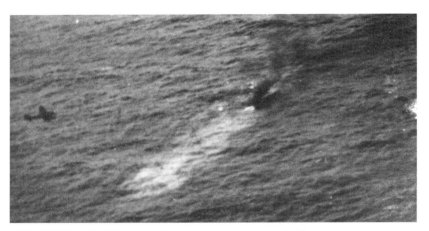

The 1404 Flt Hampden crashes into the sea on 2 August 1943.

Norman Gerrard of 10 Squadron RAAF, who had survived a series of attacks on 8 August only to be shot down in the same recently repaired Sunderland on the 11th. Possibly claimed by V/KG 40 (although no pilot was credited with the Sunderland's kill), it is also possible that this aircraft was the victim of *Hptm* Bruno Stolle, the recently appointed *Gruppen Kommandeur* of III/JG 2. On this day, he remembers having a combat with a Sunderland but, despite inflicting heavy damage, he was never credited with its destruction as the aircraft was lost in cloud.

As a side issue, the Focke Wulf FW 190s of both 8/JG 2 and 1/128 were still active over the Bay but more and more of their time was being devoted to air operations over the mainland. Nevertheless, kills during August were recorded on the 7th, when *Ofw* Fritz May of 8/JG 2 shot down a Beaufighter of 248 Squadron, the 22nd, when the *Staffel Kapitän* of 1/128, *Oblt* Heinz Wurm, shot down a 307 Squadron Mosquito, and most spectacularly on the 25th. On that day 143 Squadron, which had only just arrived at St Eval from North Coates, on the eastern coast of England, and had been operating over the North Sea, lost four out of a formation of six Beaufighters to *Oblt* Heinz Wurm (who had recently been awarded the *Deutsche Kreuz in Gold* for his exploits over the Bay), *Lt* Erich Stain, *Lt* Herbert Jarmer and *Ofw* Friedrich Jost of 1/128 – a very painful and sad introduction to life over the Bay of Biscay. Although the German single-engined pilots did not know it, they were responsible for the destruction of a further Beaufighter on 16 August:

The 192 Squadron Mosquito tries to get away but to no avail; its remains are seen
burning on the water.

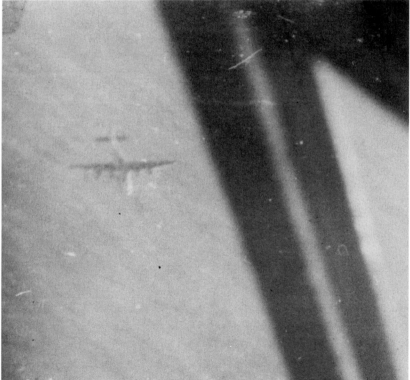

This series of shots shows some Sunderlands trying to get away, and some that were unlucky. *Hommel*

Flying Officer Fred Lacy

As a Beaufighter pilot serving with 'A' Flight, 248 Squadron, in 1943, I was tasked on 16 August to fly aircraft 'J', serial JM343, from our base at Predannack to Talbenny in Wales, where 'B' Flight was presently on detachment, undertaking pilot gunnery training.

Despite the aircraft's full combat weight plus loaded spares and their guardian passenger, I experienced no difficulty in climbing away although the take-off run might have been a little longer than usual. It was a glorious hot summer's afternoon, and as soon as we had crossed the north coast of Cornwall I swooped down to some 20 feet above the calm waters of the outer Bristol Channel en route northwards past Lundy Isle.

Suddenly, after about 20 minutes' flight, the port engine shuddered to a halt and the blades of the propeller stopped in a coarse cruising flight condition instead of continuing to windmill as was normally the case with engine failure. An attempt to restart the engine failed and to my horror the propeller refused to feather. This meant that the paddle blades were face on to the direction of flight instead of edge on, causing considerable drag, and in no time the aircraft slowed down from its cruising speed of 180 knots to 100 knots and I quickly discovered, while trying to gain height, that this speed was only a few knots above the heavily laden aircraft's stalling speed.

I explained the situation to my navigator and we agreed to continue to fly to Carew Cheriton near Tenby in South Wales rather than try to return to Predannack. During the next 20 minutes or so I was able to climb the aircraft very carefully to about 100 feet with the starboard engine roaring flat out and becoming somewhat overheated by dint of the slow forward speed. Fearing that this engine might fail, I decided to attempt a straight-in approach to Carew Cheriton as it slowly came into view. I selected undercarriage down, at the same time losing height rapidly to maintain the aircraft above the stall, but the increased drag from the lowering undercarriage began to rapidly consume all remaining height and to avoid crashing short of the runway I selected undercarriage up and attempted to go round again. We must have passed along the runway about 100 feet up, but as the undercarriage was slow in retracting the aircraft became inexorably committed landwards. I aimed towards a field straight ahead and the aircraft landed on its belly and slithered along the ground. Unfortunately, an electricity power line was in its path and a collision of the port wing with one of the line's wooden poles caused the aircraft to swing sharply left and go sideways through a hedge, over a minor road and through its far hedge into another field where it came to rest – on fire.

My unfortunate passenger was quickly out of the top hatch and he went to extricate the navigator who had been rendered temporarily dazed. I found that my headset leads had become trapped in cockpit wreckage and in all the dense smoke that surrounded me I failed to think of freeing myself by slipping my helmet off! A third attempt to snap the leads succeeded – fear lent me brute force – and I leapt from the aircraft, urging the other two to run clear as quickly as possible. When we had got about 100 yards away, there was a tremendous explosion as some 500-odd gallons of fuel exploded and the aircraft was subsequently almost completely destroyed.

During the investigation into the crash, the remains of what transpired to have been a German cannon shell were found inside the airscrew reduction gear housing of the port engine. On its previous flight, the aircraft had been damaged by enemy aircraft in combat off the Biscay coast.[1]

Another shell had smashed the aircraft's windscreen during this combat and my flight to Talbenny was in part a test flight after repairs during which the offending shell had remained undetected. It had jammed solid the intermeshing gears for the propeller blades in such a way as to prevent them suddenly from continuing to rotate or from being feathered to reduce drag.

Sgt Harry Graham was killed when he and his crew from 547 Squadron were shot down by *Oblt* Horstmann on 18 August 1943; all six crew were killed.

Fred Lacy (back left) is seen with (left to right) Tom Scott, Les Cobbledick and Bill Voce. *Randle*

14/KG 40 takes off on another mission. *Gmelin*

Fg Off Frederick Jenkins and his crew from 58 Squadron were shot down by *Hptm* Morr on 16 August 1943; there were no survivors. *King*

Meanwhile, for V/KG 40 the battles continued to rage for the remainder of the month, the most successful days being 15 and 18 August, when the German pilots shot down a total of two Sunderlands, four Wellingtons, one Halifax and one B-24D without loss. However, following those successes, the remaining thirteen days saw only three confirmed kills, even though for most days there were inconclusive combats:

Flight Sergeant Bob Cherry

On 21 August at Davidstow Moor, myself and crew in Wellington 'Y' of 547 Squadron were to carry out a patrol in the Bay of Biscay. The weather was good with moderate cloud cover.

At about 1630 hours, eight Ju 88s were spotted approximately 3 miles astern manoeuvring to fly four on either side and above our aircraft – a well-known tactic. As the first Ju 88 came in from the port side, all depth charges were dropped and evasive action taken to port. At the same time the second Ju 88 came in from the starboard. Evasive action was taken to the east and we immediately entered cloud. It was then full throttle and climb through cloud, breaking cover at around 10,000 feet. No Ju 88s were seen and we headed for home base.

We certainly fired no shots in the short skirmish; the Ju 88s might have done but no hits were found on the aircraft. The front gunner had the perfect chance to fire at the first Ju 88 as it passed, but when I questioned him he said he felt we were in for a prolonged fight and thought it was best to conserve ammunition!

Oblt Kurt Necesany of 14/KG 40 and seven other German aircraft had already encountered a Sunderland of 228 Squadron before encountering Bob Cherry and his crew and, before returning, had unsuccessfully attacked a Halifax of 58 Squadron. Those three RAF crews were lucky to return to Cornwall unscathed. The following day was a different story when just one Wellington was encountered and Kurt Necesany made sure it was shot down, causing the deaths of its crew of six.

Again, it was the turn of the 479th ASG to be on the receiving end when, on the 23rd of the month, 1/Lt K. H. Dustin of the 4th Squadron was attacked by about ten Ju 88s; what followed proved to be a monumental air battle:

14 *Staffel*. Left to right, they are *Lt* Messerschmidt, *Oblt* Hintze, *Oblt* Necesany, unknown, and *Fw* Kasch. *Gutermann*

Entry from 4th Squadron 479th ASG Combat Diary

Lt Dustin had a contact dead ahead, at approximately the same altitude, of three Ju 88s at 2 miles climbing and heading for him. These were followed by four others in formations of two. As he began to turn, three more were sighted at 10 o'clock to the plane's original course; he turned into them, beginning a diving turn to the left. One Ju 88 passed under, another under to the left, and one under to the right of the nose, and a cannon shell from the right Ju 88 entered left side, slightly wounding the pilot in the head. A cannon shell from the middle plane entered the radio compartment, slightly wounding a crew member in the leg. The fuselage was also hit by combined cannon and 7.9 machine gun fire. Nose and top turret gunners fired on the attackers and saw hits on the centre plane. The pilot, despite his wounds, recovered and completed a 180 degrees turn to the left, increasing speed to 200mph. Enemy aircraft them assumed positions either side of the B-24 and began a series of attacks from either side; all attacks were directed towards the waist and nose.

After beating off about five attacks by making enemy aircraft break off at 600 yards, a Ju 88 attacked towards left nose from 300 feet above, scoring hits on Number One engine and diving under; engine had to be feathered. Another enemy aircraft disappeared beneath the aircraft and, as the B-24 was making evasive turns, the gunner was able to see an enemy aircraft crash into the water...

The combat lasted nearly 2 hours, with V/KG 40 stalking the damaged B-24 into and out of the cloud. Finally, at 1000 hours, and after two of the crew had hacked the bomb doors open with axes in order to jettison the depth charges, the B-24 managed to lose its attackers. Meanwhile, the crew of the Ju 88, seen to crash into the sea, had managed to clamber into a dinghy and hoped that they would soon be rescued. *Lt* Ulrich Hanshen, *Uffz* Josef Vojacek and *Ofw* Otto Bonn from 15 *Staffel* had all suffered minor injuries in the ditching, but for the moment were as comfortable as they could be. Back at Lorient, nine available aircraft from both 13 and 14 *Staffeln* were scrambled at 1040 hours to search for Hanshen in the area 50 kilometres south of the Scillies towards Brest. Because of the risk of meeting Coastal Command fighters, four Messerschmitt Bf 110s of *Hptm* Karl-Heinrich Mattern's II/*Zerstörergeschwader* 1 and three FW 190s from

Fw Herrmann stands between an unknown airman and *Lt* Ulrich Hanshen (right) of
15/KG 40. *Baumann*

1/128 escorted a solitary Do 24 of 1 *Seenotstaffel*, and at 1400 hours
rescued the three Ju 88 crew men just 4 hours and 25 minutes after
they had been shot down – a rare successful rescue for V/KG 40.

At this stage it should be mentioned that the *Luftwaffe* had
recently moved II/ZG 1 from Italy to Brest on or about 5 August to
add extra fire power against the increasing volume of Allied anti-
submarine aircraft. II/ZG 1 had in fact replaced the Messerschmitt
410s of 7/ZG 1; this *Staffel* lasted less than a month over the Bay and,
having made no impact on the air war there, was recalled to Germany
for air defence duties at the end of July 1943. The Messerschmitt Bf
110 G-2s of II/ZG 1 had already scored their first kill, having shot
down a Liberator flown by the Commanding Officer of 311 Squadron
on 21 August. However, in the months that followed, successes were
rare and losses, particularly against RAF Spitfires, were heavy.[2]

Being based at Brest, II/ZG 1 had little impact on V/KG 40's
operations further out into the Bay, as was proved when four days later
the Ju 88 *Gruppe* participated in a new type of mission. Seven aircraft
from 15 *Staffel* took off from Bordeaux just after midday to escort

A Do 24 of 1 *Seenotstaffel. Metges*

twelve Dornier Do 217 E-5s of II/KG 100, each Dornier carrying a new weapon – the Henschel Hs 293A glider bomb, which was destined for ships of the RN sailing just off the Spanish coast. The attack was not a total success, with just one ship badly damaged and a further two lightly damaged. Nevertheless, the following day 15 *Staffel* took off again to locate potential targets and, having found six warships, on 27 August escorted fourteen Do 217s to attack the ships of the First Support Group. The sloop *Egret* became the first ship ever to have been sunk by a glider bomb, the victim of the *Geschwader Kommodore, Maj.* Fritz Auffhammer, and *Oblt* Otto Paulus, while the Canadian destroyer HMCS *Athabascan* was badly damaged by a glider bomb dropped by *Hptm* Wolfgang Vorpahl, *Staffel Kapitän* of 5/KG 100.

The final days of the month saw a return to more normal operations and, despite losing two Ju 88s (one in combat and another in what was presumed to be an accident), the penultimate day of the month saw another Sunderland being shot down:

A Do 217 E-4 of II/KG 100 seen during one of the attacks with the Hs 293 glider bombs. *Ernst*

Unteroffizier **Heinz Hommel**

During a *Freie Jagd* on 30 August 1943, we saw an enemy plane, type Sunderland, and I shot it down in my fifth attack. I came out of the sun and attacked from the front and from above. The enemy plane tried to hide in a thin layer of cloud below but we could see it very well. At 200 metres I opened fire with cannons and machine guns and I watched hits in the cockpit, fuselage and port wing. After my attack, the enemy plane climbed steeply, turned on its port wing and crashed into the sea. No survivors were seen.

September 1943 saw no relaxation from either side, and for the first week a series of combats solely with both British and American Liberators resulted in the deaths of 29 Allied aircrew and the loss of five Liberators for just two Ju 88s and six German aircrew. On 11 September there was a rare victory against a Mosquito, even if the probable victorious German pilot, *Uffz* Franz Huber, was shot down by two other Mosquitoes from 307 Squadron. However, the most intriguing combat of the month took place on 18 September and involved, of all things, a glider.

Uffz Heinz Hommel in his office. *Hommel*

A V/KG 40 Ju 88 C-6 returning to base. *Gutermann*

Another victim – a 461 Squadron Sunderland flown by Fg Off Dudley Marrows, shot down on 16 September 1943. *Hommel*

On 15 August 1943 the Halifaxes of 295 Squadron had begun ferrying Horsa gliders to North Africa, the gliders being intended for operations in the Mediterranean. The route that the gliders and their tugs had to take was from Portreath in Cornwall, through the Bay and on to Salé in Morocco. In just over a month a total of 15 Horsas had been successfully delivered, but as the 23rd glider/tug combination took off at 0740 hours on 18 September, both sets of crews had little idea of what was waiting for them over the skies of the Bay.

In the Halifax 'tug', Fg Off Arthur Norman was setting off on what was his second trip towing a Horsa, and carried the same crew as on his first trip. Sitting in the Horsa, Lt John Prout immediately had concerns about the long flight ahead when the undercarriage failed to drop away after take-off, while the line intercom between glider and tug also failed; communication for this trip would have to be by Aldis lamp between him and his crew and the Halifax's rear gunner, Sgt John Grant.

Being a Mark V Halifax with just the one turret, John Grant had the added responsibility of being the only means of defence should both glider and tug be attacked. 295 Squadron had met with the *Luftwaffe* over the Bay twice already. On 14 June W/O Bill McCrodden and his crew were shot down and killed by two FW 200s of 7/KG 40 flown by *Hptm* Georg Schabert and *Oblt* Ludwig Progner; the glider managed to cast off and its three-man crew was eventually picked up by a Spanish fishing boat 11 days later. The second loss occurred on 21 July when a returning Halifax was shot down by *Hptm* Hans Morr, *Staffel Kapitän* of 15/KG 40; the Halifax crew's final desperate radio transmission of 'We are being attacked by Ju 88s!' was heard by Squadron personnel back in the UK and served as a stark reminder of what could be waiting for crews over the Bay.

Initially, the combination was escorted by four Beaufighters from 248 Squadron, which, upon reaching the limit of their endurance, bade farewell and headed back towards Cornwall. All alone, the glider and its tug set course for Cap Roca on the Portuguese coast; they were not destined to be alone for long:

Lieutenant John Prout

We sighted twelve twin-engined aircraft on our starboard beam; I soon recognised them as Ju 88s. At that time Sgt Hill was flying the aircraft, Sgt Flynn was in the second pilot's seat and I was standing in the doorway. The enemy aircraft did not at first come in to the attack but flew on a course parallel to ours.

Fg Off Arthur Norman (second from right) and his crew in 1944. *Norman*

A 295 Squadron Halifax shot down by III/KG 40 on 14 June 1943. *via Hall*

Hptm Georg Schabert (fourth from left) and his crew, who were involved in shooting down the Halifax; all were reported missing over the Bay of Biscay in December 1943. *via Hall*

As we were in a clear patch, the tug pilot increased the speed to 160mph in an endeavour to reach cloud cover, which was about 1 mile ahead. Owing to the intercom failure, we were unable to communicate with the tug.

When I saw the first aircraft coming in to the attack from the starboard beam, I decided it was impossible for both the glider and tug to reach the cloud so I gave the order to cast off and Sgt Flynn carried out my instructions immediately. By this time, the attacking aircraft had opened fire on us but the fire passed safely in front of our nose.

After we had cast off, Sgt Hill put on flap and did a series of steep turns in order to evade enemy attacks. Meanwhile, Sgt Flynn proceeded aft to get the dinghy ready while I collected together things that I considered we should need. Shortly after, we were attacked by another enemy aircraft but again we escaped damage. As it was a rough sea, Sgt Hill approached across the

Opposite and page 130: A remarkable set of photos showing the glider and tug under attack, the Halifax after the glider had cast off, the Horsa in the water, and, finally, breaking up.

line of the waves and made a perfect landing. Sgt Flynn then climbed on to the wing through the top hatch, which we had opened on the way down, and I passed the dinghy up to him. By this time Sgt Hill had come back from the cockpit and we both climbed onto the wing taking with us our water bottles, tins of food, groundsheets, compasses, binoculars, etc. We inflated the dinghy on the wing, launched it and got into it. While we were ditching, one Ju 88 remained near us, the others having gone after the Halifax. While we were getting out of the glider, it circled low over us and flew away.

Sergeant John Grant

The Ju 88s quickly broke formation with four aircraft climbing above us, possibly expecting the return of our Beaufighter escort, while the other eight started their attacks. Two attacked from the rear and immediately our very gallant glider pilots pulled off to give us a better chance of defending ourselves. Our wireless operator, Sgt Chidley, sent off a glider ditching report to Portreath and our glider pilots were picked up by the RN later in the day.

We had innumerable attacks on our aircraft, mostly from head on and each beam, and the Ju 88s kept well clear of our tow rope, which was swinging wildly and, with the heavy metal connectors, would have done considerable damage if they had hit it! After what seemed a very long time, we eventually reached some thin cloud which gradually thickened.

Flying Officer Arthur Norman

The first attack developed before cloud could be reached, one Ju 88 attacking from the port beam, another being engaged by the rear gunner on the port quarter while a third was preparing to attack from the starboard bow. Corkscrewing evasive action was immediately commenced while still attempting to reach cloud. Fire from the rear turret caused the port quarter attack to be broken off and smoke from the enemy aircraft's port engine was seen. The enemy aircraft on the port beam failed to bring accurate fire to bear on us and I attempted to turn in towards the attack from the starboard bow, which was being pressed home determinedly. It was cannon and machine gun fire from this aircraft that hit the starboard wing, fuselage, rudder and tailplane.

The Rear Gunner got a burst in at this aircraft as it broke away below and on the port side. While attempting to maintain a tight turn in cloud, the controls were felt to be damaged and it became difficult to keep the aircraft in a steep turn to port. Cloud was broken occasionally in the next 2 to 3 minutes and the Rear Gunner reported wild fire from long range while several enemy aircraft could be seen milling around about 1,500 feet above and slightly behind the present position of the Halifax.

Cloud was re-entered, broken again, and one enemy aircraft passed directly overhead without apparently seeing us, and we then made for further cloud away to the south-east. Finally, good cloud cover was reached, three enemy aircraft last being seen circling 6 miles dead astern. Course was then resumed for Cap Roca while the Flight Engineer assessed the damage.

The starboard outer oil pressure and temperatures had dropped to zero. Numbers Five and Six tanks on the outer side were losing fuel, the rudder trim control was useless and the starboard rudder, tailplane and elevators had all been damaged. All other damage to the starboard wing, fuselage and rear turret was superficial as far as could be ascertained. However, I could only hold the aircraft in a straight course by holding full port rudder and aileron; this improved as speed reduced and as fuel was used from the leaking starboard tanks – all weight in the aircraft was also transferred to the port side and it gradually became easier to maintain a steady course...

Amazingly, the Halifax managed to make it to Salé, and for their parts in this remarkable combat Arthur Norman was awarded the DFC while John Grant was awarded the DFM. On the German side, the credit for 'shooting down' the Horsa was given to *Lt* Dieter Meister, but why he and such other experienced pilots as *Oblt* Hermann Horstmann, *Lt* Knud Gmelin and *Uffz* Heinz Hommel failed to shoot down the relatively undefended Halifax must be due to the flying skills of Arthur Norman and gunnery skills of John Grant; if ever two gallantry awards were ever deserved, it was theirs.

The remainder of September 1943 was an anticlimax, even though on the 21st V/KG 40 lost a 13 *Staffel* Ju 88 to an *Instep* patrol, while 14 *Staffel* shot down yet another Sunderland. The combat fought on the 25th was a rare occasion when neither side emerged as the clear winner and also showed a chivalry so often lacking over the Bay:

Lt Dieter Meister's Ju 88 R-2 in September 1943. *Gmelin*

A clearer view showing the BMW 801 engines of the Ju 88 R-2. Left to right are *Lt* Barzel, *Oblt* Horstmann and *Lt* Meister. *Gmelin*

Unteroffizier **Hans-Georg Ernst**

On this day we scrambled at 1528 hours from Bordeaux[3] for a *Freie Jagd* mission over the Bay of Biscay, our formation numbering some seven aircraft. After flying for about 2 hours we met a British fighter formation made up of Mosquitoes and Beaufighters superior in numbers to us and flying on a northerly course. The British planes coming out of the sun had seen us first and attacked at once because they were superior in speed and climbing, and because of this we formed a defensive circle. Flying in this way, the radio operator and observer could keep enemy aircraft away, preventing attacks from behind, and we scored effective hits that caused a fire in one of the enemy fighters. After that, we were able to out-manoeuvre and shoot down another plane that had climbed faster than we had. During the following attacks, we used up all of our ammunition and tried to reach a cloud bank to the east. It turned out to be very thin and suddenly a British fighter appeared to our starboard side and came very near. Certainly this plane had run out of ammunition too and after flying on a parallel course for a while and saying goodbye, it disappeared north. After 4 hours and 5 minutes flying time, we landed again at Bordeaux and found six bullet holes in our plane's fuselage and wing.

The Gäbler crew: Ernst, Gäbler and Wober. *Ernst*

One of the Ju 88 C-6s lost in the attack on Lorient on 23 September 1943 was *Werk Nummer* 3060381 of 13 *Staffel*. *Kasprowiak*

Warrant Officer Frantisek Jankowiak

25 September 1943 was quite a day. Four Mosquitoes from 307 Squadron took off from Predannack on an *Instep* patrol. The crews were Sqn Ldr Jerzy Damsz and Flt Lt Ignacy Szponarowicz, W/O Ludwik Steinke and F/S Stanislaw Sadowski, the British crew F/S Leslie Lowndes and F/S Ivor Cotton and myself with F/S Jerzy Karais.

Over the Bay of Biscay we encountered eight Ju 88s above us in broken cloud. When they spotted us they began to attack. Meantime, we tried to gain height and get into a better position ourselves.

When we returned to our base, we were sure we had destroyed seven aircraft but the British crew did not return. The RAF Intelligence Officer was not quite so generous and the official count was two destroyed, two probable and three damaged.

In addition to the 307 Squadron Mosquito, a Beaufighter of 235 Squadron had its tail shredded by cannon fire and lost its hydraulic system, which resulted in it crash-landing back in Cornwall. The Intelligence Officer was correct to reduce the claim to two destroyed, as only *Lt* Erhard Kromer from 14 *Staffel* and *Stfw* Kurt Linden from 15 *Staffel* both failed to return.

Frantisek Jankowiak just after joining 307 Squadron in 1941.

What should be mentioned at this point is that during the summer of 1943 a new camouflage for V/KG 40's Ju 88s began to emerge. Instead of the usual green camouflage, aircraft arrived on the *Gruppe* painted pale blue/grey. This change in colours did not escape the notice of the Allied aircrew who believed that a 'white' Ju 88s indicated that it was the aircraft of an executive officer or an aircraft designated as a tactical controller during air combats. It would appear that the actual reason was that the Ju 88 C-6s were arriving from the factory in standard night fighter colours of light and medium grey, which was found to be suitable for operations over the Bay. The existence of 'white' Ju 88s did not escape the interest of crews from other *Luftwaffe* units:

Leutnant Karl Geyr

I remember seeing a *Schwarm* of white-painted Ju 88 Cs from V/KG 40 when I was on low-altitude training west of La Rochelle.[4] We knew about the *Zerstörer* fellows from Bordeaux-Mérignac. I do not remember which version of the 'C' they had but I do remember that they [the aircraft] had hard noses full of guns but, contrary to night fighters, had no deer-like antennae.

Lt Geyr's comment about not having antennae was not strictly true. Trials with the FuG 200 *Hohentwiel* search/navigation radar had

14 *Staffel* aircraft sporting their new camouflage. *Gutermann*

started in July 1943, and by late summer 1943 an unspecified number of aircraft in each *Staffel* carried *Hohentwiel* in an attempt to improve operational and mission effectiveness over the Bay.

The old camouflage. *Gmelin*

With the arrival of autumn, encounters between V/KG 40 and Allied aircraft dropped off dramatically, with only one confirmed kill being recorded in October 1943, and that was by *Oblt* Kurt Necesany on the 4th of the month. However, during a confused series of combats with both the Beaufighters of 143 Squadron, two Liberators of 311 Squadron and a B-24 D of the 480th ASG on 7 October, the three German pilots were lost, one of which was the popular *Oblt* Gustav Christner, who shot down a Beaufighter of 143 Squadron. German records say that two of the three losses were caused by Liberators, while Allied claims were two Ju 88s damaged (311 Squadron), one Ju 88 damaged (480th ASG) and two Ju 88s destroyed, one damaged (143 Squadron), so it cannot be said for certain who got whom.

For much of the month of October 1943 *Staffeln* had been depleted when an undisclosed number of Ju 88s were detached to the airfields of Juvincourt and Guyancourt in the north of France. These

The *Hohentweil* aerial is just visible on the leading edge of F8 + YZ of 15/KG 40. *Ernst*

aircraft were then tasked to shadow enemy bomber formations attacking Germany in daylight. Although a number of missions were flown, including one on the 14th of the month when the ball-bearing factories at Schweinfurt were attacked, no combats resulted, and at the end of the month all aircraft returned to duties over the Bay of Biscay.

The detached crews returned to a changed *Gruppe*. On 13 October V/KG 40 was redesignated I *Gruppe/Zerstörergeschwader* 1 – the Ju 88s were no longer part of a bomber *Geschwader* but were now part of a heavy fighter *Geschwader*. Command of the *Gruppe* was formally handed to *Hptm* Horst Grahl, while *Oblt* Kurt Necesany was moved from *Staffel Kapitän* of 2/ZG 1 to be the *Gruppe Ia*; his place as *Staffel Kapitän* was taken by *Oblt* Albrecht Bellstedt. *Hptm* Hans Morr went to form a new Ju 88 C *Staffel*, 7/ZG 1, and leadership of 3 *Staffel* was given to *Oblt* Hans Schuster. Furthermore, recognition of the efforts of V/KG 40 was shown in the award of the *Deutsche Kreuz in Gold* to *Lt* Dieter Meister and *Hptm* Morr on 17 October, with *Oblt* Albrecht Bellstedt receiving the same award on 14 November. It should be stressed that, despite the efforts and sacrifices made by the Ju 88 C

crews of V/KG 40 and, latterly, I/ZG 1, only six gallantry awards were awarded to its personnel during the entire period of its existence. In addition to the three pilots already mentioned, only *Oblt* Hermann Horstmann, *Ofw* Ernst Mündlein and *Ofw* Kurt Gäbler were awarded the *Deutsche Kreuz in Gold,* even if *Ofw* Mündlein's award came mainly as a result of service with another unit. The rest of the aircrew, including such an accomplished pilot as Kurt Necesany, just had to make do with getting the award of the *Frontflugspange* – little recompense for their efforts.

Oblt Gustav Christner and his crew, killed on 7 October 1943. *Gmelin*

F/S Josef Kuhn was the pilot of a 311 Squadron Liberator badly damaged in combat with V/KG 40 on 7 October 1943. *Popelka*

F/S Frantisek Veverka was Kuhn's rear gunner; he damaged one of the attackers despite being wounded, for which he was awarded the DFM. *Popelka*

Despite the relative inactivity of October, November 1943 would prove to be a little more exciting. The month began with a number of uneventful *Freie Jagd* and escort missions for FW 200s. Then on 10 November *Oblt* Albrecht Bellstedt, the *Staffel Kapitän* of 2/ZG 1 of just two days, was responsible for the first kill for the *Gruppe* for more than a month.

The German submarine *U-966* had received the attention of a number of Allied aircraft, and by 10 November the U-boat's captain, *Oblt zS* Ekkehard Wolf, had decided to scuttle the damaged vessel in Spanish territorial waters. What happened next is related by an unidentified German sailor:

> After the *U-966* sank, an enemy Sunderland flying boat circled over us as we were swimming in the water, several times and at low altitude. An RAF crew man leaned out of the cockpit and photographed or filmed us for a long time. Every now and again he would swing his arm as if he was waving to us. Suddenly, three Ju 88s appeared from the direction of the

An unidentified 14/KG 40 Ju 88 C-6 after a landing accident. *Gutermann*

Oblt Kurt Necesany (left) hands over command of 2/ZG 1 to *Oblt* Albrecht Bellstedt, much to the amusement of French workers standing behind them. *Gutermann*

Ofw Kurt Gäbler; the *Deutsche Kreuz in Gold* is seen on his right breast. *Ernst*

Although never seen on its aircraft, I/ZG 1 did have its own unofficial shield. *Gmelin*

Oblt Hans Schuster (right) with (left to right) *Hptm* Morr, *Oblt* Isslinger and *Lt* Baumann. *Baumann*

Spanish mainland. The lead pilot immediately engaged the flying boat, fired at it several times and shot it down in flames. The flying boat crashed into the sea several hundred metres from us and was still burning long after we had been rescued by Spanish fishermen. The victorious Ju 88 then followed the other two aircraft and disappeared over the sea, presumably in pursuit of the Liberators that had attacked us previously.

There were no survivors from the 228 Squadron Sunderland captained by Fg Off Arthur Franklin, and only three bodies were ever recovered. For the remainder, their deaths were marked by the Sunderland's tail, which had broken off on impact; even that eventually floated off and, on fire, sank without trace.

Seven days later another Sunderland was shot down, and two days after that two Wellingtons from 15 OTU on their way to North Africa were chased and shot down in quick succession by two pilots from 2/ZG 1. In the only encounter with RAF fighters during the month, which occurred on 20 November, the new *Staffel Kapitän* of 3/ZG 1, *Oblt* Hans Schuster, was the only casualty in a fierce dogfight off the Spanish mainland, despite the two RAF squadrons involved, 157 and 248, claiming two Ju 88s destroyed and five damaged. I/ZG 1 had been tasked with looking after a Junkers 290 of *2/Fernaufklärungsgruppe 5* (2/FAG 5) and a FW 200 of 7/KG 40, but was unable to prevent both aircraft being shot down by 157 Squadron and 248 Squadron respectively.

In addition to searching for survivors of the previous day's combats, another escort sortie for aircraft carrying glider bombs was flown on 21 November. II/KG 40 had recently been equipped with the Heinkel 177 A-5, and this was its first mission. Twenty aircraft, each carrying two Hs 293s, attacked a convoy in the Bay, which resulted in one ship being damaged and the loss of three He 177s, two of them due to getting lost in bad weather.

The last two days of the month saw combats with Sunderlands – one was shot down on the 29th, while the one attacked on the 30th managed to return home badly damaged but not before it had shot down *Uffz* Hermann Fischer and his crew. It was the loss of Fischer that was partly responsible for the series of missions and combats the following day.

At 1000 hours on 1 December 1943 eight Ju 88s had taken off to search for the downed Ju 88 of *Uffz* Fischer. At 1135 hours they

This page and opposite above: Ju 290s of *FAG 5* seen over the Bay of Biscay in the autumn of 1943. *Griehl*

On 17 November 1943 a 15 OTU Wellington tries to get away, but to no avail.
Gutermann

spotted and attacked a 228 Squadron Sunderland, which managed to escape into the cloud. Meanwhile, further north, Typhoons of 193 and 266 Squadrons, which were escorting Mosquitoes of 487 Squadron, were having a field day shooting down a Ju 52 of 1/*Minensuchgruppe 1* and a Ju 88 of *Wekusta* 51, and damaging a further Ju 88 from *Wekusta Oberbefehlshaber der Luftwaffe*. The Mosquitoes of 157 Squadron, sent in advance of 487 Squadron's shipping strike, then came across the Ju 88s of I/ZG 1 and immediately bounced them.

The German formation immediately broke up, and in the space of 20 minutes one Ju 88 was seen to dive vertically into the sea in a ball of flames, a second ditched, and although a dinghy was seen no survivors were spotted, while a third, flown by *Uffz* Anton Meierl, ditched and the crew successfully got into a dinghy. RAF losses totalled one Mosquito, which was shot down by the *Bordfunker* of a 2/ZG 1 Ju 88.

The surviving Ju 88s returned to Lorient, leaving just one to circle *Uffz* Meierl's dinghy as long as its fuel, the recently returned 228 Squadron Sunderland and the surviving 157 Squadron Mosquitoes allowed it. Making a note of the position, this Ju 88 then headed back to France and shortly afterwards was relieved by two more Ju 88s from the unit. The trouble was that by the time these Ju 88s got to the dinghy, it was being circled by five Beaufighters of 235 Squadron. A short inconclusive dogfight ensued before the Ju 88s were ordered to return to base. The reason for the recall was that considerable effort was being expended to find survivors from the three other non-I/ZG 1 losses, which was fortuitous for one RAF pilot:

Flying Officer Sam Blackwell

I was a pilot of a Typhoon [from 266 Squadron] that took off from Predannack at about 1000 hours on 1 December 1943 escorting Mosquitoes whose mission was to attack enemy shipping off Lorient. I was shot down at about 1130 hours by a Ju 88 about 20 miles off the French coast. I abandoned my aircraft and got into the dinghy and was in the dinghy until about 1700 hours, when I was picked up by a Do 24 seaplane that had an escort of six Ju 88s. I was flown to the seaplane base in the Bay of Poulmic where I was put into a fairly large hospital at what was probably the air-sea rescue base.

I spent the night in the hospital. A medical orderly, who had been in the Do 24 and spoke some English, asked me my name, rank and number. He was anxious to find out if my

U-515 is greeted by I/ZG 1 on 9 November 1943. *Gmelin*

Squadron had shot down two Ju 88s that day, probably because the Germans were looking for the crew. I myself had shot down a Ju 52, and the Ju 88 that shot me down had been brought down by another of our aircraft.[5]

In addition to Sam Blackwell, all but one crew member from the Ju 52 from *1/Minensuchgruppe* and only the pilot of the *Wekusta 51* Ju 88, were rescued. As for *Uffz* Anton Meierl, his dinghy was seen by Mosquitoes of 157 Squadron later that day and again by 248 Squadron Beaufighters the next day; sadly for the three Germans, no sign of them or the other three German crews was ever found in the days that followed. A further crew from 2/ZG 1 was also lost on 1 December when it was shot down by an American bomber over the Eifel region of Germany while presumably engaged in a shadowing flight. Five crews had now been lost in two days, resulting in the deaths of 15 experienced aircrew, and if that was not bad enough worse was to follow later in the month.

For the next 11 days the I/ZG 1 crews were relatively inactive, but with an improvement in the weather over the Bay on the morning of 12 December 1943, six Ju 88s from 1 *Staffel* took off just after midday to protect reconnaissance aircraft returning from a mission. After less than 30 minutes one of the Ju 88s suffered an engine failure and *Oblt* Hermann Horstmann instructed a second Ju 88 to escort this aircraft back to Lorient. Shortly after 1400 hours the Ju 88s were confronted by the nightmare of an enemy fighter formation that had a two-to-one advantage over the German fighters:

I/ZG 1 performs close escort for a KG 40 FW 200. *Ernst*

Uffz Gerhard Zimmermann

We were four Ju 88s when we met eight Beaufighters. We attacked and soon two 'Tommies' were shot down by my pilot, *Lt* Gmelin, and *Oblt* Horstmann. Soon after that, *Oblt* Horstmann and *Lt* Maeder were shot down too. While we were chasing a second Beaufighter, our *Rottenflieger*, a very young crew, was also shot down. We had another combat with a third Beaufighter but had to withdraw because we were

The He 177. *via Bohn*

He 177s of II/KG 40 at Bordeaux. Hs 293 glider bombs can be seen underneath the wings, outside the engines, of the four aircraft on the left. *Griehl*

short of fuel, so, only just, we came home flying on one engine. It is understandable that nobody in our *Staffel* can forget this day knowing *Oblt* Horstmann's popularity within the *Staffel* and the whole *Geschwader.*

Lt Friedrich Maeder, killed in action on 12 December 1943. *Gmelin*

Uffz Gerhard Zimmermann. *Gmelin*

Uffz Hans Frank (far right) was the third casualty on 12 December 1943. To his right is
Uffz Rolf Johenneken and *Gefr* Werner Goebler; the latter was also killed on this day.
Johenneken

Oblt Hermann Horstmann has received a soaking as a result of a practical joke played on him by his *Staffel* in the summer of 1943. *Hommel*

Although he went down fighting against a numerically superior enemy, the loss of the 25-year-old Hermann Horstmann, and for that matter the other two crews, was a severe blow to both the effectiveness and the morale of I/ZG 1. Hermann Horstmann had made an immediate impression, shooting down his first enemy aircraft shortly after arriving at V/KG 40 in January 1943, and the following month was given command of a *Staffel*. He had led his aircrew throughout the bitter battles of the summer only to die when he had no alternative but to fight a numerically superior enemy, a tactic that he had always tried to avoid when previously confronted with such a situation.

For the last few weeks of the year it appeared that I/ZG 1 had not got over the shock of the loss of the popular *Staffel Kapitän*. Hampered by poor weather, only sporadic escort and fighter sweep missions were flown by the Ju 88s, while further out into the Atlantic the He 177s of II/KG 40 were actively involved against Allied shipping, especially in the days immediately following Christmas Day 1943. The shorter-range Ju 88s could do little to influence the air battles that raged, and accordingly II/KG 40's effectiveness was limited. It must have been with a feeling of impotency in the face of a far more technically and numerically superior enemy that the crews saw in 1944; if they thought the tide was turning in the latter half of 1943, 1944 would herald the beginning of the end for I/ZG 1.

Chapter Six

Butchered
January-August 1944

1944 arrived with a vengeance for I/ZG 1 when, five days after the start of the new year, American bombers paid a visit to Bordeaux. For members of the crew of one of the attacking B-17s, it was the start of an eventful 60 days:

2nd Lieutenant Larry Grauerholz

For the 10-man crews off the 337th BS stationed at Snetterton, it was to be a bad day, a day that would cost the Squadron seven of the 21 planes put up. The first clue was at morning 'chow' – in days of scarce fresh eggs, it was a two-egg mission. That meant no milk run.

At briefing, the wall map was uncovered. Target: the airfield just west of Bordeaux, well beyond the range of fighter escort. The airfield was being used as a base for German planes to raid Allied shipping in the Bay of Biscay.

After rendezvous, the bombers cruised south from England across the vineyards and farms of western France. About 2 hours into the mission the escorting fighters peeled off with a farewell wing-dip and headed home. The clumsy bombers were on their own.

For a time as the planes droned on it seemed difficult for crews to realise that this was anything more than a routine practice mission. At the same time, we realised the defenders were tracking the planes and had probably figured out the intended target. Soon, as Bordeaux approached, ugly black puffs of smoke began to appear in the sky ahead. Jerry and his flak guns were ready.

The B-17s began to buck and swerve as the formation took evasive action to foil the anti-aircraft gunners, but the flak began to claim its toll. Here and there an engine began to smoke and the plane began to make a slow downward spiral.

Flak took a heavier toll over the target, as the planes were forced to fly straight and level for the bomb run. Manifold pressure on one of our starboard engines faded and the

The crew of 'Lucky Lady' – Larry Grauerholz is second from the right, bottom row. *Grauerholz*

propeller was feathered. A B-17 could fly as well on three engines as on four – so we had often been assured!

But 'Lucky Lady' was not able to keep in formation as the Squadron turned away from Bordeaux west to the Atlantic to escape the AA guns. A bomber that cannot keep formation was a sitting duck, clay pigeon or whatever metaphor you prefer. The cripple was the target the German fighters looked for, and soon they were upon us and the air battle was on.

Within minutes, another engine was knocked out, the oxygen system went kaput, meaning we could not maintain altitude, and a gunner was wounded. The pilot, realising the situation was hopeless, lowered the landing gear as the international sign of surrender. By that time 'Lady' was well out over the Atlantic, so he turned back, intending to try a ditching in the water or crash-landing close to the shore if he could make it. He nearly made it.

We surviving crew members owe our lives to 2/Lt Richard Stakes who threaded the bomber through the trees to set 'Lucky Lady' down on a mud bank near the point the Gironde empties into the ocean. German fighters buzzed us as we evacuated the plane and tried to set it on fire. Setting a fire isn't much of a task, but getting a B-17 to burn when it's half submerged isn't so simple. Finally, using a gasoline-soaked parachute as a wick, we converted 'Lucky Lady' into a column of smoke and flame to prevent salvage by the enemy.

While this was going on, two crew men went to a farmhouse to summon aid for our wounded gunner. After the war we learned that he had received medical attention but had died in a prison hospital. The rest of the crew struggled through the marsh and headed in the general direction of Spain.

Although the vast majority of defending German fighters were from JG 2, a number of I/ZG 1's Ju 88s had managed to get airborne before the airfield was bombed. It was one of these that probably shot down 'Lucky Lady':

Unteroffizier Hans-Georg Ernst

While we were taking off from Bordeaux, the first bombs were

hitting the ground a short distance away. We climbed at once and saw the enemy bombers were attacking in three waves. One of the lead B-17s had been hit by flak and was showing a white smoke trail and was flying behind its unit. We wanted to attack this plane, but in the meantime several of our single-engined fighters attacked and the bomber went down in a steep spin,

Uffz Hans-Georg Ernst. *Ernst*

two crew members baling out. We thought that it would crash without further attacks, and in fact this bomber crashed into the Bay of Arcarchon at 1058 hours, burning on impact.

After that we climbed again and chased the bombers. They were flying 20-30km west of Bordeaux over the Bay of Biscay and were turning onto a northerly course. One of the planes left the unit to the east, presumably to give protection to some of the other bombers lagging behind because of battle damage. We immediately went into an attack position from below and behind. The B-17 was hit and black smoke came out of the left wing, possibly the inner engine. While attacking, we saw some of our fighters, which also tried to attack, so we fired the recognition signals of the day. We pressed home a further six attacks from the right and behind and we could see effective hits in the fuselage and wings; the enemy plane was losing height constantly. The American pilot was very experienced and was able to bring the plane under control and ditched the B-17 on a lake in front of him. This happened at 1107 hours, the place being the middle of the eastern edge of the Lac d'Hourtin Carcans. The plane finally settled on the beach and four or five crew were seen on the fuselage and wings.

Two days later it was the turn of the recently formed 7 *Staffel* both to be blooded and to get its first kill. Whilst on an *Instep* with three other Mosquitoes from 157 Squadron, Fg Off Philip Huckin and F/S Robert Graham spotted two Ju 88s. These were chased until the nearest one was overtaken, attacked and sent into the sea. However, accurate return fire from *Fw* Johann Pütz's Ju 88 disabled both of the Mosquito's engines and the pilot was forced to ditch 170 miles south-west of Land's End.

Both crew members managed to get into their dinghies but the future looked bleak. However, at noon the next day they were spotted by four Mosquitoes from their Squadron led by Sqn Ldr 'Taps' Tappin. The four Mosquitoes circled until relieved by five Beaufighters, all of which stimulated the flagging spirits of the two cold and wet aircrew. At about 1300 hours a Warwick of 280 Squadron dropped an Airborne Lifeboat and Fg Off Huckin swam across to it. A minute or so later his navigator brought his dinghy alongside in style and, without getting excessively wet, boarded the lifeboat; after a few preparations, they started the engines and headed towards England.

103 hours after ditching, the two aircrews were picked up, not particularly worse for wear, and for their efforts in downing the Ju 88 as well as surviving the subsequent ditching and the days that followed, they were awarded the DFC and DFM respectively.

The remainder of the month was uneventful but saw a number of crews moving from Bordeaux to Marseilles-Istres by both air and bus to start escort sorties for anti-shipping operations in the Mediterranean. Even though the move by air was uneventful, the move by bus during the night of 16 January 1944 was not. At about 0200 hours the bus was attacked by the French Resistance and two of its passengers wounded. One of the casualties was the *Gruppen Kommandeur*, *Hptm* Horst Grahl, who was slightly wounded. For the other casualty, *Oblt* Herbert Hintze, his wounds were far more serious. Hit in the leg by 'dum-dum' bullets, he was destined to spend the remainder of the war in a series of hospitals, and never again flew operationally.

Oblt Herbert Hintze, recovering after wounds received on 16 January 1944. *Hintze*

The first mission over the Mediterranean took place on 1 February 1944. *Lt* Robert Baumann had recently moved from 3/ZG 1 to help form the new 7/ZG 1, and 1 February saw him flying his 59th mission. He had flown to Istres earlier that day and hoped that evening to be flying back to Bordeaux:

Leutnant **Robert Baumann**

On 1 February we were tasked to escort a mixed bomber formation attacking a convoy near Oran. The bombers consisted of He 177s with guided bombs, Ju 88s with torpedoes and He 111s with torpedoes and bombs. Taking off at 1615 hours, at 1800 hours we met five Beaufighters and there was an air battle. During this combat, a Beaufighter and a Ju 88 were shot down.

When we were attacked head-on, our starboard engine was hit and started leaking coolant. My over-zealous *Bordfunker* threw off the canopy and I was forced to ditch. After ditching, the plane floated for a few seconds and sank, taking the *Beobachter* with it.

Some minutes later the English plane ditched too. My *Bordfunker* had lost his dinghy and, as I had seen something yellow in the distance, I gave him mine and swam to this yellow thing, which turned out to be another one-man dinghy.

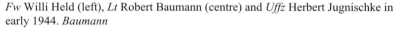

Fw Willi Held (left), *Lt* Robert Baumann (centre) and *Uffz* Herbert Jugnischke in early 1944. *Baumann*

A He 111 H-6 armed for anti-shipping missions. *via Igelbrink*

During the night I could hear my *Bordfunker* calling out –
he was not able to get into the dinghy and later drowned. One
of our aircraft flying back home flew so low over me that I
could see the exhaust flames, but as my signal pistol did not
work I was not able to draw attention to myself.

The next morning, English planes were searching for the
Beaufighter crew and found them. It was about midday when
an Allied boat appeared and I was picked up; a few minutes
later the English crew were also picked up and we had a short
talk. Then I was brought to Algiers.

7/ZG 1 had been intercepted by Beaufighters of 39 Squadron.
Essentially trained for ground attack missions with rockets, the
Beaufighters had been easily placed to go the convoy's aid, despite
not being well versed in the finer points of air combat:

Flight Sergeant Freddie Cooper

Six of us took off to head off a German formation that was said to
be threatening an Allied convoy about 100 miles out in the Med.
We flew in a port echelon and I was Number Six. We sighted
about 50 German aircraft at some distance at 2 o'clock low and
turned to attack. We did not know anything about the Ju 88

The rescue of *Lt* Baumann. *Cooper*

The RAF crew are rescued shortly afterwards. *Cooper*

fighter escort but I found out when tracer started to stream past the cockpit. Things then got a bit chaotic for we were wholly involved with the Ju 88s and could not get near the bombers.

I found myself in a head-on situation with a Ju 88 and let loose with my four cannon from fairly long range and just kept on firing. His port engine then blew up and I saw him ditch. By this time my navigator was shouting that our port wing was on fire and I saw flames streaming back. Tracer streamed past the port side and then intercom went dead.[1] I turned steeply to port

F/S Freddie Cooper and F/S Bridle. *Cooper*

F/S Bridle in front of 'F for Freddie', the aircraft lost on 1 February 1944. *Cooper*

and found myself in the company of three Ju 88s, but no other soul in sight. The four of us just went round in ever decreasing circles while the fire in the port wing burned ever brighter. In the end I realised that my only hope of survival was to put the aircraft in the water before the wing tanks blew up. Without any intercom, I had to hope that my navigator would realise what was happening when I jettisoned the top hatch. The water was like glass, the tracer was still coming past the cockpit and, in my anxiety, I forgot to lower the flaps. It seems a miracle that we ditched without mishap.

The cockpit immediately began to fill with water and I scrambled out, leaving my parachute, dinghy, helmet and a bag contacting a 9mm Beretta pistol and sealed tins of water behind. Fortunately, the five-man dinghy housed under a thin plywood cover in the port wing had self-inflated by an impact switch, had burst through its cover and was floating about 20 feet away. My navigator got out, together with his parachute pack. He also threw out the big emergency ration pack, but it was riddled with holes and promptly sank. The Beaufighter reared up its tail and sank without a trace. With absolute silence, a cloudless blue sky, a limitless horizon and water like glass, I had never felt so helpless.

Darkness was beginning to fall and we were cold, wet and frightened. We huddled together under the parachute silk and heard the sound of engines both overhead and, we thought, on the surface, but saw nothing. Throughout the night we heard cries of 'Hilfe, Hilfe!' and we realised that there was a German crew – our crew – in the vicinity, but there was nothing that we could do.

Unknown to us, our CO had sent out Squadron aircraft to look for us from first light onwards and an RAF rescue launch had set out from Algiers on the previous evening in the vague hope of finding something. At about 1400 hours a Beaufighter appeared low overhead and we fired a flare from the dinghy pack. The Beau climbed high above us and circled, homing in on the rescue launch. When we climbed aboard, I was introduced to a blond young man dressed in khaki battledress as, 'This is a friend of yours.' He was the pilot of the Ju 88 we had shot down and he had actually been sighted before us. He only had a one-man dinghy and although his [two] crew members had hung on for as long as they could, they had both slipped away and drowned in the night. My schoolboy German was scarcely up to fluid conversation, but we got on well and, when we arrived at Algiers, he gave me his flying helmet (which I still have) as a memento. The ripped-off radio plug was evidence of his anxiety to leave the sinking aircraft and the last time I saw him he was immaculately dressed in his light blue uniform on the breast of which was his Iron Cross.

Following the brief Mediterranean interlude, it was back to business as usual over the Bay for the remainder of October 1943, a month that also saw the continued build-up of III/ZG 1. Essentially III/ZG 1 would be employed on the same duties as I/ZG 1 with the exception of one *Staffel*. Towards the end of 1943 two experimental units were formed under the direct command of *Fl.Fü. Atlantik*. *Sonderkommando Rastedter*, commanded by *Hptm* Siegfried Rastedter, operated a mix of one FW 200, an He 111 and Ju 88s and 188s whose duties were to observe, investigate and jam Allied radio and radar traffic. The task of *Sonderkommando Kunkel*, commanded by *Hptm* Fritz Kunkel, was to use Ju 88 Cs and, more recently, the R-2 version, equipped with the FuG 202 *Lichtenstein* and FuG 227 *Flensburg* airborne interception radar against Allied aircraft over the Bay during the night. In particular, they were after the RAF mine-laying aircraft. Drawing experienced crews from I and III/ZG 1, particularly *Lt* Arthur Ewert and *Ofw* Kurt Gäbler, the *Kommando* was officially formed on 15 January 1944, but it is believed that the first operations were flown on 1 December 1943. By March 1944, the *Kommando* had been redesignated *9(Nacht)/ZG 1* and formed the third *Staffel* within III/ZG 1.

A Ju 88 C-6 of *Kommando Kunkel* showing the *Lichtenstein* aerials on the nose and the *Flensburg* aerials on the leading edges of both wings. *Ernst*

Hptm Fritz Kunkel (centre with hat). *Ernst*

An He 111 of *Kommando Rastedter* destroyed in a bombing raid on Bordeaux, probably on 5 January 1944. *Griehl*

Weather for much of February 1944 hampered the operations of ZG 1 over the Bay while assisting both the Allied aircraft still on patrol. However, for one USN crew from VB-103, an improvement in the weather on 14 February spelled disaster:

Aviation Machinists Mate 1C William Middleton

We started our patrol about 0600 hours on 14 February. Our patrol was pretty routine all the way to a spot off the coast of Portugal and we started the return trip to England. We noticed many fleecy white clouds in a blue sky but it was not until late in the afternoon that we saw two Ju 88s in the clouds on our starboard side. Everyone was then alert and ready.

We didn't have to wait too long for the action. They peeled off and started their approach. We were ready for them as the gun positions were manned at all times but they only made one pass and we knew we had taken some hits. The two starboard engines began to cut out and the pilots feathered them and we still kept firing at the Ju 88s as they went by and disappeared behind us. Soon our plane became hard to control and we were losing altitude – we usually flew at about 1,000 feet so we couldn't afford to lose much altitude and we were going down! It was late in the afternoon and the sun was low to the southwest, and we were afraid they would come back out of the sun but they never did. We fired many rounds back towards the sun just in case they were lurking there but they never showed up again; if we had hit them, we didn't know for sure.

After about 15 or 20 minutes the plane commander, Lt Ken Wright, told everyone to take their ditching stations. Everyone did so and the pilot set us down on the water about 150 miles out from Land's End and about the same distance from Brest. I was standing behind the pilot's armour plate under the escape hatch, which was now open. The compartment soon filled with water and I went up and out and saw the co-pilot, Lt (jg) Petersen in the water. It was my job to get out the life rafts, so I got up on the wing then up to the fuselage and opened to two hatches, got the rafts out and handed them down to Lt Petersen. He inflated them and began rounding up the crew. I then slid down off the wing into one of the rafts, then tied the two rafts together. We got everyone we could find in the water into the rafts and started counting noses.

The two radio men were missing and, after the plane sank a minute or so later, we all kept hollering their names hoping that they were nearby in the water but there was no response. They probably never got out of the plane. The tail gunner, though apparently not injured, was not talking. He said very little and laid down in the raft so we covered him with our coats, even though they were wet, to try to keep him warm. The next morning he was dead, having died during the night. We all had cuts and bruises but otherwise we were OK.

The night was fairly uneventful – the sea was fairly calm and we discovered that one of the rafts was leaking so we had to pump it up every 30 minutes. The next day we saw several planes but they were all too far away. About noon on the 15th we saw a four-engined plane pass close to us – I think it was a Sunderland.[2] We fired a flare and they saw it. In response they waggled their wings and started circling over and around us. They stayed over us for several hours and kept us in sight. At about 1600 hours a motor launch arrived and picked us up.

The combat with the Ju 88s had only lasted 30 seconds and only the lead Ju 88 had attacked. With just one burst of fire the PB4Y-1's top turret was put out of action, the elevator controls had been damaged, the radar and compass put out of action and both the Number One and Four engines hit; shortly afterwards both stopped. It had been a devastating attack by the German pilot, who was probably *Oblt* Kurt Necesany. He had experienced little luck in air combats since his transfer to the *Gruppen Stab*, but it was on this day that he was reported missing in combat in the approximate position that the attack on the VB-103 plane took place. Although the top and tail gunners estimated hits on the attacking aircraft, no claim was made. Similarly, as the PB4Y-1 was not seen to crash, no claim was filed by any German pilot.

The loss of yet another 'old hand' would have been a severe blow to the I/ZG 1 pilots, especially just two months after the death of *Oblt* Hermann Horstmann. Twenty-three-year-old Kurt Necesany had flown his first operational sortie in September 1942 and had continued to fly operationally without a rest until his death. He had officially been credited with five kills, and his kill on the day of his death was unknowingly his sixth; for his efforts, he had received scant reward from the *Luftwaffe*. Attempts were made the following day to search for *Oblt* Necesany and his crew, but apart from finding a 10 Squadron

RAAF Sunderland that was damaged and returning with a dead rear gunner, no trace of the Ju 88 or its crew was ever found.

The remainder of February 1944 was very much an anticlimax. Apart from the occasional fighter sweep, *Freie Jagd* and uninteresting task of escorting BV 222s of 1/129, only one further combat occurred when *Uffz* Fritz Gilfert of 3/ZG 1 shot down another PB4Y-1, this time from VB-105. The radio operator from Lt Raymond North's crew managed to send a distress signal saying that they were under attack by enemy aircraft, but a search of the area given only revealed a large oil slick and two dinghies, one of which could have belonged to *Fw* Heinz Baldeweg's Ju 88, which was believed to have been shot down by the PB4Y-1's gunners.

ZG 1's morale by this stage must have been very low. Losses of experienced crews, virtually each time that they shot down an enemy aircraft, must have been galling. Furthermore, the chances of being picked up in the Atlantic had proved to be slim, and in any case, should they have survived a ditching; staying alive in a dinghy at that time of the year reduced the odds of not surviving even further. With Bordeaux now unusable following the attack on 5 January, the Ju 88 crews were being moved from Lorient to Vannes or Istres almost daily, and even those airfields regularly came under attack from Allied single-engined aircraft that, to date, ZG 1 had luckily been able to avoid in combat. How much longer the Ju 88s of ZG 1 could survive no one could say, but the future was starting to look bleak.

March 1944 saw another Mediterranean interlude with the usual tragic results. During a *Freie Jagd* on 8 March in and around the Balearic Islands, three Ju 88s, one flown by the popular *Oblt* Edgar Podzimek, fell victim to Beaufighters of 153 Squadron. 2/ZG 1 claimed to have shot down a Beaufighter that was flown by F/S Alan Applegate, but even this was cold comfort.

The following day saw the scene of battle returning to the Bay of Biscay. The Japanese submarine *I 29* was entering the Bay and the Germans committed considerable air and surface assets to ensure its safe arrival at Lorient. During the afternoon of 9 March two German torpedo boats and two destroyers had set sail to meet up with the submarine. Meanwhile, aircraft from ZG 1 had moved to the airfield at Cazeaux towards the south of the Bay. Operating from there would allow the German fighters to remain longer on patrol for both the German warships and Japanese submarine, which were now off the north coast of Spain.

Oblt Edgar Pozimek is second from left; to his left are *Lt* Friedrich Maeder and *Lt* Knud Gmelin. *Gmelin*

The sudden burst of activity in the Bay did not go unnoticed by the RAF, so on 10 March four Mosquitoes from 248 Squadron escorting two *Tsetse* Mosquitoes from 248 Squadron's Special Detachment were sent to attack the submarine and its escorts. *Tsetse* was the code name for a 57mm cannon carried by Mosquitoes, which had the potential to do serious damage to any submarine, surface vessel or, for that matter, Ju 88.

The RAF formation found the ships off Cape Penas being circled by eight Ju 88s. Immediately the fighters tried to draw the German fighters away from the ships, allowing the *Tsetse* Mosquitoes to attack unhindered. Individual and confused dogfights ensued and 248 Squadron claimed to have shot down three Ju 88s and to have damaged the submarine. In reality, only one Ju 88 was lost and the submarine sailed on undamaged.[3] One RAF pilot, Sqn Ldr Tony Phillips, DFC, even claimed to have shot down one of the Ju 88s using his 57mm cannon, but this cannot be proven.

As the Mosquitoes withdrew, so did the Ju 88s, only to be replaced by a further formation of Ju 88s, one of which was flown by the *Geschwader Kommodore* of ZG 1, *Obstlt* Lothar von Janson. Thirty-six-year-old *Obstlt* von Janson was a pre-war regular officer

Left to right: George Forrest, Jimmy Carlin, Johnny Green, Jimmy Orchard, Stan Nunn, Tom Scott, unknown, and Wg Cdr Tony Phillips. *Randal*

who had joined up in 1928. He had served with JG 132 and in the Spanish Civil War with J88, followed by a series of ground and Staff appointments before being given command of I/JG 133 (later I/JG 53), which flew the Bf 109. He was still the *Gruppen Kommandeur* of I/JG 53 at the start of the war and handed over command after the Battle of France. Then followed a series of jobs at the *RLM* and War Academy before serving on the staff of *Luftflotte* 1 and 2 *Fliegerdivision*. Despite having no operational experience on the Ju 88, let alone the Ju 88 C, he was given command of ZG 1 on 4 November.

The second escort sortie of 10 March 1944 was incident-free and, low on fuel, they headed back for Lorient. However, it is believed that the Ju 88 being flown by the *Geschwader Kommodore* either became separated or he decided to get back to Lorient early. Whatever the reason, it was a fatal mistake. Two sections of two Mosquitoes from 157 Squadron had taken off from Predannack on an *Instep* patrol north and north-east of where 248 Squadron had carried out its attack earlier that day:

Nearest the camera is Lothar von Janson, seen here with I/JG 53 in early 1940.

A Mosquito of 157 Squadron. *Smyth*

Flight Lieutenant John Smyth

We were flying low over the sea, returning to Predannack, when, fortunately for us, I saw him coming up at an angle behind us, against the sun shining on the sea. I broke R/T silence to tell Lt Sandiford, RN, 'Turn port!' and as he did the Ju 88 began to weave and allowed Sandiford and I about two deflection shots, after which he dived into the sea. I took a couple of cine pictures of the wreckage and we returned home.

Obstlt von Janson took no evasive action until it was too late, and even his gunners did not have time to fire at their attackers. His Ju 88 burst into flames along the fuselage and engines and, on diving into the sea, blew up. All that was left in the water was burning wreckage and a dinghy; no signs of any survivors, or for that matter bodies, were seen.

For the remainder of the month, missions were flown purely over the Bay of Biscay, but now there was an added new task – an

Flt Lt John Smyth (right) with his regular navigator, Plt Off Laurie Waters. *Smyth*

On the left is *Fw* Josef Mrechen, *Bordfunker* of the only Ju 88 to be lost in the combats off Cape Penas on 10 March 1944. *Ernst*

increasing number of missions closer to England looking for signs of an Allied invasion fleet. Nevertheless, a *Freie Jagd* on 23 March resulted in the new *Staffel Kapitän* of 1/ZG 1, *Hptm* Günther Moltrecht, formerly the *Kapitän* of the *Zerstörer-Ergänzungsgruppe* at Chateaudun, shooting down a 461 Squadron Sunderland and the rest of the *Staffel* damaging a further Sunderland from the same squadron. Eight days later I/ZG 1 shot down two PB4Y-1s from VB-110 without loss, and almost could have got a third from VB-103:

Lieutenant Bruce Higginbotham

During our briefing for the 31 March 1944 mission, we were advised that enemy aircraft were in the patrol area, so the three PB4Y-1s flew to their assigned areas in formation so we could have greater fire power. After we broke off to go to our own areas, I was attacked by two Ju 88s. One German plane pulled alongside my plane so close that I could see the pilot staring at the bow ERCO turret to determine what armament we had. Then the two planes pulled quickly ahead and made a bow attack. My turret gunner claimed a hit on the lead plane. They then broke off the attack and headed west. Shortly after, we

Lt Bruce Higginbotham, second from right. *via Cummings*

intercepted a message from one of the other VB-103 PB4Y-1s
that he was under attack, then heard from the third that they
too had come under attack. Both later reported they were safe.
However, while a VB-105 plane was attacking a submarine,
two VB-110 aircraft homed in on the action and unfortunately
communicated by radio. The Ju 88s homed in on the
transmission and shot down the two aircraft with all hands lost.

April 1944 was to see the beginning of the end for the Ju 88s of ZG
1. The month began quietly, but the 11th would prove to be a day of
carnage, the carnage being brought about by the arrival off Sainte
Nazaire of *U-255*. What happened next was recorded in the U-boat
Captain's diary:

Oblt zS Erich Harms

Picked up our escort – four minesweepers and one
Sperrbrecher at 0730 hours. Ten 88s are flying close escort.

At 0935 hours there is suddenly an air combat between the
Ju 88s and enemy aircraft. We are attacked by aircraft
weapons. As far as possible, I try to take cover near the
minesweepers. The impacts of heavy weapons are short. One
aircraft attacks with cannon, coming from starboard. By
ordering full power ahead, I am able to get shelter near the

U-255 seen on 11 April 1944. *Gmelin*

leader of the escorts. Some impacts are as near as 20 metres behind our stern. The Ju 88s and the enemy planes are in a terrific dogfight. You can never say which plane is an enemy one and which is one of ours. The attackers are also twin-engined and I reckon there are at least ten. Three crashes are noticed, if friend or foe cannot be ascertained. The *Sperrbrecher* has been hit and burning, leaves the convoy.

By 1020 hours, all of the planes have disappeared. Again, we have got out of a very difficult situation very well. No hits, now we come in with maximum speed escorted by only two minesweepers.

Two *Tsetse* Mosquitoes of 248 Squadron's Special Detachment had been tasked to attack the *U-255* and its escort. Six other Mosquitoes, led by Wg Cdr Oswald Barron, DFC and Bar, gave close escort to the *Tsetses* while top cover was provided by four Mosquitoes from 151 Squadron led by Wg Cdr Geoff Goodman, DFC. The mission

A Mosquito of 248 Squadron. *via Scott*

did not start particularly well when one of the 248 Squadron Mosquitoes crashed shortly after take-off, killing both of its crew. Nevertheless, undeterred, the formation spotted their intended quarry and at 0935 hours attacked:

Sergeant Len Newens

We suddenly came across the U-boat and flak ships and Wg Cdr Barron immediately wheeled to attack the flak ships while the *Tsetse* Mosquitoes attacked the U-boat. My Skipper was taken by surprise at the sudden change of direction and we were left a little behind the rest. We saw Wg Cdr Barron getting hit and going into the sea in a sheet of flames and the same happened to another Mosquito. They also went in flames. As we went down to attack the flak ships, we were hit by flak and suddenly we were aware of Ju 88s all around. A general dogfight ensued and we fired at a Ju 88 and were under the impression that we had shot it down but we were suddenly aware that our starboard engine was on fire. We tried to extinguish the flames in the engine by pressing the extinguisher and feathering button but the prop kept windmilling and the vibration was such that my Skipper could not keep the aircraft in the air. We crashed into the sea at around 300 knots without flaps so we were very fortunate to get away with it.

I managed to get the top canopy open and the two dinghies out. I inflated my Mae West once in the water and swam around waiting for Ken to join me. Unfortunately, he had one foot caught in the rudder bar but managed to free himself by leaving his flying boot behind.

The aircraft floated very much nose down and had broken off half way along the fuselage. We eventually got into our dinghies, tied them together and eventually let off a flare to attract attention. After a couple of hours a French fishing vessel came in sight and we were hauled aboard.

Unusually for the unit, I/ZG 1 was in an ideal position to bounce 248 Squadron. However, the men did not see 151 Squadron above them; it was no wonder that the crews of *U-255* and its escorts had difficulty in identifying who was who in the furious dogfight that ensued:

Unteroffizier Gerhard Zimmermann

We were flying close escort for a U-boat and for minesweepers in the Loire Estuary; our strength was ten aircraft. Four planes were flying just above the water, another group of four at medium height and two Ju 88s high above in the clouds. We had just changed our position when, a minute later, we sighted a group of about nine Mosquitoes diagonally below us. My pilot, *Lt* Gmelin, attacked immediately and was able to shoot down a 'Tommy' right away. Our *Rottenflieger* – young and inexperienced – kept flying close to our plane. Now the Mosquitoes started moving and one of them attacked our *Rottenflieger* in a turn and the Ju 88 was hit and burned. Simultaneously, I succeeded in shooting at this Mosquito with my machine gun and set it on fire; both planes crashed in the sea. Now another Mosquito attacked from the rear. *Lt* Gmelin pulled the control column and, as a result of this and its higher speed, the Mosquito appeared in front of us. *Lt* Gmelin pushed the control column a little bit, opened fire and the 'Tommy' went down. Right afterwards, another Mosquito attacked head on and again *Lt* Gmelin was able to shoot it down. Then we were attacked from below but this time our plane was hit – the fin and tailplane were damaged and the stowage for the dinghy opened and it was lost. After that, we dived and finally we got home flying low level. Our *Staffel* had lost three planes. *Hptm* Moltrecht crashed into the sea trying to pull out of a dive and another crew was also shot down. Most of our losses occurred because these crews had only recently joined the *Staffel* and were inexperienced.

Lt Gmelin and *Uffz* Zimmermann, photographed after their return on 11 April 1944. *Gmelin*

Lt Gmelin's claims of three Mosquitoes for himself and one for his *Bordfunker* were optimistic, as only three Mosquitoes were lost, a further Mosquito being written off crash-landing back in England. Nevertheless, he was awarded the *Ehrenpokal* for shooting down four Mosquitoes and his claims were allowed to stand. *Uffz* Josef Horvath of 1/ZG 1, who was acting as *Lt* Gmelin's *Rottenflieger*, also claimed a Mosquito, but his claim was never confirmed, something that Horvath's *Bordfunker* feels strongly about:

Unteroffizier Hans Namhoff

We took off from Lorient at 0702 hours and were assigned to *Lt* Gmelin as his *Rottenflieger*. His strict orders for our 'young' crew were to stay close to his plane and to keep formation even when enemy contact was made. This was an order an experienced crew never followed and it proved to be our undoing. During attacks from the rear, I had to get the pilot to turn towards the enemy plane so that we could bring into action the rear guns. As a result of staying in formation, the Mosquitoes were able to pound our plane to pieces without any problems. After they attacked, they dived under our planes and climbed again in front of *Lt* Gmelin's Ju 88 and all he had to do was push the buttons. So he was rewarded with three kills. Although we managed to shoot down one Mosquito – it was

The tail of *Lt* Gmelin's Ju 88 lists all of his kills including the four Mosquitoes. *Gmelin*

on fire – soon our left engine was on fire and our pilot was forced to ditch, a manoeuvre carried out excellently by *Uffz* Horvath. Werner Herrmann and myself surfaced shortly after each other but for *Seppl* Horvath, we waited in vain.

We could not reach the plane's big dinghy because it was too far away, so only my one-man dinghy was available. Because Werner had been wounded more seriously, he climbed in and as a precaution I tied myself to the dinghy. So we waited for a few hours and between 1400 and 1500 hours we were fished out by a crew of a small boat with an outboard motor, the crew being a Frenchman and a German soldier. Apparently a soldier on coastal watch duties watched our ditching and ordered our rescue.

German losses are hard to assess because of a second series of combats later that day. However, 151 Squadron claimed two destroyed, one probable and one damaged, while 248 Squadron claimed one destroyed

Fg Off Tom Scott and Fg Off Gerry Yeates of 248 Squadron destroyed a I/ZG 1 Ju 88 on 11 April 1944. *Scott*

Proof of their kill – a Ju 88 hits the sea. *Scott*

and one probable. Combined with the claims made by the RAF in the afternoon, it seems likely that on this day the RAF underclaimed!

However, because of the loss of Fg Off Keith Kemp and his navigator F/S Jim Maidment of 151 Squadron, who had been heard to say they were ditching, four Mosquitoes of 151 Squadron took off again later that afternoon to try and find them. Sadly, they failed, but instead found I/ZG 1 looking for their crews shot down in the morning:[4]

Warrant Officer George Kelsey

We reached the vicinity of the search at 1532 hours and sighted and reported to the Leader three twin-engined aircraft, which looked like Ju 88s in the 9 o'clock position at a range of about 3 miles. My pilot was ordered to lead the attack but as we turned to port to investigate, and as they approached, we saw a total of three sections of four aircraft with a further two in the box. On sighting us, the enemy aircraft turned for home in an easterly direction but, having seen them first, we had a good speed advantage.

On closing in on the first enemy aircraft we were hit by return fire from the rear gunner, which damaged our Mosquito's nose and my side of the cockpit. This did not impair our combat capability and I took up a rear-facing position to give my pilot a running commentary on the tail-end activities. We opened fire at a range of about 600 yards and the first few rounds hit the rear cockpit and appeared to lift the gunner and his canopy out of the aircraft. The next burst was at a range of 300 yards closing to 150 yards, and strikes were seen on the port engine, cockpit and wing roots. The enemy aircraft then fell into the sea, burning fiercely.

We then broke away to port and fired at a Ju 88 crossing from starboard to port. Hits were seen on the fuselage but the combat was broken off to go to the aid of a Mosquito that appeared to be in trouble with one engine failing and being fired at by an enemy aircraft on its tail. The Ju 88 was given a burst of fire at about 250 yards, closing rapidly to 100 yards. Hits were seen on the fuselage and tail and the rudder assembly then came away from the target aircraft, just missing us, this debris being followed by the aircraft's elevators. This engagement had to be broken off because another Ju 88 had got onto our tail and its firing accuracy was getting too close for comfort.

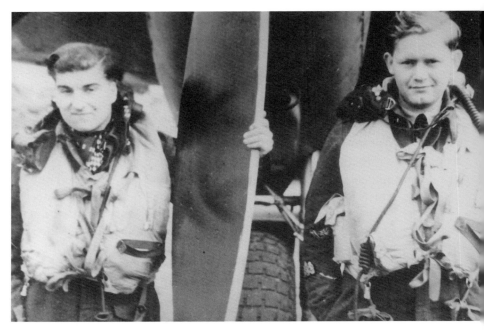

F/S Jack Playford and W/O George Kelsey of 151 Squadron. *Kelsey*

I kept this attacking Ju 88 under observation and when it
had closed to 400 yards my skipper carried out a very severe
turn to port just above sea level. The enemy did not follow
this manoeuvre, and after about one and a half orbits we got
onto his tail. A short burst of fire was given but after about 1
second the guns stopped and we had no alternative but to set
course for base. We were later told that the Ju 88, which had
been attacked and we had seen to be partly disintegrated, had
crashed into the sea.

A further three Ju 88s were claimed destroyed and two damaged in
this combat. I/ZG 1 claimed four Mosquitoes, but only the Mosquito
flown by W/O William Penman failed to return, while George
Kelsey's Mosquito was written off on return when it was found how
accurate the German rear gunner had been in their first combat.

I/ZG 1 had lost a total of seven aircraft and at least two damaged
in just one day. The cost in human terms was fifteen killed,
including yet another *Staffel Kapitän*, and five wounded. As one of
the survivors remembered:

The funerals of a crew from ZG 1, spring 1944. *Ernst*

Uffz Berzborn with his pilot, *Uffz* Rolf Dickel, and observer, *Uffz* Gunther Matzke, in February 1944. *Berzborn*

Unteroffizier Aegidius Berzborn

It was a dreadful air battle. I cannot remember for sure how many German and for that matter British crews were shot down.

Such losses could not be sustained without experienced replacements, and unfortunately for ZG 1 experienced replacements were just not available. It must have given both of the *Gruppen* a severe morale problem for the surviving crews to see so many faces missing from the crew room, and it is doubtful whether the celebrations for the 1,000th operational sortie of 2 *Staffel* on 15 April could have given the survivors a much-needed morale boost.

Things seemed to get worse. *Kommando Kunkel* suffered its first loss on 17 April when one of its aircraft crashed into the Bay after suffering engine failure. Then on the 20th four more crews from both I and III/ZG 1, including *Oblt* Martin Reuter, the *Staffel Kapitän* of 7/ZG 1, were shot down during another escort sortie over the Mediterranean. From then until 6 June 1944 priorities and missions changed.

This page and overleaf: Celebrations for the 1,000th operational mission, 15 April 1944.
Gutermann

Firstly, *9(Nacht)*/ZG 1 began flying regular nocturnal missions, and on a number of occasions was scrambled to intercept enemy aircraft. However, even though claims were filed on at least three occasions, the kills were not confirmed as no evidence of the destruction of the enemy aircraft was found. Secondly, detachments to the airfield at Salon to fly missions over the Mediterranean became more permanent. A number of missions were flown from Salon, predominantly *Freie Jagd*, and although a mixture of Allied aircraft were encountered, such as Marauders and Lightnings, only one loss occurred, and that was during an escort sortie on 11 May 1944 when *Uffz* Heinrich Lang and his crew from 8/ZG 1 were shot down, possibly by friendly fire.

However, it was obvious that an invasion was imminent in northern France. As a result, *X Fliegerkorps*, as *Fl.Fü. Atlantik* had been redesignated on 1 April 1944, tasked ZG 1 to undertake reconnaissance missions looking for signs of the invasion fleet. At the same time, the crews began practising low-level flying (much to the annoyance of the local populace, as one *Bordfunker* remembers) in preparation for attacks on both Allied shipping and ground targets. When the invasion came on 6 June 1944 it came as no surprise to the aircrew of ZG 1 when, later in the day, they were thrown into action:

Unteroffizier Aegidius Berzborn

The days before the invasion began, there had been permanent air attacks on our bases so that we were often forced to move to other airfields. Then came the 'Longest Day' – the Invasion. I do not remember how many missions we flew to the Orne Estuary, and for these missions our planes had been carrying bombs under the wings. Our losses during these attacks on the Allied bridgeheads were enormous. I had seen how my comrades were butchered. These combats were so cruel and the enemy's air superiority was overwhelming.

During the first day's actions, four Ju 88s were shot down and possibly a fifth managed to crash-land behind German lines. The following day was no better when six crews were lost and a further two aircraft were shot down by Allied fighters – because of Allied air superiority, it was rapidly becoming a slaughter. Losses on 7 June included *Oblt* Ulrich Hanshen, the *Gruppen Adjutant* of III/ZG 1, and *Lt* Kurt Löw, the *Staffel Kapitän* of 7/ZG 1 – both were experienced pilots and the loss of such men heralded the death knell of ZG 1.

Oblt Martin Reuter (right), *St Kap* of 7/ZG 1, with (left to right) *Lts* Kurt Löw and Robert Baumann. *Gutermann*

To prevent discovery by Allied aircraft, a I/ZG1 Ju 88 tries to blend in. *Ernst*

On 8 June ZG 1 was being forced to move from Lorient to Nantes following yet another Allied air attack on the airfield. The next mission was scheduled for just after dawn on the 9th:

Unteroffizier Gerhard Zimmermann

On 9 June we took off at 0428 hours for a low-level attack with bombs and guns against the British bridgehead near Caen. Although suffering from a very bad cold, *Lt* Gmelin flew this mission. Our attack strength that day was 15 aircraft, and because 1 *Staffel* had Ju 88 R-2s, we flew behind the formation.

Because of a compass error, we crossed the coast too far east near Bouville. Then we flew very low along the coast to the west, climbing up to 100 metres over the Orne Estuary, flying under a layer of cloud. It was then that we saw the first Allied fighters. These were three Mustangs but they obviously didn't see us. When we reached the Orne, we received heavy defensive fire from the light British four-barrelled flak guns. Well, I didn't get worked up easily, but at that time I did not think I would be coming home again.

We dropped our retarded incendiary bombs and attacked several flak positions with our guns, flying very low. It had lasted only a short time when *Lt* Gmelin said, 'I am wounded! I have to make an emergency landing!' He turned and prepared the landing. *Uffz* Dunker threw off the canopy roof but then *Lt* Gmelin lost consciousness and he didn't succeed in making a good emergency landing – we crashed into a wood near our front line. Because of the crash I was thrown out of the plane, but at once I ran back.. The plane's left wing had been torn off, the cockpit broken and shifted. I managed to free our *Beobachter* who had been caught in the canopy and together we took our unconscious pilot to the wing and began to dress his wounds. A .50 calibre bullet was in his hip, and even though there was not much blood it was obvious that he was bleeding internally. A short time later he regained consciousness and sent *Uffz* Dunker for help.

Below and overleaf: One of the June casualties – a III/ZG 1 Ju 88 after crash-landing behind German lines. *Ernst*

The Ju 88 in
which *Lt* Knud
Gmelin met his
death – *Werk
Nummer* 750897.
Gmelin

In the meantime, the British artillery was shelling our lines. We saw the shell bursts and thought that our own artillery was shelling the Allied bridgehead, so *Uffz* Dunker went the wrong way. Hardly had he left when we were machine-gunned by a German tank – even today, I am surprised that we were not hit. I dragged *Lt* Gmelin into a ditch and also took cover. As a result of this, two German soldiers came and together we carried *Lt* Gmelin back on a strip of canvas. Soon he lost consciousness again and by the time we crossed the German lines it was too late.

Everything had lasted just half an hour. The crash happened at 0615 hours at Epron, north of Caen. At 0655 hours it was over – he was unconscious for his last 15 minutes. He did not think that he was going to die – quite the opposite – he was convinced he would be saved. Although I knew the seriousness of his wounds, I could not believe it when the doctor told me that he was dead.

Later we went to the central dressing station south of Caen where he was buried that evening in the grounds of Château Lourigny. Some wild flowers were put on his grave and there was a simple cross in the shape of an *Eiserne Kreuz*. As he was being buried, 'Tommy' shelled a nearby village with naval artillery – it was as if they were shooting three blank rounds over his grave.

Only one other Ju 88 was lost and another seriously damaged during this attack, one of the losses being an experienced crew from the *Ergänzungsgruppe*/ZG 1. The following day, a further two Ju 88s were lost on what would be the last mission of ZG 1 over the beachhead; two days later, the survivors flew south to Cazeaux:

Unteroffizier Aegidius Berzborn

The combats had been so cruel and the enemy's superiority so overwhelming that we were pulled out of action after a few days, having suffered about 75% losses.

Apart from the occasional sortie escorting Ju 290s over the south of the Bay, by the end of June 1944 there was no longer a job for the day elements of ZG 1 to do. It was thought, however, that there was still a job for the night fighters of *9(Nacht)*/ZG 1, but even they were not immune to Allied aircraft:

Flight Lieutenant Jeremy Howard-Williams

We took off from Manston in a Mosquito Mark XII of the Fighter Interception Unit at 0055 hours on the morning of 28 June 1944 to patrol Orleans/Bricy and Chateaudun airfields. We arrived at Orleans at 0211 hours after having been delayed by following a contact on what turned out to be a Liberator. The Orleans airfield perimeter lights were on, but apart from seeing a beacon flashing 'BC' 10 miles to the north-west of the airfield, we flew on to Chateaudun where we obtained a contact on an aircraft flying west. We climbed from 2,000 feet to 4,000 feet and closed in on target, which was identified, without doubt, as a Ju 88. I increased range to 200 yards, pulled up dead astern and fired a 2-second burst, aiming at the port wing root. A large flash and many strikes were observed and the enemy aircraft lurched to port but continued to fly straight and level. A further 2-second burst was fired at the starboard engine and a large flash and pieces coming off were noticed. Enemy aircraft then went into a slight climb and, as it still refused to burn, a further 2-second burst was fired at the port engine. The enemy aircraft then burst into flames and pulled sharply up and stalled off to port into the ground, where it burned fiercely.

Flt Lt Jeremy Howard-Williams (second from right) and his navigator, Fg Off 'Jock' Macrae (third from left), were the last Allied aircrew to shoot down a Ju 88 from ZG 1. *Mrs Howard-Williams*

The Ju 88 C-6 in which *Uffz* Migge and his crew met their deaths on 28 June 1944.
Ernst

Jeremy Howard-Williams's kill was a Ju 88 C-6 of *9(Nacht)*/ZG 1
and resulted in the deaths of *Uffz* Werner Migge and his crew. It was
to be the final loss for the Ju 88s of ZG 1, as in the days that
followed all the crews were posted away to other units and
eventually, on 5 August 1944, after having flown no further
operational sorties, I and III/ZG 1 were disbanded.

Epilogue

The war did not end there for the survivors of ZG 1. Depending on flying ability and whether they had ended up flying day or night missions, crews were posted to either single-seat day fighters or night fighters.

For 9(*Nacht*)/ZG 1 the transition was easy and they became I/NJG 4 on 10 July 1944, while some of the pilots from the other *Staffeln* were posted to other *Nachtjagdgeschwaden*. For example, *Fw* Heinz Hommel, after receiving training as a night fighter pilot, would end the war flying with 7/NJG 2, while *Oblt* Willi Deuper was posted to (and later killed in action with) *Stab* IV/NJG 6. Such pilots as these were, in the main, the luckier ones.

The majority of pilots went to form II (*Sturm*)/JG 4 to fly the FW 190, and by January 1945 eight former ZG 1 pilots have been traced as being killed in action with this unit, including *Deutsche Kreuz in Gold-*

Above: Aircrew of 13/KG 40. Left to right, they are *Uffz* Martin Schroeder, unknown, *Uffz* Rudolf Lucht, *Uffz* Walter Schedle, *Uffz* Heinz Hommel, *Uffz* Karl Brambora, unknown, *Uffz* Hans-Dieter Koch, unknown, *Uffz* Hans Andreas, *Uffz* Walter Bach, *Uffz* Hans Becker (killed on 8 March 1944), unknown, *Uffz* Ernst Goetz, and *Uffz* Gerhard Zimmerman. *Hommel*

A Ju 88 C-6 of 14/KG 40. *Gmelin*

holder *Ofw* Fritz Mündlein; countless others were shot down, wounded. The more able pilots went to executive posts within other existing *Jagdgeschwaden*. Of the four surviving V/KG 40 and I/ZG 1 *Deutsche Kreuz in Gold*-holders, three were converted to single-seat fighters and were dead within three months. *Hptm* Hans Morr lasted just four days as *Gruppen Kommandeur* of IV/JG 53, while *Oblt* Dieter Meister lasted a little longer – just over two months as *Staffel Kapitän* of 10/JG 2 – before he too was shot down and killed, having flown a total of more than of 200 operational missions. The third, *Oblt* Albrecht Bellstedt, was killed as *Staffel Kapitän* of 9/JG 2 on 21 October 1944. It is therefore not surprising that very few survivors are still alive today, and the history of V/KG 40 has become lost in the mists of time.

Lt Friedrich Maeder looks out over what would become his grave – the Bay of Biscay.

With the benefit of hindsight, more than 50 years since the unit was disbanded, did V/KG 40, and latterly I and III/ZG 1, play a major part in both the Battle for the Atlantic and its associated air war? I now believe that the answer must be yes. Initially the Ju 88 C-6 was ideally suited in its role, inflicting a heavy toll on Allied aircraft. For example, in their two-year existence C-6s shot down 109 Allied planes, the majority of which were engaged in anti-submarine operations. Accordingly, the Allies had no alternative but to divert other aircraft to counter this 'Junkers Menace', particularly RAF night fighters, which could have been better employed shooting down German bombers attacking Britain. Therefore I think it can safely be said that they did succeed in both making an impact on the air and submarine war in the Atlantic and, indirectly, had a passing impact on other war zones.

From a German viewpoint, was the effort and bloodshed all worthwhile? First of all, the Ju 88 C-6 was initially suited to its role of maritime reconnaissance and long-range fighter, but when confronted by RAF Beaufighters and the far superior Mosquito the Germans had no alternative but to either increase formation sizes, retreat or try and fight it out. Thus missions had to be planned to take this into consideration, and as a result the effectiveness of the unit began to decrease from the summer of 1943 onwards, by which time the Allies had got the upper hand in the U-boat war. The decision to then throw the Ju 88 C-6 and R-2 into the air battle over the invasion beaches in

Fw Paul Gruner in a Ju 88 H-1 of 3/123 tries to get away from Mosquitoes of 248 Squadron on 31 July 1944. *Scott*

Like so many other German aircraft and their crews, this is all that marks the death of Gruner and his crew. *Blanchard*

Normandy was nothing more than murder, and to then convert pilots, most of whom were originally bomber and reconnaissance trained, to single-seat fighters and pit them against far superior Allied aircraft was criminal. But at that stage of the war, did the *Luftwaffe* have much of an alternative? The answer is probably no.

Therefore the answer was that the effort was worthwhile up to the summer of 1943, but at a terrible cost. At least 222 personnel died in action flying the Ju 88, 58 were killed in accidents, seven were taken prisoner and 51 suffered wounds or injuries of varying degrees. Little did I think nearly 30 years ago that, while I was enjoying the sunshine and playing on the beaches near Bordeaux, many airmen of many nationalities had fought and died off those French beaches. For most of those who died, many in their early twenties, their remains lay, as they do today, within the wreckage of their aircraft somewhere at the bottom of the Bay of Biscay – bloody Biscay.

Bibliography

Published sources

Bishop, Clifford, *Fortresses of the Big Triangle First*, Bishops Stortford, 1986

Dierich, Wolfgang, *Die Verbände der Luftwaffe, 1935-45*, Stuttgart, 1976

Filley, Brian, *Junkers Ju88 in Action, Part 2*, Caroltown, Texas, 1991

Franks, Norman, *Conflict Over the Bay*, London, 1986
   Search, Find & Kill, London, 1995

Hendrie, Andrew, *Short Sunderland*, Shrewsbury, 1994

Hummelchen, Gerhard, *Der Fliegerführer Atlantik*, Herford, 1972

Kaufmann, Johannes, *Flugbericht, 1939-45*, Schwabischhall, 1989

Neitzel, Soenke, *Der Einsatz der Deutschen Luftwaffe uber dem Atlantik und der Nordsee, 1939–45*, Bonn, 1995

Richards, Dennis, and Saunders, Hilary St John, *Royal Air Force, 1939–45, Vols I–III*, London, 1972

Scherzer, Viet, *Die Träger des Deutschen Kreuz in God der Luftwaffe, 1941-45*, Bayreuth, 1992

Schoenfeld, Max, *Stalking the U-Boat*, Shrewsbury, 1995

Documentary sources

Air Historical Branch, London (various)

Bundesarchiv-Zentralnachweisstelle, Aachen (various)

Bundesarchiv/Militarchiv, Freiburg (various)

Bundesarchiv/Bildarchiv, Koblenz

Deutsches Dienststelle (WASt), Berlin (various)

Deutsches Schiffahrtsmuseum, Bremerhaven

D.(Luft) T.2088 C-6 Teil 12A/Ju88 C-6 Flugzeug Handbuch

Einzelmeldung der Luftflotte 3 (various)

Imperial War Museum, London (Oberbefehlshaber der Luftwaffe Genst. Gen. Qu./Abt/40.g.Kdos IC)

Kriegstagebuch der Seekriegsleitung

Public Records Office (various)

US Air Force Historical Research, Maxwell AFB (Operational records of 479th Anti-Submarine Group)

US Navy Historical Research Centre, Washington (Operational records of Fleet Air Wing 7 and associated combat units)

Appendix A

Gruppen Kommandeure, Staffel Kapitän and Executive Officers of V Gruppe/Kampfgeschwader 40 and I and III Gruppen/Zerstörergeschwader 1, July 1924-August 1944

V/KG 40: I/ZG 1

Gr Kdr	*Hptm* Gerd KORTHALS	1/7/42-3/11/42 +
	Hptm Helmut DARGEL	12/11/42-30/12/42 +
	Hptm/Maj Alfred HEMM	1/7/42-13/11/42
	(deputy): Mar – Sep 43	
	Hptm Horst GRAHL	10/10/43-5/8/44
Gr Adj	*Oblt* Siegfried RAMSAUER	15/2/43-15/11/43
	Lt Lothar WOLFF	15/2/44-15/6/44
Gr Ia	*Hptm* Horst GRAHL	27/5/43-10/43
	Oblt Kurt NECESANY	8/11/43-14/2/44 +
Dep Gr Adj	*Lt* Lothar WOLFF	
	Oblt Gustav CHRISTENER	-7/10/43 +
Gr NO	*Oblt* Ernst-Heinrich SCHICKEDANZ	
Gr TO	*Hptm* STEFFEN	
	Oblt Siegfried RAMSAUER	Apr-Aug 44
Maj Beim Stab	*Maj* SINNING	
13/KG 40	*Hptm* Carlhanns WEYMAR	22/7/42 +*
1/ZG 1	*Hptm* Paul HEIDE	20/8/42-9/9/42 +
	Hptm Georg ESCH	-24/3/43 +
	Oblt Hermann HORSTMANN	-12/12/43 +
	Hptm Günther MOLTRECHT	15/1/44-11/4/44 +
	Lt Knud GMELIN	*St Fhr*-9/6/44 +
14/KG 40	*Hptm* Hans William REICKE	9/42-30/1/43 +
2/ZG 1	*Oblt* Kurt NECESANY	7/2/43-7/11/43 (to *Gr Ia*)
	Oblt Albrecht BELLSTEDT	8/11/43-5/8/44 (21/10/44 + as *St Kap 9/JG 2*)
15/KG 40	*Hptm* Hans MORR	12/9/42-Summer 43 (to *7/ZG 1*)
3/ZG 1	*Oblt* Hans SCHUSTER	-20/11/43 +
	Lt Alfred KLAUS (Deputy)	
	Oblt Dieter MEISTER	1/44-5/8/44 (21/11/44 + as *St Kap 10/JG 2*)

III/ZG 1

Gr Kdr	*Hptm* Hans MORR	7/3/44-5/8/44 (29/10/44 + as *Gr Kdr IV/JG 53*)
Gr Adj	*Lt/Oblt* Ulrich HANSHEN	4/2/44-7/6/44 +
Gr TO	*Lt* Artur EWERT	
Gr Ia	*Oblt* SCHMIDT	
7/ZG 1	*Hptm* Hans MORR	late 1943-6/3/44 (to *Gr Kdr III/ZG 1*)
	Oblt Martin REUTER	7/3/44-20/4/44 +
	Lt Kurt LÖW	*St Fhr*-7/6/44 +
8/ZG 1	*Hptm* Heinz SCHOCKER	(11/9/44 + with *11/JG 4*)
9(NJ) St **	*Hptm* Fritz KUNKEL	11/43–10/7/44

+ Killed

* Possibly the first *St Kap* but was still on the strength of *Zerstörer Kommando/KG 6* at the time of his death.

** Formed from *Kommando Kunkel* 26 June 1944; renamed *1/NJG 4* on 10 July 1944.

Appendix B

Aircrew identified as having flown with V *Gruppe/Kampfgeschwader* 40 and I and III *Gruppen/Zerstörergeschwader* 1, July 1942–August 1944

Surname	Name	Rank	Role	Crew	Unit	+	Date	Notes
Altenhöner	Herbert	*Uffz*	FF		3/ZG 1	+	13-03-44	
Andreas	Heinz	*Fw*	BF		13/KG 40; 1/ZG 1		?	
Andrians	Wilhelm	*Fw*	FF		14/KG 40	+	22-02-43	
Angermayr	Erich	*Lt*	FF		ErgSt/ZG 1	+	02-05-44	
Apel	Friedrich	*Lt*	FF		15/KG 40	+	23-03-43	
Bach	Walter	*Uffz*	BO	Klose crew	13/KG 40		survived	?
Baldeweg	Heinz	*Fw*	FF		3ZG 1		?	
Barion	Karl-Heinz	*Uffz*	*FF*		*13/KG 40*			
Bart	Heinrich	*Ogefr*	BF	Lausser crew	I/ZG 1	+	23-11-43	
Barthelmes	Walter	*Fw*	BF	Reicke crew	14/KG 40	+	30-01-43	
Bartling	Heinrich	*Uffz*	BO	Schuster crew	III/ZG 1	+	20-11-43	
Bartsch	Dietrich	*Lt*	FF		III/ZG 1	+	09-02-45	12/JG 54
Bass	Karl	*Uffz*	FF		III/ZG 1	+	?	
Bauer	Karl	*Fw*	FF		7/ZG 1	+	10-03-44	
Baumann	Karl	*Uffz*	BF	Hensgen crew	15/KG 40	+	17-05-43	
Baumann	Robert	*Lt*	FF		15/KG 40; 3 & 7/ZG 1		POW 01-02-44	
Baumer	Herbert	*Ogefr*	BO	Maeder crew	13/KG 40; 1/ZG 1	+	12-12-43	
Baumrucker	Ernst		FF		I/ZG 1			-JG 4
Becker	Hans	*Uffz*	BO	Podzimek crew	I/ZG 1	+	08-03-44	
Bellstedt	Albrecht	*Oblt*	FF, *St Kap*		14/KG 40; 2/ZG 1	+	21-10-44	-*St Kap* 9/JG 2
Benz	Phillipp	*Uffz*	BO	Neumann crew	15/KG 40	+	15-05-43	

Surname	First name	Rank		Crew	Unit		Date	
Berger	Walter	*Lt*	FF	Knapp crew	13/KG 40	+	01-11-42	
Bergs	Franz	*Fw*	BO	Paschoff crew	V/KG 40	W	29-11-42	
Bernhard	Norbert	*Ogefr*	BF	Kelle crew	15/KG 40	+	29-01-43	
Berns	Kurt	*Uffz*	BF		7/ZG 1	+	20-04-44	
Bersch	Hans	*Ogefr*	BF	Ludwig crew	15/KG 40	+	07-09-43	
Berchthold	Willy	*Uffz*	BF	Dettmer crew	15/KG 40	+	09-02-43	
Berzborn	Aegidius	*Uffz*	BF	Dickel crew	13/KG 40, 1/ZG 1		survived	-11/ZG 26
Besdziek	Horst	*Uffz*	FF		7/ZG 1	+	20-04-44	
Beyer	Wilhelm	*Ogefr*	BF	Forell crew	1/ZG 1	+	11-04-44	
Bichler	Heinz	*Lt*	FF		10/ZG 1	+	14-02-44	
Bilger	Alfred	*Ogefr*	BO	Paschoff crew	15/KG 40	+	29-01-43	
Bindzus	Erich	*Ofw*	FF		I/ZG 1	+	23-11-43	
Bittner	Josef	*Uffz*	BO	Pütz crew	7/ZG 1	+	07-01-44	
Blach	Georg	*Ogefr*	BF	Baldeweg crew	3/ZG 1	+	26-02-44	
Blam	Willi	*Gefr*	BO	Mühlbauer crew	V/KG 40	W	03-01-43	
Blankenberg	Gerhard	*Lt*	FF		13 & 15/KG 40	+	04-09-43	
Blume	August	*Uffz*	BF	Klose crew	13/KG 40; 1/ZG 1		survived	
Blumenröther	Friedrich	*Uffz*	BF	Reuter crew	7/ZG 1	+	20-04-44	
Bogdan		*Uffz*	FF		2/ZG 1		?	
Boldt	Walter	*Ogefr*	BO	Baumann crew	15/KG 40	W(+)	03-01-43	
Boldt	Willi	*Ofw*	BO	Reichelmann crew	2/ZG 1	+	11-04-44	
Bongers	Ernst	*Uffz*	BF	Döhler crew	3/ZG 1	+	07-03-44	
Bonn	Otto	*Ofw*	BO	Hanshen crew	14/KG 40	W	23-08-43	
Boseker	Paul	*Ogefr*	BF	Schneidewind crew	V/KG 40	+	05-06-43	
Brambora	Karl	*Uffz*	BF	Meister crew	13 & 14/KG 40		survived	
Bromel	Günther	*Uffz*	BF	Schwarz crew	3/ZG 1	+	20-04-44	
Bruchling		*Lt*			I/ZG 1		?	
Budde	Hermann	*Gefr*	BO	Gehre crew	3/ZG 1	W	13-03-44	
Bücken	Erwin	*Uffz*	BF	Besdziek crew	7/ZG 1	+	20-04-44	

Surname	First name	Rank	Role	Crew	Unit	Date	Fate	Note
Bückinger	Hermann	*Ogefr*	BM	Schneidewind crew	V/KG 40	05-06-43	+	
Bückle	Wilhelm	*Uffz*	BF	Linden crew	15/KG 40	25-09-43	+	
Buxbaum	Wilhelm	*Fw*	BO	Baldeweg crew	3/ZG 1	26-02-44	+	
Chlond	Herbert	*Uffz*	FF		2/ZG 1	06-06-44	W	-5/JG 4
Chraust	Alois				13/KG 40; 1/ZG 1	?		
Christner	Gustav	*Oblt*	FF		14/KG 40	07-10-43	+	
Clemens	Lothar	*Fw*	BF	Necesany crew	2/ZG 1	14-02-44	+	
Cox	Hans	*Flg*	BO	Engeln crew	7/ZG 1	10-06-44	POW	
Dargel	Helmut	*Hptm*	FF*Gr Kdr*		Stab V/KG 40	30-12-42	+	
Derr	Waldemar	*Uffz*	FF		13/KG 40	20-06-43	+	
Dettmer	Heinrich	*Ofw*	FF		15/KG 40	09-02-43	+	
Deuper	Willi	*Oblt*	FF		13 & 10/KG 40	15-02-45	+	
Dickel	Rolf	*Uffz*	FF		13/KG 40; 1/ZG 1	survived		-*Adj* IV/NJG 6
Dietermann	Günther	*Uffz*	BF	Moltrecht crew	1/ZG 1	11-04-44	+	-11/ZG 26
Dietler	Ludwig	*Uffz*	BF	?	2/ZG 1	09-06-44	+	
Dobslaff	Rudi	*Ofw*	BO	Theiss crew	3/ZG 1	07-06-44	W	
Dock	Heinz	*Ogefr*	BO	Frassek crew	15/KG 40	12-07-43	POW	
Döhler	Heinz	*Fw*	FF		3/ZG 1	07-03-44	+	
Doss	Kurt	*Fw*	FF	Esch crew	13/KG 40	16-09-42	W	
Drebing	Albert	*Uffz*	BF		13/KG 40	survived		
Dressler	Erich	*Gefr*	BO	Strobel crew	3/ZG 1	07-06-44	M	
Drewes	Werner	*Ogefr*	BF	Lang crew	8/ZG 1	11-05-44	+	
Drumm	Herbert	*Gefr*	BO	Ludwig crew	15/KG 40	07-09-43	+	
Dürr	Roland	*Ogefr*	BF	Schulz crew	2/ZG 1	03-11-43	W	
Dunker	Wilhelm	*Uffz*	BO	Gmelin crew	1/ZG 1	09-06-44	W	
Ebeling	Werner	*Uffz*	FF		ErgSt/ZG 1	26-08-44	+	-12/JG 4

Surname	First name	Rank	Role	Crew	Unit	Fate	Date	Later unit
Eistert	Gerhard	Ogefr	BS	Wagner crew	13/KG 40	+	08-10-42	
Engeln	Erich	Uffz	FF		7/ZG 1	+	10-06-44	
Eppendahl	Fritz	Uffz		Berger crew	13/KG 40	+	01-11-42	
Erler	Albert	Uffz	FF		2/ZG 1	+	18-12-44	5/JG 4
Ernst	Hans-Georg	Uffz	BO	Gäbler crew	15/KG 40; 9(NJ)/ZG 1		survived	-I/NJG 4
Esch	Georg	Hptm	FF, St Kap		13/KG 40	+	24-03-43	
Ess	Werner	Uffz	BF	Maeder crew	13/KG 40; I/ZG 1	+	12-12-43	
Ewert	Artur	Lt	FF, TO		14/KG 40; 9(NJ)/ZG 1		?	-I/NJG 4
Ewert	Karl-Heinz	Uffz	BO	Leonhardt crew	2/ZG 1	+	23-03-44	
Exner		Uffz	BF	Gutemann crew	14/KG 40		?	
Fehr	Paul	Fhj Fw	FF	Angermayr crew	3/ErgZerstGr ZG 1	+	16-03-44	
Fetterroll	Eduard	Gefr	BF		ErgSt/ZG 1	+	02-05-44	
Feuerberg	Ernst	Ogefr	BF	Neumann crew	2/ZG 1	+	01-12-43	
Fichterer		Lt			13/KG 40		?	
Fiedler	Ernst				13/KG 40; I/ZG 1		?	
Fischer		Uffz			14/KG 40; 2/ZG 1		?	
Fischer	Hermann	Uffz	FF		2/ZG 1	+	30-11-43	
Flothmann	Hermann	Lt	FF		14/KG 40	+	01-11-42	
Forell	Hermann	Uffz	FF		1/ZG 1	+	11-04-44	
Francois	Karl-Hermann		FF		1/ZG 1		?	-/JG 4
Frank	Hans	Uffz	FF	Wittmer crew	13/KG 40; I/ZG 1	+	12-12-43	
Frank	Hugo	Uffz	BF		14/KG 40	+	08-08-43	
Frassek	Georg	Uffz	FF		15/KG 40	POW	12-07-43	
Freiwald	Edmund	Fw	FF		2/ZG 1	M	07-06-44	
Friedlein	Peter			Rakow crew	14/KG 40		?	
Fritz	Franz	Ofw	BF	Korthals crew	Stab V/KG 40	+	03-11-42	
Fritz	Gerhard	Uffz	FF		2/ZG 1	+	11-04-44	

Surname	First name	Rank	Role	Crew	Unit		Date	Notes
Gäbler	Kurt	*Ofw*	FF		15/KG 40; 9(NJ)/ZG 1	W	04-03-45	*-1/NJG 4*
Galuba	Kurt	*Uffz*	BF	Hartmann crew	Stab/ZG 1		survived	
Gärtner		*Uffz*			13/KG 40		?	
Gah	Wilhelm	*Gefr*	BF	Müller crew	14/KG 40	+	07-10-43	
Gall		*Oblt*			13/KG 40		?	
Gargulak	Friedrich	*Uffz*	BO	Döhler crew	3/ZG 1	+	07-03-44	
Gebicke	Rudolf	*Fw*	BF	Freiwald crew	2/ZG 1	M	07-06-44	
Gehre	Heinz	*Ogefr*	FF		3/ZG 1	W	13-03-44	*-5/JG 4*
Geissler	Werner	*Uffz*	BO	Bindzus crew	1/ZG 1	+	23-11-43	
Gerlach		*Uffz*			13/KG 40		?	
Gesenberg	Manfred	*Gefr*	BO	von Heinburg crew	V/KG 40	+	26-11-42	
Giessuebel	Vincenz	*Ofw*	FF		13/KG 40		survived	
Gilfert	Fritz	*Uffz*	FF		3/ZG 1		?	*-12/JG4*
Gmelin	Knud	*Lt*	FF, *Stfhr*		13/KG 40; 1/ZG 1	+	09-06-44	
Göbler	Werner	*Gefr*	BF	Frank crew	1/ZG 1	+	12-12-43	
Götz	Ernst	*Uffz*	BO	Hommel crew	13/KG 40; 1/ZG 1		survived	*-7/NJG 2*
Goganzer	Wilhelm	*Uffz*	BS	Flothmann crew	14/KG 40	+	01-11-42	
Göhler	Rudolf	*Ogefr*	BF	Huber crew	V/KG 40	+	11-09-43	
Goos	Stephan	*Uffz*	BO	Kelle crew	7/ZG 1	M	20-04-44	
Gottwald	Heinrich	*Fw*	BO	Vieback crew	13/KG 40	+	20-05-43	
Grahl	Horst	*Maj*	FF, *Gr Kdr*		Stab V/KG 40 & ZG 1		survived	
Grass	Emmerich	*Uffz*	BF	Passier crew	13/KG 40	+	17-09-42	
Greiner		*Uffz*			1/ZG 1		?	
Grimmer	Ottmar	*Uffz*	BF	Passier crew	13/KG 40	W	17-09-42	
Gröll	Willibald	*Uffz*	BO	Andrians crew	14/KG 40	+	22-02-43	
Grötzinger	Hans	*Uffz*	BO	Moltrecht crew	1/ZG 1	+	11-04-44	
Gründler	Karl	*Fw*	BS	Heide crew	13/KG 40	+	09-09-42	
Gruntz	Hans-Ulrich	*Uffz*	BF	Meier crew	3/ZG 1	+	01-12-43	
Gutermann	Wilhelm	*FF*	FF		14/KG 40; 2/ZG 1		survived	*-St Kap 6/JG 4*
Haarberger	Gerd	*Oblt*	BO	Hintze crew	14/KG 40		?	

Surname	First name	Rank	Role	Crew	Unit	Fate	Date	Notes
Haas	Erich	*Uffz*	BF	Leonhardt crew	2/ZG 1	+	23-03-44	
Hadatschek	Rudolf	*Uffz*	BF	Stohl crew	2/ZG 1	+	01-12-43	
Hänel	Fritz	*Uffz*	FF		3/ZG 1; 2/ZG1	+	09-06-44	
Hanshen	Ulrich	*Oblt*	FF, *Adj*		15/KG 40; Stab III/ZG 1	M	07-06-44	
Harms	Ernst	*Uffz*	FF		13/KG 40	+	24-09-42	
Hartmann	Wilhelm	*Oblt*	FF		Stab/ZG 1		survived	
Hass	Günther	*Lt*	FF		V/KG 40	+	18-04-43	
Haugh		*Uffz*	BF	Wolff crew	15/KG 40		?	
Hegele	Leo	*Uffz*	BO	Klose crew	13/KG 40; I/ZG 1		?	
Hegemann	Hermann	*Uffz*	BF	Schlegel crew	7/ZG 1	+	01-02-44	
Heicke	Jürgen	*Uffz*	FF		13/KG 40	+	21-09-43	
Heide	Paul	*Hptm*	FF, *St Kap*		13/KG 40	+	09-09-42	
Hein	Friedrich	*Ogefr*	BO	Kriedel crew	V/KG 40	+	29-01-43	
von Heinburg	Arno	*Lt*	FF		V/KG 40	+	26-11-42	
Heinze	Helmuth	*Uffz*	BF	Frassek crew	15/KG 40	POW	12-07-43	
Held	Willi	*Fw*	BO	Baumann crew	13 & 15/KG 40; 7/ZG 1	+	01-02-44	-III/KG 40
Hemm	Alfred	*Maj*	FF, *Gr Kdr*		Stab V/KG 40		?	
Henke	Christian	*Gefr*	BF	Harms crew	13/KG 40	+	24-09-42	
Henrichs	Bernhard	*Ofw*	BO	Blankenberg crew	13/KG 40	+	04-09-43	
Hensgen	Werner	*Lt*	FF		15/KG 40	+	17-05-43	
Hermes	Kurt	*Gefr*	BO	Angermayr crew	ErgSt/ZG 1	+	02-05-44	
Hermann	Walter	*Uffz*	FF		2/ZG 1	M	06-06-44	
Hermann	Werner	*Uffz*	BF	Horvath & Hanshen crews	1/ZG 1	W	11-04-44	
Herzog			FF		Stab III/ZG 1 1/ZG 1	M	07-06-44	
Hess	Edwin	*Gefr*	BO	Reichelmann crew	2/ZG 1	W	05-04-44	
Heuer	Georg	*Ofw*	FF		14/KG 40	+	30-01-43	
Heym	Klaus		FF		1/ZG 1	+	08-08-44	-JG 4
Heymann	Heinrich	*Uffz*	BF	Röder crew	2/ZG 1	M	07-06-44	

Surname	First name	Rank	Role	Crew	Unit	Symbol	Date	Note
Hiebsch	Fritz	Fw	FF		15/KG 40	+	11-06-43	
Hiesinger	Alfons	Uffz	BF		3/ZG 1	W	11-04-44	
Hildebrand	W.		BF	Sprang crew	14/KG 40; ErgSt/ZG 1		?	
Hillenbrand	Otto	Uffz	BS	Mündlein crew	2/ZG 1	+	08-03-44	
Hintze	Herbert	Oblt	FF	Rauschke crew	14/KG 40; 2/ZG 1		survived	
Hinz		Flg			10/ZG 1		?	
Hissbach	Heinz-Horst	Hptm	FF		14 & 15/KG 40	+	14-04-45	-Gr Kdr II/NJG 2
Hobusch	Heinz	Gefr	BF	Itzigehl crew	13/KG 40	+	30-08-43	
von Hoensbroech	Wolfgang Graf	Lt	FF		13/KG 40	+	08-09-42	
Hoffmann	Werner	Uffz	BO	Thies crew	14/KG 40	+	22-03-43	
Hoffmann	Peter	Uffz	BO	Hiebsch crew	15/KG 40	+	11-06-43	
Hofrichter	Walter	Ogefr	BO	Heuer crew	14/KG 40	+	30-01-43	
Hollerith	Josef	Fw	FF		7/ZG 1	+	07-06-44	
Holstein		Ogefr		Sukowski crew	10/KG 40		?	
Homm	Anton	Ofw	BF	Mlodoch crew	13/KG 40, 1/ZG 1	+	02-09-42	
Hommel	Heinz	Uffz	FF		13/KG 40; 1/ZG 1		survived	-7/NJG 2
Horstmann	Hermann	Oblt	FF, St Kap		14 & 13/KG 40,1/ZG 1	+	12-12-43	
Horvath	Josef	Uffz	FF		1/ZG 1	+	11-04-44	
Hössel	Alfred	Ogefr	BS	Steurich crew	14/KG 40	+	22-03-43	
Huber	Franz	Uffz	FF		V/KG 40	+	11-09-43	
Isslinger	Franz	Oblt	FF		15/KG 40	+	09-02-43	
Itzigehl	Ernst	Uffz	FF		13/KG 40	+	30-08-43	
von Janson	Lothar	Obstlt	FF, Kdre		Stab/ZG 1	+	10-03-44	
Jarmer	Herbert	Lt	FF		10/ZG 1	+	11-02-44	
Jöckel	Hans	Gefr	FF		9.(NJ)/ZG 1	M	17-04-44	
Johenneken	Rolf	Uffz	BO	Dickel, Frank & Klose crews	13/KG 40; 1/ZG 1		survived	-11/ZG 26

Surname	First name	Rank	Position	Crew	Unit		Date	Notes
Jugnischke	Herbert	*Uffz*	BF	Baumann crew	7/ZG 1	+	01-02-44	
Jung	Georg	*Gefr*	BS		13/KG 40	W	27-09-42	
Kabiall	Erwin	*Uffz*	FF		2/ZG 1	+	11-09-44	5/JG 4
Kablitz		*Ogefr*	BM		2/ZG 1		?	
Kallenbach	Willi	*Ogefr*	BO	Schlatter crew	V/KG 40	+	27-02-43	
Kaltenbrunner	Johann	*Uffz*	FF		13/KG 40	+	05-10-42	
Kasch	Richard	*Fw*	Bf	Hintze crew	14/KG 40; 2/ZG 1		?	
Kaudelka	Günther		FF		1/ZG 1		?	
Kaufmann	Hans				13/KG 40		?	
Kaufmann	Johannes	*Hptm*	FF, *St Kap*		10/KG 40; ErgSt/ZG 1		survived	-*St Kap* 9/JG 4
Kelle	Walter	*Uffz*	FF		7/ZG 1	M	20-04-44	
Keller	Erich	*Uffz*	FF		2/ZG 1	+	01-01-45	-5/JG 4
Kessel	Günter	*Gefr*	BF	Jöckel crew	9.(NJ)/ZG 1	M	17-04-44	
Klaus	Alfred	*Oblt*	FF		15/KG 40; 3/ZG 1		?	
Klein	Hermann	*Uffz*	BF	Gutermann crew	14/KG 40	W	19-06-43	-II/KG 40
Klose	Herbert	*Fw*	FF		13/KG 40; 1/ZG 1		?	
Klöster		*Gefr*			13/KG 40		?	
Knapp	Wilhelm	*Ofw*	FF		V/KG 40; ErgSt/ZG 1	W	29-11-42	
Knefeld	Alfred	*Uffz*	BO	Christner crew	14/KG 40	+	07-10-43	
Koch	Hans-Dieter	*Uffz*	BF	Hommel crew	13/KG 40; 1/ZG 1		survived	
Köhler	Hans Joachim	*Ogefr*	BS	Migge crew	9.(NJ)/ZG 1	+	28-06-44	
König	Günther	*Uffz*	FF		V/KG 40	W	24-07-43	
Körner	Gerhard	*Gefr*	BO	Besdziek crew	7/ZG 1	M	20-04-44	
Kohal	Karl	*Uffz*	BS	Müller crew	14/KG 40	+	07-10-43	
Kommar	Helmut	*Uffz*	BF	Altenhöner crew	3/ZG 1	+	13-03-44	
Korczowy	Rudolf	*Fw*	BO	Horstmann crew	I/ZG 1	+	12-12-43	
Korthals	Gerhard	*Hptm*	FF, *Gr Kdr*		Stab V/KG 40	+	03-11-42	
Kotek	Anton	*Uffz*	BF	Schlatter crew	V/KG 40	+	27-02-43	

Surname	First name	Rank	Role	Crew	Unit	Fate	Date	Notes
Kothmann	Bernhard	*Uffz*	BF	Schülli crew	14/KG 40	+	07-10-43	
Kraml	Othmar	*Uffz*	BF	Keller crew	2/ZG 1	W	06-06-44	
Kramer	Erhard	*Lt*	FF		14/KG 40	+	25-09-43	
Kriedel	Johannes	*Ofw*	FF		V/KG 40	+	29-01-43	
Kubutat	Heinrich				13/KG 40		?	
Kuhlmann	Josef	*Uffz*	BF	Vieback crew	13/KG 40	+	20-05-43	
Kuhn					ErgSt/ZG 1		?	
Kuhnert	Hubert	*Uffz*	BO	Forell crew	I/ZG 1	+	11-04-44	
Kunkel	Fritz	*Hptm*	FF, *St Kap*		9.(NJ)/ZG 1		survived	-1/NJG 4
Kuntz	Georg	*Ofw*		Morr crew?	15/KG 40		?	
Kunz	Georg	*Fw*	BF	Horstmann crew	I/ZG 1	+	12-12-43	
Kurschatke	Georg	*Uffz*	BO	Wittmer crew	14/KG 40	+	08-08-43	
Lamla	Erwin	*Gefr*	BO	Schmidberger crew	9.(NJ)/ZG 1	+	10-06-44	
Landhoff	Wilfried	*Gefr*	BF	Vetter crew	2/ZG 1	+	01-12-43	
Lang	Heinrich	*Uffz*	FF		8/ZG 1	+	11-05-44	
Lausser	Otto	*Fw*	FF		I/ZG 1	+	23-11-43	
Lengemann	Heinz	*Uffz*	BF	Serke crew	15/KG 40	+	30-12-42	
Lechner	Johann	*Uffz*	BF	Hollerith crew	7/ZG 1	+	07-06-44	
Lengfeld	Wilhelm	*Uffz*	BO	Sprang crew	3/ZG 1	+	11-04-44	
Lentz	Ulrich	*Uffz*	BO	Itzigehl crew	13/KG 40	+	30-08-43	
Lenz	Karl	*Uffz*	BO		V/KG 40	W	08-07-43	
Leonberger	Richard	*Ofw*	FF		ErgSt/ZG 1		survived	
Leonhardt	Rolf	*Uffz*	FF		2/ZG 1	+	23-03-44	
Lepper	Karl	*Uffz*	FF		10/KG 40	+	31-08-43	
Leubner	Edmund	*Fw*	BF	Christner crew	14/KG 40	+	07-10-43	
Licht	Hubert	*Gefr*	BO	Lang crew	8/ZG 1	+	11-05-44	
Liebig	Erich	*Fw*	BF	Knapp crew	V/KG 40	W	29-11-42	
Lienert	Phillipp	*Ofw*	FF		ErgSt/ZG 1		?	

Surname	First name	Rank	Position	Crew	Unit	Fate	Date	Notes
Linden	Kurt	*Stfw*	FF		15/KG 40	+	25-09-43	
Lindner	Rudolf	*Ogefr*	BO		V/KG 40	W	17-05-43	
Löbs		*Fw*			/ZG 1		?	
Löw	Kurt	*Lt*	FF, *StFhr*		15/KG 40; 7/ZG 1	M	07-06-44	
Lollognon		*Ogefr*			13/KG 40		?	
Lübbers	Paul	*Fw*	BF	Müller crew	14/RG 40	+	31-08-43	
Lucht	Rudolf	*Uffz*	BO	Schröder crew	14/KG 40		survived	
Ludwig	Heinz	*Uffz*	FF		15/KG 40	+	07-09-43	
Ludwig	Rudolf	*Uffz*		Kramer crew	13/KG 40	+	25-09-43	
Luttenberger	Eugen	*Uffz*	BO	Freiwald crew	2/ZG 1	M	07-06-44	
Löckenhoff	Friedhelm	*Uffz*	BF	Horstmann crew	13/KG 40		survived	
Maeder	Friedrich	*Lt*	FF		13/KG 40; I/ZG 1	+	12-12-43	
Mahlmeister	Georg	*Fw*	BF		Kdo Kunkel/9/ZG 1	POW	?	I/NJG4
Malik					/ZG1		?	
Martin	Rudolf	*Gefr*	BS	Fischer crew	2/ZG 1	+	30-11-43	
Masmeier	Heinz	*Uffz*	BF	Schmidberger crew	9(NJ)/ZG 1	+	10-06-44	
Mathaei	Josef	*Ogefr*	BO	Derr crew	13/KG 40	+	20-06-43	
Matzke	Günther	*Uffz*	BO	Dickel crew	I/ZG 1		?	
May		*Uffz*			13/KG 40		?	
Meyer	Wilhelm	*Uffz*	BF	Neumann crew	15/KG 40	+	15-05-43	
Mayerhofen	Fritz	*Ofw*	BF	Esch crew	13/KG 40	+	24-03-43	
Meier	Anton	*Uffz*	FF		3/ZG 1	+	01-12-43	
Meinz	Wilhelm	*Uffz*	BS	Neumann crew	2/ZG 1	+	01-12-43	
Meister	Dieter	*Oblt*	FF, *St Kap*		13 & 15/KG 40; 3/ZG 1	+	21-11-44	
Melzer	Hans	*Uffz*	BF	Wolff crew	15/KG 40	W	08-07-43	
Messerschmidt	Helmut	*Lt*	FF		14/KG 40; 2/ZG 1	+	11-04-44	
Metzger					V/KG 40; /ZG 1	?	?	
Michael	Horst	*Ogefr*	BF	Migge crew	9.(NJ)/ZG 1	M	28-06-44	-*St Kap* 10/JG 2

Surname	First name	Rank	Position	Crew	Unit	Fate	Date	Notes
Migge	Werner Horst	Uffz	FF		9.(NJ)/ZG 1	+	28-06-44	
Mlodoch	Hans	Ofw	FF		13/KG 40	+	02-09-42	
Mölder	Eberhard	Uffz	BF	Gehre crew	3/ZG 1	W	13-03-44	
Moller		Gefr	BO	Hommel crew	13/KG 40		?	
Moller	August	Ofw	BO	Stöffler crew	III/KG 40	+	20-07-42	
Mogall					ErgSt/ZG 1		?	
Mohrwinkel	Paul	Uffz	BF	Podzimek crew	I/ZG 1	+	08-03-44	
Moltrecht	Günther	Hptm	FF, St Kap		Stab IV/KG 40 & I/ZG 1	+	11-04-44	
Morr	Hans	Hptm, St Kap, Gr Kdr	FF		15/KG 40; 3,7.& Stab III/ZG 1	+	29-10-44	-Gr Kdr IV/JG 53
Mrechen	Josef	Fw	BF	Bauer crew	7/ZG 1	+	10-03-44	
Mroz	Franz	Gefr	BS	Schlegel crew	7/ZG 1	+	01-02-44	
Mueller	Herbert	Uffz	BO	Ulbricht crew	III/ZG 1		survived	
Mühlbauer	Kurt	Ogefr	FF		V/KG 40	W	03-01-43	
Müller				Kaufmann crew	10/KG 40; ErgSt/ZG 1		?	
Müller	Alfred	Uffz		Kramer crew	13/KG 40	+	25-09-43	
Müller	Heinz	Uffz	BO	Reuter crew	7/ZG 1	+	20-04-44	
Müller	Hermann	Lt	FF		14/KG 40	+	07-10-43	
Müller	Horst	Lt	FF		14/KG 40	+	31-08-43	
Müller	Klaus	Ogefr	BO	Lausser crew	I/ZG 1	+	23-11-43	
Müller	Willi		FF		13/KG 40; 1/ZG 1		?	-/JG 4
Münch	Franz	Ogefr	BO	Runge crew	Z/Kü.Fl.Gr 106	+	20-08-42	
Mündlein	Johannes	Ogefr	BS	Lepper crew	10/KG 40	+	31-08-43	
	Ernst	Ofw	FF		10 & 14/KG 40; ErgSt/ZG 1	+	11-09-44	-9/JG 4
Mützel (Muetzl)		Fw	FF		13/KG 40, 1/ZG 1, 5 JG/4		?	
Namhoff	Hans	Ogefr	BF	Horvath & Mützel crews	1/ZG 1	W	11-04-44	-7/NJG 2

Surname	First name	Rank	Role	Crew	Unit		Date	Note
Necesany	Kurt	Oblt	FF, St Kap, Ia		13 & 14/KG 40; 2/ZG 1; Stab I/ZG 1	+	14-02-44	
Neininger	Georg	Uffz	BO	Huber crew	/KG 40	+	11-09-43	
Nepomucky	Herbert	Fw	BO	Meier crew	3/ZG 1	+	01-12-43	
Neumann	Gerhard	Lt	FF		2/ZG 1	+	01-12-43	
Neumann	Hans	Lt	FF		15/KG 40	+	15-05-43	
Neustadt	Otto	Uffz	BO	Apel crew	15/KG 40	+	23-03-43	
Nicolai	Karl Heinz	Uffz	BO	Müller crew	14/KG 40	+	31-08-43	
Nohe	Werner	Uffz	BF	Berger crew	13/KG 40	+	01-11-42	
Olbrecht	Heinz	Oblt	FF		14 & IV/KG 40		survived	-/JG 4 (?)
Olszowski	Alois	Ofw	BF	Schuster crew	3/ZG 1	+	20-11-43	
Opitz					ErgSt/ZG 1			?
Orte	Ulrich	Gefr	BF	von Hoensbroech crew	13/KG 40	+	08-09-42	
Otto	Herbert	Uffz	BF	Ulbricht crew	III/ZG 1	+		
Oxfort		Lt	FF		7/ZG 1		?	
Paschoff	Paul	Uffz	FF		15/KG 40	+	29-01-43	
Passier	Henny	Fw	FF		13/KG 40	W	17-09-42	
Paul		Uffz			1/ZG 1		?	
Peterburs	Hans	Ofw	FF		10/KG 40; ErgSt/ZG 1		?	
Peters	Karl-Ludwig	Uffz	BF	Leonberger crew	1/ZG 1		?	
Petzold	Wolfgang	Ogefr	BO	Weide crew	V/KG 40	+	09-05-43	
Pflüger	Hermann	Uffz	BS	Stohl crew	2/ZG 1	+	01-12-43	
Pluntke		Lt			10/KG 40		?	
Podzimek	Edgar	Oblt	FF		13/KG 40; 1/ZG 1	+	08-03-44	
Pohl	Gerhard	Ofw		Mlodoch crew	13/KG 40	+	02-09-42	
Pütz	Johann	Fw	FF		7/ZG 1	+	07-01-44	

Purvin	Egon	*Fw*	BF	Theiss crew	3/ZG 1	+	07-06-44	
Quapp	Fritz	*Ofw*	BO	Hanshen crew	15/KG 40; Stab III/ZG 1	M	07-06-44	
Rakow	Hans	*Ofw*	FF		14/KG 40		survived	
Ramp		*Uffz*			13/KG 40		?	
Rams	Lothar	*Gefr*	BF	Herrmann crew	2/ZG 1	+	06-06-44	
Ramsauer	Siegfried	*Oblt*	FF, *Adj*, TO		14/KG 40; Stab V/KG 40 & ZG 1		?	-Stab/5. Jagd-Div
Rankl	Richard	*Uffz*	BF	Andrians crew	14/KG 40	+	22-02-43	
Rathgeber				Morr crew (?)	15/KG 40		?	
Rauer	Helmut	*Uffz*	BS	Vetter crew	2/ZG 1	+	01-12-43	
Rauschke	Gerd	*Uffz*	FF		2/ZG 1	+	08-03-44	
Reichelmann	Hans	*Uffz*	FF		2/ZG 1	+	11-04-44	
Reicke	Hans-William	*Hptm*	FF, *St Kap*		14/KG 40	+	30-01-43	
Reinl	Karl	*Gefr*	BS	König crew	V/KG 40	W	24-07-43	
Reuter	Martin	*Oblt*	FF, *St Kap*		7/ZG 1	+	20-04-44	
Reuter		*Uffz*			I/ZG 1		?	
Richter	Albert	*Fw*	BF	König crew	V/KG 40		24-07-43	
Richter	Georg	*Uffz*	BF	Dargel crew	Stab V/KG 40	+	30-12-42	
Richter	Hans	*Uffz*	BO	Heicke crew	13/KG 40	+	21-09-43	
Rieger	Helmut	*Ogefr* BO		Hollerith crew	7/ZG 1	+	07-06-44	
Riess					ErgSt/ZG 1		?	
Riske					ErgSt/ZG 1		?	
Rodert	Ludwig	*Uffz*	BF	von Weymar crew	Z.St/KG 6	+	22-07-42	
Röder	Hans	*Uffz*	FF		2/ZG 1	M	07-06-44	
Röger	Wolfgang				13/Kg 40		?	
Rönsch	Heinrich	*Uffz*	BF	Rauschke crew	2/ZG 1	+	08-03-44	
Rüger	Werner	*Fw*	BO	Necesany crew	2/ZG 1	+	14-02-44	

Runge	Adolf		FF		Z/Kü.Fl.Gr. 106	+	20-08-42	
Sandermeier	Fritz	*Gefr*	BF	Keller crew	2/ZG 1	W	06-06-44	
Sauer		*Gefr*	BF		13/KG 40		?	
Sause	Paul	*Fw*	BF	Thies crew	14/KG 40	+	22-03-43	
Schadow	Wilhelm	*Uffz*	BF	Wagner crew	13/KG 40	+	08-10-42	
Schedle	Walter	*Uffz*	BF	Schröder crew	14/KG 40		survived	
Schickedanz	Ernst-Heinrich	*Oblt*	NO		Stab V/KG 40		?	
Schillings	Hans				13/KG 40		?	
Schirmacher	Lothar	*Gefr*	BO	Röder crew	2/ZG 1	M	07-06-44	
Schlatter	Karl	*Uffz*	FF		/KG 40	+	27-02-43	
Schlegel	Helfried	*Uffz*	FF		7/ZG 1	+	01-02-44	
Schlüter	Wilfried	*Uffz*	FF		10/KG 40	+	31-08-43	
Schmatz	Hermann	*Uffz*	BO	Ewert crew	9(NJ)/ZG 1		?	-/NJG 4
Schmidberger	Xaver	*Uffz*	FF		9(NJ)/ZG 1	+	10-06-44	
Schmidt		*Oblt*	FF		10/KG 40		?	Stab III/ZG 1
von der Schmidt	Ernst	*Uffz*	FF	1/ZG 1		?		
Schmidt	Karl	*Uffz*	BO	Schwartz crew	2/ZG 1	+	06-06-44	
Schneider	Walter	*Uffz*	BF	Strobel crew	3/ZG 1	M	07-06-44	
Schneidewind	Helmuth	*Uffz*	FF		/KG 40	+	05-06-43	
Schocker	Heinz	*Hptm*	FF, *St Kap*		8/ZG 1	+	11-09-44	-*St Kap* II/JG 4
Scholdei	Heinz	*Uffz*	BO	von Janson crew	Stab/ZG 1	+	10-03-44	
Scholz	Heinz	*Uffz*	BS	Kaltenbrunner crew	13/KG 40	?	24-09-42	
Schramm	Karl-Heinz	*Gefr*	BS	Harms crew	13/KG 40	+	survived	
Schröder	Arthur	*Oblt*	FF		13/KG 40		survived	
Schröder	Karl-Fritz	*Fw*	BF	Kaufmann crew	10/KG 40; ErgSt/ZG 1	+	07-10-43	
Schülli	Hellmut	*Lt*	FF		14/KG 40	+	11-04-44	
Schüssler	Hans	*Uffz*	BO	Messerschmidt crew	2/ZG 1	+	20-04-44	
Schulte	Helmut	*Uffz*	BO	Schwarz crew	3/ZG 1	M		

Surname	First name	Rank	Pos	Crew	Unit	Fate	Date	Transfer
Schultz	Heinz	Uffz	BF	Kaltenbrunner crew	13/KG 40	+	05-10-42	
Schulz	Hans	Lt	FF		2/ZG 1	+	03-11-43	
Schulze			BF		ErgSt/ZG 1		?	
Schulze	Heinz	Uffz	BO	Serke crew	15/KG 40	W	30-12-42	
Schulzky	Hans	Uffz	FF		14/KG 40	W	07-10-43	-9/JG 4
Schuster	Hans	Oblt	FF, St Kap		15/KG 40; 3/ZG 1	+	07-10-44	
Schwandner	Franz	Ogefr	BW	Jöckel crew	9(NJ)/ZG 1	+	20-11-43	
Schwartz	Kurt	Uffz	FF		2/ZG 1	+	17-04-44	
Schwarz	Josef	Lt	FF		3/ZG 1	+	06-06-44	
Schwarz	Kurt	Ogefr	BF	von Heinburg crew	V/KG 40	+	20-04-44	
Schwarzrock	Hans	Uffz	BF	von Janson crew	Stab/ZG 1	+	26-11-42	
Schweigert	Manfred	Ogefr	BO	Reicke crew	14/KG 40	+	10-03-44	
Seidel	Erwin	Uffz	BF	Hiebsch crew	15/KG 40	+	30-01-43	
Seifert	Heinrich	Uffz	BF	Löw crew	7/ZG 1	+	11-06-43	
Seifert	Rudolf	Uffz	BO	Hensgen crew	15/KG 40	M	07-06-44	(came back)
von Selle	Erich	Obstlt	FF, Kdre		Stab/ZG 1	+	17-05-43	
Selzer		Uffz	BF	Ewert crew	9,(NJ)/ZG 1		survived	-Stab/7. Jagd-Div
Semmelmann	Rudolf	Uffz	BF	Weide crew	V/KG 40	+	?	-1/NJG 4
Serke	Günther	Lt	BF		15/KG 40	W	09-05-43	
Sieger	Artur	Uffz	BO	Zimmer crew	2/ZG 1	M	30-12-42	
Simon	Wilhelm	Ofw		Apel crew	15/KG 40	+	08-03-44	
Sinning(?)		Maj			Stab V/KG 40 (?)		23-03-43	
Sommer	Josef	Gefr	BF	Schlüter crew	10/KG 40	+	31-08-43	
Sommer	Otto	Uffz	BF	Engeln crew	7/ZG 1	+	10-06-44	
Specklin	Karl	Ogefr	BF	Fischer crew	2/ZG 1	W	30-11-43	
Sprang	Fritz	Uffz	FF		3/ZG 1	+	11-04-44	
						+	16-02-45	
von Sprinzenstein	Franz Felix (Graf Freiherr)	Lt	FF		I/ZG 1	+	04-08-44	-II/JG 4

Surname	First name	Rank	Role	Crew	Unit	Fate	Date	Notes
Sprunkel	Günter	*Uffz*	BF	Fehr crew	15/KG 40 & 3/ErgZerstGr ZG 1	+	16-03-44	
Staas	Helmut	*Uffz*	BO	Altenhöner crew	3/ZG 1	+	13-03-44	
Stabentheimer	Florian	*Gefr*	BO		14/KG 40	+	24-03-43	
Starkert	Wilhelm	*Fw*	BF	Schwartz crew	2/ZG 1	+	06-06-44	
Steffen	Ulrich	*Hptm*	FF, TO		Stab V/KG 40; I/ZG 1		?	
Stellmayer	Johannes	*Uffz*	BS	Kaltenbrunner crew	13/KG 40	+	05-10-42	
Steurich	Werner	*Uffz*	FF		13 & 14/KG 40	+	22-03-43	
Stich	Siegfried		Wart		13/KG 40		?	
Stöffler	Karl	*Lt*	FF		III/KG 40	+	20-07-42	
Stöpel	Helmut	*Gefr*	BF	Lepper crew	10/KG 40	+	31-08-43	
Stohl	Walter	*Fw*	FF		14/KG 40; 2/ZG 1	+	01-12-43	
Streng	Fritz	*Uffz*	BF	Runge crew	Z/Kü.Fl.Gr 106 V/KG 40	+	20-08-42	
Strobel	Rurt	*Uffz*	FF		3/ZG 1	M	07-06-44	
Strütt		*Ogefr*	BO	Gutermann crew	14/KG 40	W	?	
Stumpf	Rolf	*Uffz*	BO	Gutermann & Messerschmidt crews	14/KG 40 / 2/ZG 1	W / +	19-06-43 / 11-04-44	
Sucht		*Uffz*			13/KG 40		?	
Sundermann	Albert	*Ogefr*	BO	Dettner crew	15/KG 40	+	09-02-43	
Sukowski		*Lt*	FF		10/KG 40			-11/ZG 26
Taberthofer	Max	*Fw*	BF		14/KG 40	+	24-03-43	
Temke	Karl-Heinz	*Uffz*	BO	Bauer crew	7/ZG 1	+	10-03-44	
Theiss	Günther	*Fw*	FF		I/ZG 1	W	07-06-44	-5/JG 4
						+	05-09-44	
Thies	Artur	*Lt*	FF	Linden crew	14/KG 40	+	22-03-43	
Thimm	Walter	*Uffz*	BO		15/KG 40	W	25-09-43	
Trutt	Otto	*Uffz*	BO		V/KG 40	+	08-07-43	
Uhde	Konstantin	*Ogefr*	BO	Schulz crew	2/ZG 1	+	03-11-43	
Uhsemann	Klaus	*Lt*	FF		9,(NJ)/ZG 1	+	11-04-44	

Surname	First name	Rank	Role	Crew	Unit	Status	Date	Notes
Ulbricht	Karl	*Lt*	FF		III/ZG 1		survived	*St Kap* 12/JG 4
Ullmann	Paul	*Uffz*	BO	Fritz & von Sprinzenstein crews	I/ZG 1	W	11-04-44	
					I/ZG 1	W	20-05-44	
Unger	Manfred	*Gefr*	BS	Hermann crew	2/ZG 1	M	06-06-44	
Ustarbowski				Sukowski crew	10/ZG 1		?	
Utlaut	Kurt	*Uffz*	BF	Pütz crew	7/ZG 1	+	07-01-44	
Vetter	Max	*Ogefr*	FF		2/ZG 1	+	01-12-43	
Vieback	Hans	*Lt*	FF		13/KG 40	+	20-05-43	
Vojacek	Josef	*Uffz*	BF	Hanshen crew	14/KG 40	W	23-08-43	
Wachs	Werner	*Uffz*	BF	Derr crew	13/KG 40	+	20-06-43	
Wagner	Helmut	*Fw*	FF		13/KG 40	+	08-10-42	
Wagner	Otto	*Fw*	BF	Isslinger crew	15/KG 40	+	09-02-43	
Wagner	Walter	*Gefr*	FF		ErgSt/ZG 1	+	?	-5/JG 4
Walter	Artur	*Ogefr*	BS	von Hoensbroech crew	13/KG 40	+	08-09-42	
Warnemünde	Walter	*Gefr*	BF	Heicke crew	13/KG 40	+	21-09-43	
Wawris	Otto	*Uffz*	BF	Blankenberg crew	13/KG 40	+	04-09-43	
Weber	Franz	*Uffz*	BO	Isslinger crew	15/KG 40	+	09-02-43	
Weber	Fritz	*Uffz*	BF	Heuer crew	14/KG 40	+	30-01-43	
Weber	Gerhard	*Ogefr*	BS	Bindzus crew	2/ZG 1	+	06-06-44	
Wegmann	Karl	*Fw*	BF		I/ZG 1	+	23-11-43	
Weide	Heinz	*Lt*	FF		/KG 40	+	09-05-43	
Weissbrod	Hermann	*Ogefr*	BF	Reichelmann crew	2/ZG 1	W	05-04-44	
						+	11-04-44	
Wenz	Karl	*Fw*	BO	Schülli crew	14/KG 40	+	07-10-43	
Werner	Werner	*Uffz*	FF		I/ZG 1	+	?	
Werner	August	*Ofw*	BF	Stoffler crew	III/KG 40	W	20-07-42	
Wetzel	Siegfried	*Gefr*	BS	Weymar crew	Z.St/KG 6	+	22-07-42	

Surname	First name	Rank	Role	Crew	Unit		Date	Notes
Weymar	Carlhanns	Hptm	FF	Heide crew	Z.St/KG 6	+	22-07-42	
Wiencke	Rudi	Ogefr	BF	Kriedel crew	13/KG 40	+	09-09-42	
Winkelmann	Felix	Uffz	BF	Esch crew	/KG 40	+	29-01-43	
Winkelmann	Karl-Friedrich	Uffz	BO	Korthals crew	13/KG 40	+	24-03-43	
Winteler	Heinz	Uffz	BF	Zimmer crew	Stab V/KG 40	+	03-11-42	
Winter	Nikolaus	Uffz	BF	Frank crew	2/ZG 1	M	08-03-44	
Wirth	Adolf	Uffz	BO		I/ZG 1	+	12-12-43	
Wittmer	Max	Lt	FF		14/KG 40	+	08-08-43	
Wöber	Leo	Ogefr	BF	Gäbler crew	15/KG 40; 9(NJ)/ZG 1	?	-1/NJG 4	
Wöhle		Gefr	BO	Chlond crew	2/ZG 1	?		
Wolf	Dietrich	Ofw	FF		2/ZG 1	+	07-06-44	
Wolf	Josef	Uffz	BO	Fehr crew	15/KG 40 & 3/ErgZerstGr ZG 1	+	16-03-44	
Wolff		Uffz	BO	Gmelin crew	13/KG 40		?	
Wolff	Lothar	Oblt	FF, Adj		15/KG 40; Stab I/ZG 1		survived	-Adj II/JG 4 & St Kap 15/JG 4
Zimmer	Wilhelm	Fw	FF		2/ZG 1	M	08-03-44	
Zimmermann	Gerhard	Uffz	BF	Gmelin crew	13/KG 40; I/ZG 1		survived	
Zink		Uffz	BF	Chlond crew	2/ZG 1		survived	
Zunker	Wolfgang	Uffz	BF	Dargel crew	Stab V/KG 40	+	30-12-42	

Appendix C

German identification drawings
of British aircraft

England ·

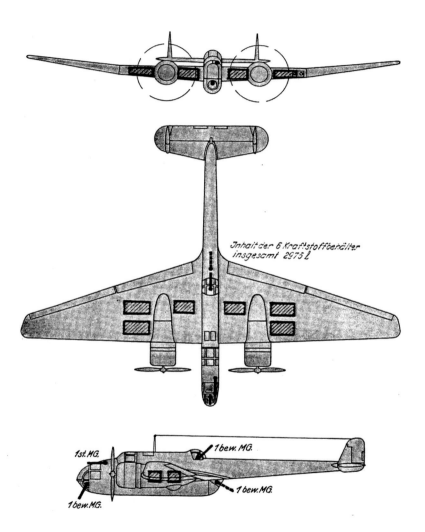

Jnhalt der 6 Kraftstoffbehälter
insgesamt 2975 L

1st. MG.

1 bew. MG.

1 bew. MG.

1 bew. MG.

Handley-Page „Hampden"
Kampfflugzeug

1 starres ungesteuertes MG. im Rumpfbug, je 1 bewegliches Doppel-MG. auf Rumpfoberseite und im rückwärtigen Teil des unteren Rumpfstockwerks, 1 bewegliches MG. in der Unterseite des Rumpfbugs, das normal vollkommen eingezogen ist und nur ein sehr beschränktes Schußfeld nach vorn unten besitzt. Panzerung des Flugzeugführersitzes und des rückwärtigen unteren MG.-Standes. Neuerdings geschützte Kraftstoffbehälter.

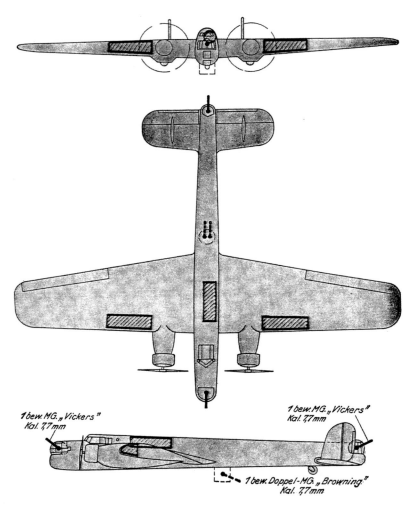

Armstrong-Whitworth „Whitley"

Kampfflugzeug

*Bei den Mustern „Whitley II" und „Whitley III" (kenntlich an den luftgekühlten Sternmotoren) im Rumpfbug und im Rumpfheck hinter dem Leitwerk je 1 bewegliches MG. in einem handbetätigten „Armstrong-Whitworth"-Drehturm, 1 bewegliches Doppel-MG. in ausfahrbarem, handbetätigtem Drehturm an Rumpfunterseite. Bei den Mustern „Whitley IV und Whitley V" (kenntlich an den flüssigkeitsgekühlten 12 Zyl.-V-Motoren) 1 bewegliches MG. im Rumpfbug, 1 bewegliches Vierfach-MG. im Rumpfheck in hydraulisch betätigtem Drehturm, 1 bewegliches Doppel-MG. in ausfahrbarem, handbetätigtem Drehturm an Rumpfunterseite. Antrieb des hydraulisch betätigten Drehturmes im Rumpfheck von einer Pumpe am **rechten** Motor.*

England

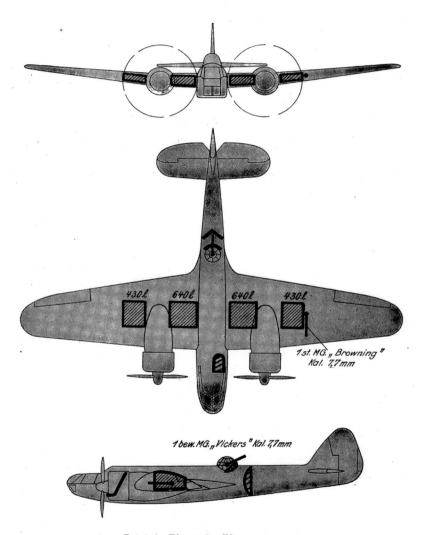

1st. MG. „Browning"
Kal. 7,7mm

1 bew. MG. „Vickers" Kal. 7,7mm

Bristol „Blenheim IV" (*„Long-nosed")* [1]
Kampfflugzeug und Aufklärer

1 starres ungesteuertes MG. im linken Flügel, 1 bewegliches MG. oder Doppel-MG. in halbausfahrbarem, hydraulisch betätigtem Drehturm mit 360° Drehbereich. Neuerdings geschützte Kraftstoffbehälter.

[1] Desgl. Muster **„Blenheim I"** *(kurznasig).*

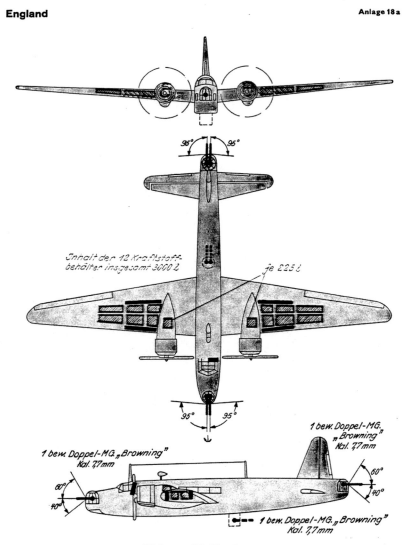

95°   95°

Inhalt der 12 Kraftstoff-
behälter insgesamt 3000 ℓ

je 225 ℓ

95°   95°

1 bew. Doppel-MG. „Browning"
Kal. 7,7mm

1 bew. Doppel-MG. „Browning"
Kal. 7,7mm

60°
40°

1 bew. Doppel-MG. „Browning"
Kal. 7,7mm

60°
40°

Vickers „Wellington"
Kampfflugzeug

Im Rumpfbug und im Rumpfheck hinter dem Leitwerk je ein bewegliches Doppel-MG. in einem hydraulisch betätigten „Nash &
Thompson"-Drehturm. Bei neuerer Ausführung Vierfach-MG. im Heckturm. Antrieb des Bug- und Heckturmes von Pumpe am
linken Motor. Bei einigen Flugzeugen des Musters Vickers „Wellington" weiterhin 1 bewegliches Doppel-MG. in ausfahrbarem,
handbetätigtem Drehturm an Rumpfunterseite (s. Abbildung). Die 8 inneren Kraftstoffbehälter sind vorn und hinten durch eine
Panzerplatte von 4,5 mm Stärke geschützt. Neuerdings geschützte Kraftstoffbehälter.

Appendix D

Air combat victories for
III/IV/V *Gruppe/Kampfgeschwader* 40 and
I and III *Gruppen/Zerstörergeschwader* 1,
July 1942-July 1944

15 Jul 42   Wellington shot down by *Fw* Henny Passier, IV/KG 40

Wellington Z1155/F of 311 Sqn. F/S H. Dostal, Sgt R. Pancir, Flt Lt M. Cigler, Sgt J. Holub, Sgt F. Novak, Sgt V. Orlik, all M

20 Jul 42   Two Wellingtons shot down by *Lt* Karl Stoeffler, III or IV/KG 40, NNW La Coruna, 1210hrs

Wellington HX518 of 15 OTU. Took off 0650hrs in transit to the Middle East. Plt Off A. R. E. Houston – P, Sgt W. E. Konigkramer – P, Sgt G. R. Halliwell – WOp, Plt Off J. H. Kinsey – O, Sgt E. Lister – AG, all M

Wellington HX423 of 15 OTU (F/S Smallwood) damaged

20 Aug 42   Handley Page shot down by *Fw* Vincenz Giessuebel, 13/KG 40, *PlQ* 14W/8415, 1652hrs. Crashed in Spain – shared by *Oblt* Adolf Runge, Z/Kü.Fl.Gr 106/IV/KG 40, who was also shot down

Lancaster R5543 of 61 Sqn. Crashed at Pontedorna, near Cabana, Spain. Plt Off J. E. Madsen – P, Plt Off T. L. Wilson – O, Plt Off J. H. Harrad, Sgt H. Allen – AG, Sgt V. J. Watson – WOp, Sgt T. L. Boland – AG, Sgt R. H. Linton, all +

1 Sep 42   Sunderland shot down by *Hptm* Hans William Reicke, *St Kap* 14/KG 40, *PlQ* 14W/7542, 2117hrs (shared with *Hptm* Heinz-Horst Hissbach, 14/KG 40)

Sunderland T9113 of 461 Sqn. Fg Off R. H. H. Hosband – P, Fg Off Emrys-Jones, Plt Off O. L. Wennholm – P, Plt Off D. I. Stewart – O, Sgt N. J. Alecock – FMEAG, Sgt R. V. Chinnery, Sgt R. Eva – WOp/AG, Sgt C. E. Hayward – FMEAG, F/S S. King – WOp, Sgt D. M. Bowd – WOp/AG, Sgt J. I. White – AG, all M

8 Sep 42   Hampden shot down by *Lt* Wolfgang Graf Von Hoensbroech, 13/KG 40, *PlQ* 14W/7811, 1155hrs

Probably Hudson AM909 of 500 Sqn. Shot down S of Scilly Islands, 1100hrs. F/S B. H. H. Wilson – O, +; Sgt S. K. Pearce – P, Sgt J. Blankley – WOp, Sgt S. F. Norton – WOp, Sgt R. T. Smith – WOp, all POW

9 Sep 42   Whitley shot down by *Hptm* Paul Heide, *St Kap* 13/KG 40 (*Hptm* Heide shot down in combat and +)

Whitley Z9209/G of 77 Sqn. Sgt W. J. Hilton, Plt Off J. Kenworthy, Plt Off L. W. Hawkes, Sgt J. Ferguson, Sgt P. Johnson, F/S R. F. Smith, all M. Last message 1353hrs

11 Sep 42   Wellington shot down by *Lt* Kurt Necesany, 13/KG 40, *PlQ* 14W/8843, 1450hrs (shared by *Lt* Willi Deuper and *Fw* Henny Passier, 14/KG 40)

Apparently crashed in sea but probably Wellington HD988/U of 311 Sqn (Sgt Mazuruck), which fought a combat with Ju 88s, 1335hrs, but returned to base

15 Sep 42   Whitley shot down by *Uffz* Johann Kaltenbrunner, 13/KG 40, *PlQ* 14W/6813, 1620hrs (shared by *Lt* Dieter Meister; crew seen in dinghy)

Whitley shot down by *Fw* Henny Passier, 13/KG 40, *PlQ* 14W/9885, 1847hrs

Whitley Z9365/A of 502 Sqn. Shot down over Bay of Biscay. Sgt A. B. Coburn – P, Plt Off A. E. Coates, Sgt H. A. Roberts – O, Sgt W. Harvey – WOp, Sgt J. R. Ellam – WOp, all M; Sgt T. J. Edwards – WOp, POW.

Wellington shot down by *Lt* Willi Deuper, 13/KG 40, *PlQ* 14W/9855, 1732hrs

Wellington HD982/Y of 311 Sqn. Took off 0959hrs. Fg Off J. Nyvlt – P, Sgt J. Neradil – P, Flt Lt A. Gabriel – O, Fg Off R. K. Matejicek – WOp, Sgt J. Simko – WOp, Sgt O. Jebacek – WOp, all M

Hudson shot down by *Lt* Willi Deuper, 13/KG 40. *PlQ* 14W/9869, 1832hrs

No Hudsons lost in this area on this day but Wellington T, 311 Sqn (Fg Off Taiber), reported combat with two Ju 88s at 1630hrs; Wellington V, 311 Sqn (Flt Lt Eichler), reported combat with two Ju 88s at 1740hrs; Wellington L, 311 Sqn, (Sgt J. Hadravek), damaged Ju 88 1650hrs

16 Sep 42   Wellington shot down by *Hptm* Georg Esch, *St Kap* 13/KG 40, *PlQ* 14W/9826, 1712hrs (shared by *Lt* Dieter Meister, *Uffz* Ernst Harms, *Uffz* Werner Steurich)

Wellington HF836/E of 304 Sqn (Fg Off M. Targowski) badly damaged in combat, 1612hrs. Possibly Hudson V9156 of 1402 (Met) Flt. Took off 1330hrs. Sgt L. Hurn – P, Sgt O. R. O'H. Cotter – O, Sgt L. Thompson – WOp/AG, Sgt S. O. Rogers – WOp/AG, all M

17 Sep 42   Hudson shot down by *Lt* Kurt Necesany, 13/KG 40, *PlQ* 14W/8933, 1537hrs (two men seen in water)

Hudson AM587 of 500 Sqn. F/S D. B. Smith – P, Sgt R. Finklestone-Sayliss – O, Sgt A. Young – WOp, Sgt R. J. Wilson – WOp, all M

24 Sep 42   Wellington shot down by *Uffz* Heinz Scholz, 13/KG 40 (BS to *Uffz* Johann Kaltenbrunner), *PlQ* 14W/7851, 1543hrs (shared by *Lt* Kurt Necesany)

Possibly Wellington R1657/H of 304 Sqn (Sgt J. Bakanacz), which fought a combat with Ju 88s, claiming one, c1545hrs

29 Sep 42   Wellington shot down by *Lt* Walter Berger, 13/KG 40, *PlQ* 14W/8760, 1730hrs (shared by *Uffz* Johann Kaltenbrunner)

Wellington HF921/M of 311 Sqn. Ditched 10 miles S of Land's End, 1830hrs following combat with Ju 88s. Sqn Ldr J. Sejbl – P, F/S V. Kubalik – P, Fg Off K. Slama – P, Sgt J. Bajer – WOp, all rescued suffering from shock/exposure; Sgt J. Stern – AG, inj; Plt Off P. Friedlander – AG, M

30 Sep 42   Whitley shot down by *Lt* Kurt Necesany, 13/KG 40, *PlQ* 14W/7716, 1528hrs (three men seen in dinghy)

Whitley BD258/S of 51 Sqn. Shot down over Bay of Biscay. Fg Off H. E. Sullivan – P, F/S H. F. Tice – WOp, Sgt M. E. Robinson – WOp, all POW; Sgt B. F. Bushell – O, Sgt W. Green – AG, Sgt J. D. Shaw – P, all M

Whitley shot down by *Hptm* Heinz-Horst Hissbach, 14/KG 40, *PlQ* 14W/6526, 1316hrs (shared by *Lt* Hermann Flothmann, 14/KG 40)

Whitley Z9465 of 51 Sqn. F/S F. Oliver – P, Sgt S. A. W. Lea – P, Sgt J. C. Caldwell – N, Sgt F. Taylor – AG, F/S P. W. Davis – WOp/AG, Sgt J. D. Quilter – AG, all M

8 Oct 42   Whitley shot down by *Lt* Dieter Meister, 13/KG 40, *PlQ* 14W/9865, 1600hrs

Whitley AD671 of 10 OTU. Sgt L, H, Dean, Sgt C, N, Ellis, Sgt W, A, Gammon, Sgt F, D, Garrett, Fg Off D, H, Cochran, Sgt W. C. Roach, all POW (Fg Off Cochran shot by Gestapo after Great Escape)

12 Oct 42   Whitley shot down by *Uffz* Walter Stohl, 14/KG 40, *PlQ* 24W/1647, 1547hrs (shared by *Lt* Dieter Meister)

Whitley BD564/L of 502 Sqn missing (last message received 1455hrs). Sgt W. N. Moore – P, Sgt R. A. Larcombe – P, Sgt V. D. Savage – WOp, Sgt S. J. Page – WOp, Sgt R. P. Nicholls – WOp, Plt Off R. B. F. Walker – N, all M

15 Oct 42   Whitley shot down by *Lt* Heinz Olbrecht, 14/KG 40, *PlQ* 14W/9817, 1723hrs (shared by *Lt* Artur Thies and *Ofw* Hans Rakow)

Whitley Z9435 of 10 OTU. Sgt B. L. Rogers – P, Sgt S. Nicholson – P, Fg Off G. R. Tart – P, Sgt J. McDonald – AG, Sgt N. A. Revitt – O, F/S G. H. Thornley – WOp, all M

16 Oct 42   Whitley shot down by *Lt* Dieter Meister, 13/KG 40, *PlQ* 14W/0817, 1614hrs (shared by *Lt* Kurt Necesany)

Whitley Z9153 of 51 Sqn shot down 1516hrs. Sgt R. J. Benn – P, Plt Off A. H. S. Brown – P, Sgt P. M. Jones – WOp, Sgt R. S. Fielding – N, Sgt J. J. Kerr – WOp, Sgt A. A. Gillies – AG, all M

Wellington shot down by *Uffz* Werner Steurich, 13/KG 40, *PlQ* 14W/0924, 1638hrs

Wellington R1413 of 304 Sqn. Took off at 0825hrs on anti-submarine sweep. Fg Off M. Targowski DFC – P, Fg Off T. Oles – O, Sgt C. Twardoch – P, Sgt Z. Piechowiak – WOp, Sgt W. Mlynarski – AG, Sgt F. Kubiak – AG, all M

21 Oct 42   Beaufighter shot down by *Hptm* Heinz-Horst Hissbach, 14/KG 40, *PlQ* 14W/8883, 1620hrs

Beaufighter T5281/G of 235 Sqn. Plt Off W. D. Hollis and Sgt H. Taylor both M. Shot down in combat with Ju 88s, 1517hrs

1 Nov 42   Wellington shot down by *Hptm* Heinz-Horst Hissbach, 15/KG 40, 170nm WSW Brest, 1656hrs

Wellington R1716 of 304 Sqn. Took off 1330hrs. Plt Off S. Krawczyk – P, Sgt J. Rogala-Sobieszczanski, Fg Off A. Szkuta – N, Plt Off N. Wodzinski – AG, Sgt Z. Sasal – AG, Flt Lt I. Skorobahty – 2P, all M

23 Nov 42   Wellington damaged by V/KG 40

Wellington DV799/Z of 311 Sqn. Plt Off Radina and crew uninj (0854-1656hrs)

30 Nov 42   Whitley shot down by *Hptm* Hans William Reicke and *Lt* Artur Thies, 14/KG 40, 1405hrs (also claimed by *Hptm* Heinz-Horst Hissbach, 15/KG 40, *PlQ* 14W/7735)

Whitley AD961 of 10 OTU. Missing on patrol over Bay of Biscay. Sgt G. Bagshaw – P, Sgt E. O. P. Bell – P, Sgt B. Briscoe – O, Sgt W. M. Knowles – AG, F/S W. H. Mackintosh – WOp, Plt Off D. V. Smith, all M

17 Dec 42   Whitley shot down by *Lt* Artur Thies, 14/KG 40, 1215hrs

Whitley EB363 of 10 OTU. Shot down 47.50N, 08.00W. Sgt M. T. Denham – P, Plt Off P. A. Davies – P, Plt Off V. J. Wotton – B, all + and buried at Concarneau, St Breive and Dinard respectively. Plt Off R. Sword – AG, Sgt R. Rawcliffe – O, F/S T. H. Miller, all M

23 Dec 42   P-38 shot down by V/KG 40, *PlQ* 14W/9718, 1047hrs

P-38 G of 95 F/S/82nd FG. Shot down by Ju 88. *Lt* E. T. Green – E

Boston shot down by *Ofw* Georg Heuer, 14/KG 40, *PlQ* 14W/9718, 1047hrs

A-20B serial 41-3004 of 47th BG. Missing in combat with four Ju 88s. Capt D. B. Martz – P, S/Sgt A. H. Weddell – AG, S/Sgt H. A. Stewart, all M

30 Dec 42   P-39 shot down by *Ofw* Georg Heuer, 14/KG 40, *PlQ* 14W/8759, 1138hrs

P-39D of 16th Observation Sqn/68th Gp, 2/Lt V. H. Lincoln Jr M

B-17 possibly shot down by V/KG 40, *PlQ* 14W/4857, 1338hrs

Either B-17F 42-2975 of 306th BG (Capt J. B. Brady and crew M) or B-17F 42-5078 of 366th BS/305th BG (1/Lt F. E. Love and crew, M) or B-17F 41-24449 KY-C 'Short Snorter' of 401st BS/91st BG (1/Lt W. D. Bloodgood and crew, M)

30 Jan 43   Two Beaufighters shot down in combat with *Hptm* Hans William Reicke (*St Kap*), *Ofw* Georg Heuer, *Uffz* Juergen Heicke, 14/KG 40, *PlQ* 14W/0738, 1131-1142hrs (*Hptm* Reicke collided with a Beaufighter)

Beaufighter JL447/WR-G of 248 Sqn. Sgt J. Bell and Sgt A. W. Parnell, both M

Beaufighter EL321/WR-M of 248 Sqn. Fg Off E. W. Cunningham and Plt Off J. G. D. McC. Rawden, both M

4 Feb 43   Halifax shot down by *Lt* Willi Deuper, 13/KG 40, 165sm WSW of Brest (shared by *Uffz* Heinz Hommel)

Probably Halifax G/405 Sqn. Damaged by Ju 88 SW of Ushant, 1400hrs. Fg Off W. W. Colledge and crew uninj

5 Feb 43   P-39 shot down by *Oblt* Hermann Horstmann, 13/KG 40, *PlQ* 14W/9779, 1255hrs

P-39 L of 346th F/S/350th FG. Missing near Bordeaux. F/S H. M. Nelson M

9 Feb 43   Two Beaufighters claimed by *Lt* Dieter Meister, 15/KG 40, *PIQ* 14W/8657, 1455hrs and *PIQ* 14W/8658, 1500hrs

Combat fought with Beaufighters of 248 Sqn. WR-F (Flt Lt G. H. Melville-Jackson and F/S A. Umbers) slightly damaged

10 Mar 43   Whitley shot down by *Lt* Dieter Meister, 15/KG 40, *PIQ* 14W/0336.

Whitley BD202/G of 10 OTU. Sgt J. P. Ingram, Sgt J. E. L. Woollam, Sgt W. S. Young, Sgt J. Mitchell, Plt Off R. Marriot, Sgt W. Mills, all M

23 Mar 43   B-17 shot down by *Oblt* Hermann Horstmann, 13/KG 40, *PIQ* 14W/9759, 1315hrs

Fortress FK209 of 59 Sqn. Fg Off R. J. Weatherhead – P, Sgt H. W. J. Arnold – P, Fg Off W. C. Zapfe – N, F/S G. Cojocar – WOp/AG, Sgt C. L. Copping – WOp/AG, Sgt F. Spiho – WOp/AG, Sgt R. G. Montgomery – WOp/AG, Fg Off R. A. Phillips – WOp/AG, all M

Liberator shot down by *Lt* Ulrich Hanshen, 15/KG 40, *PIQ* 14W/2586, 1420hrs

Liberator AL587 of 511 Sqn. Lost in transit Gibraltar to UK. Flt Lt G. T. R. Francis – P, F/S C. E. Ferro – P, Sgt L. G. Burry – WOp/AG, Sgt R. P. Marvin – E, Fg Off J. S. Renouf – N, Fg Off R. S. Tedder – WOp, as well as the following passengers: AVM R. P. M. Whitham CB, OBE, MC, Sgt F. N. Boustead, Fg Off J. G. Green, F/S W. J. Hough, Plt Off A. H. Bowler, Fg Off F. Stuart, Fg Off O. A. Smith, Fg Off L. J. Marriott, Sgt W. A. Upston, Sgt N. R. Knight, Lt P. S. Skelton, Col J. E. Merin, Lt Col L. W. Armstrong-McDonnell, all M

24 Mar 43   Halifax shot down by *Oblt* Hermann Horstmann, *StFhr* 13/KG 40, *PIQ* 14W/9526, 0840hrs

Halifax BB277/H of 58 Sqn. Took off 0503hrs. Fg Off R. A. H. Ayles – P, Sgt T. A. Miles – P, Fg Off J. G. Smith – O, Sgt A. Watson – E, Sgt B. C. Trivett – WOp/AG, Sgt D. S. Saunders – WOp/AG, Sgt W. A. Vesely – WOp/AG, all M

17 Apr 43   Whitley shot down by *Lt* Albrecht Bellstedt, 14/KG 40, *PIQ* 24W/1640, 1510hrs

Whitley BD226 of 10 OTU. Sgt L. G. Smith – P, Fg Off C. Thwaites – P, Plt Off H. W. Barnett – B, Plt Off J. H. Reynolds – AG, Sgt W. Davis – N, Sgt K. Ray, all M

9 May 43   Halifax probably shot down by V/KG 40

Halifax HR743/N of 58 Sqn. F/S J. A. Hoather DFM – P, Sgt T. E. Hamley, Flt Lt L. R. Ott, Sgt J. Summerville, Sgt E. Ramjohn, Sgt A. Simpson, Sgt H. S. Butler, Sgt R. Y. Herd, all M

13 May 43   Liberator shot down by *Fw* Vincenz Giessuebel, 14/KG 40

Liberator FL947/R of 224 Sqn. Plt Off G. B. Willerton – P safe, F/S J. D. White, Sgt K. Hodd, Flt Lt T. Luke, Plt Off R. G. Barham – WOp, F/S H. Bell, Sgt P. Gardner, Plt Off J. R. McCall, Lt B. Church RNVR, all +

Liberator FL946/L of 224 Sqn (W/O E. J. J. Spiller) damaged in combat, 1728hrs

14 May 43   Sunderland shot down by *Oblt* Kurt Necesany/*Lt* Willi Gutermann, 14/KG 40, *PlQ* 24W/1512, 1052hrs

Sunderland DV968/M of 461 Sqn damaged in combat with Ju 88s. Sgt J. Barrow – W, Flt Lt E. C. Smith and remainder of crew uninj

15 May 43   Sunderland shot down by *Ofw* Vincenz Giessuebel, 14/KG 40, 150km N of Cap Ortegal, *PlQ* 14W/0721, 1537hrs

Sunderland DD837/V of 228 Sqn. Flt Lt G. A. Church – P, Fg Off T. A. Newbury, Fg Off A. J. Hibberd, Fg Off W. L. Leeman, Sgt R. Deacon, F/S D. Smart, F/S J. Rolfe, Sgt W. A. Jones, F/S E. Maycock, Sgt A. Morgan, Sgt C, Sheppard, all +

17 May 43   Sunderland shot down by *Hptm* Hans Morr, *St Kap* 15/KG 40, *PlQ* 14W/0567, 0820hrs

Sunderland W4004/Z of 10 Sqn RAAF. Flt Lt M. K. Kenzie – P, Fg Off K. L. Ridings – 1P, Plt Off N. J. McLeod – 2P, Fg Off R. G. Bowley DFC – N, Fg Off V. J. Corless – N, Flt Lt T. W. Patrick-arm, F/S J. E. Jackson – WOp, Sgt J. A. Pearce – WHM, Sgt J. H. Hogg – E, Sgt T. H. Doran-Fit, F/S J. C. Kelly – AG, LAC J. Murdoch – Fitter, all +. Lost 0720hrs

Sunderland damaged in combat with three Ju 88s of V/KG 40, 46.23N 09.30W, 1728hrs

Sunderland DV960/H of 461 Sqn. Fg Off J. G. P. Weatherlake and crew uninj

Whitley shot down by *Lt* Albrecht Bellstedt, 14/KG 40, *PlQ* 14W/0824, 1316hrs

Whitley BD260/P of 10 OTU. Ditched 80 miles NW of Cap Finisterre after combat with Ju 88s, 1200hrs. Crew rescued by Spanish trawler and landed at Vigo. Sgt S. J. Barnett, Sgt J. H. Pike, Sgt G. O. Sharpe, Sgt L. Whitworth, Sgt E. R. Price, Sgt H. A. Weber, all safe

20 May 43   Beaufort shot down by *Lt* Willi Gutermann, 14/KG 40, *PlQ* 14W/8835, 1200hrs

Probably Blenheim EH464 of 42 OTU. Took off from Portreath 0842hrs for Gibraltar. Fg Off E, G, Simmonds – P, Sgt S, K, Newnham – N, Sgt G. J. Holt – WOp, all M

30 May 43   Liberator possibly shot down by *Ofw* Vincenz Giessuebel, 14/KG 40, 120km WNW of Brest. Probably shot down by 5/196

Liberator BZ713/S of 224 Sqn. F/S H. V. Archer – P, Sgt J. H. Brooks, Sgt L. Horricks, Sgt J. Millward, Sgt W. E. Innes, Sgt S. Nichols, Sgt S. Rogers, Sgt A. S. Pudefin, all +

1 Jun 43   Wellington shot down by *Uffz* Heinz Hommel, 13/KG 40, *PlQ* 14W/9885, 0828hrs

Wellington shot down by *Oblt* Hermann Horstmann, *St Kap* 13/KG 40, *PlQ* 14W/8858, 0805hrs

Wellington HE961 of 420 Sqn. Fg Off G. S. McCulloch – P, Sgt K. M. Gillies – N, Sgt J. C. Nicholl – WOp, F/S G. D. McDougal – AG, LAC J. B. Leith – fitter, Plt Off P. J. Greig, LAC A. C. J. Coates, all +

Wellington HE568 of 420 Sqn. Sgt A. Sodero – P, Fg Off G. H. Hubbell – N, Plt Off W. B. King – B, Plt Off R. S. Hollewell – WOp, F/S H. L. Dowle – AG, LAC T. R. Brookes, Cpl J. F. McKenzie, all M

Liberator shot down by *Hptm* Hans Morr and *Lt* Lothar Wolff, 15/KG 40, *PlQ* 14W/0857, 1914hrs

Probably Halifax BB257/B of 58 Sqn. Reported under attack 1911hrs. F/S F. W. Gilmore, Plt Off J. R. Bickerton, Fg Off J. A. Thain, Sgt C. W. Makin, F/S S. F. Miller, Sgt L. E. Daw, Sgt S. D. Wyatt, all +

DC3 shot down by *Oblt* Albrecht Bellstedt, 14/KG 40, *PlQ* 24W/1785, 1250hrs

DC-3 coded G-AGBB of KLM/BOAC. Capt Q. Tepas, Capt D. De Koning (First Officer), Mr C. Van Brugge (radio officer), Mr E. Rosevink (engineer). Thirteen passengers: Mr I. J. Sharp, Mr F. G. Cowlrick, Mr T. M. Shervington, Mr G. T. Maclean, Mr W. J. Israel, Mr K. Stonehouse, Mrs E. P. Stonehouse, Mrs C. A. Paton, Mr L. Howard, Mr A. T. Chenhalls, Mrs Hutcheon, Miss Hutcheon, Miss Hutcheon, all M

Boston shot down by *Maj* Alfred Hemm, *Gr Kdr* V/KG 40.

No recorded losses

2 Jun 43   Sunderland shot down by *Lt* Friedrich Maeder, 13/KG 40, 300km NW Brest, *PlQ* 24W/1778, 1858hrs

Sunderland EJ134/N of 461 Sqn. Crashed off Mounts Bay, Prah Sands, Cornwall, 1858hrs. Plt Off K. M. Simpson – W, Fg Off E. C. E. Miles – E +, Flt Lt C. B. Walker and remainder of crew uninj

3 Jun 43   Hudson shot down by *Lt* Heinz Olbrecht, 15/KG 40, *PlQ* 14W/2785, 1025hrs

Hudson FK386 of 117 Sqn. Reported missing in transit from Portreath to Gibraltar. Fg Off J. B. Buckley – P, Fg Off E. J. McSherney – N, F/S D. V. Edwards – WOp. Passengers: Gp Capt R. G. Yaxley DSO, MC, DFC, Wg Cdr H. F. Burton DSO, DFC, Wg Cdr E. Paul, Wg Cdr D. T. Cotton, Sqn Ldr O. V. Hanbury DSO, DFC, Sqn Ldr J. K. Young, Wg Cdr J. Goodhead, all M

Beaufighter damaged by Ju 88, possibly Hampden claimed by *Oblt* Albrecht Bellstedt, 14/KG 40

Beaufighter JL819/W of 236 Sqn. Flt Lt H. Shannon – P, uninj; Plt Off S. I. Walters – N, W; Lt Cdr F. J. Brookes, both +

14 Jun 43   B-17 shot down by *Lt* Lothar Wolff, 15/KG 40, 90km NW of Cap Ortegal, *PlQ* 14W/0557, 2040hrs

Fortress FK212/V of 220 Sqn. Fg Off C. F. Callender, Fg Off J. W. Verney, Sgt N. Harbridge, Plt Off W. Offler, F/S E. Wright, F/S W. Comba, F/S G. Dawson and F/S S. Frost, all +

Whitley shot down by *Lt* Friedrich Maeder, 13/KG 40, 1757hrs. Possibly Mosquito DD643 of 264 Sqn, lost over Bay of Biscay, 1610hrs. W/O P. D. Hendra, F/S K. P. O'Dowd, both M

Hampden shot down by *Hptm* Hans Morr, *St Kap* 15/KG 40

Hampden X2961/S of 415 Sqn. Sqn Ldr J. G. Stronach, W/O W. A. Trask, Plt Off A. B. Clegg, Fg Off G. K. Crumming, all +

19 Jun 43 Mosquito damaged in combat with Ju 88 of 14/KG 40

Mosquito S of 151 Sqn. Damaged in combat, suffered engine failure and crash-landed at Predannack. Fg Off A. D. Boyle and Sgt H M Friesner, both uninj

22 Jun 43 Hudson damaged in combat with V/KG 40

Hudson U of 1404 Flt. Sgt Davis and crew uninj

1 Jul 43 Liberator damaged in combat with V/KG 40, *PlQ* 14W/8556-9696, 1359-1423hrs

Liberator BZ730/O of 53 Sqn. Fg Off R. T. Merrifield and crew uninj

7 Jul 43 Beaufighter shot down by *Oblt* Dieter Meister, 13/KG 40, *PlQ* 14W/9637, 0925hrs.

Beaufighter LX781 of 304 FTU. Lt W. L. Cox USAAC – P, M; Sgt E. R. Black – N, + (buried Burello, Spain). Possibly claimed by 1/128?

8 Jul 43 Liberator shot down by *Hptm* Horst Grahl, *Lt* Lothar Wolff and four others from 15/KG 40, *PlQ* 14W/0685, 1725hrs

Liberator BZ716/B of 53 Sqn badly damaged in combat with Ju 88s. Fg Off J. F. Handasyde – P, Plt Off O. G Eaves, F/S A. J. Barnes, F/S A. E. Whorlow, Sgt H. D. Lindsay, all uninj; Fg Off J. Witts, +; F/S H. A. Pomeroy – WOp/AG, W

12 Jul 43 Whitley shot down by *Oblt* Hans Schuster, 15/KG 40, *PlQ* 24W/1553, 1610hrs

Whitley BD681/N of 10 OTU. Sgt C. T. Rudman, Sgt R. B. Turner, Sgt W. A. Speller, Lt J. B. Williams and Sgt R. R. Riddle, all +

Sunderland shot down by *Lt* Ulrich Hanshen, 15/KG 40, *PlQ* 24W/1679, 1518hrs

Sunderland DV977/Y of 228 Sqn. Sgt R. Codd, Sgt R. Martin, Sgt J. Sowerby, Sgt P. Harding, Sgt D. Hamilton, F/S R. Armstrong, Sgt A. Sparks, Sgt J. Graham, Sgt D. Waterman, Sgt R. Whale, all +; Sgt E Davidson rescued

16 Jul 43 Halifax damaged in combat with V/KG 40

Halifax JD178/V of 502 Sqn. Fg Off J. G. Grant and crew uninj

17 Jul 43 Sunderland shot down by *Oblt* Siegfried Ramsauer, Stab V/KG 40, 0842hrs

Possibly Sunderland EJ145/P of 204 Sqn. Crashed during escort duties 100 miles NW of Port Etienne. Fg Off D. W. Pallett – P, Sgt A. J. Fulker – P, Sgt R. A. Adams – E, Sgt H. Adamson – N, Sgt F. Ascough – WOp/AG, Fg Off R. N. McCann – WOp/AG, Sgt W. H. Corless – WOM/AG, Sgt G. J. Davis – WOp/AG, Sgt R. B. Murray – WOp/AG, Sgt A. J. Tregallas – E, all safe

18 Jul 43   Sunderland shot down by *Oblt* Gustav Christner and *Lt* Lothar Wolff, 15/KG 40, *PlQ* 14W/0555, 1314hrs (*Lt* Knud Gmelin, 13/KG 40, involved)

Sunderland JM687 of 204 Sqn. Missing on trip from UK to Gibraltar. Flt Lt A. H. N. Gooch – P (Capt), Sgt D. G. Griffiths – P, Plt Off R. J. Quinn – AG, Sgt A. Thompson – FME/AG, Sgt A. J. Tozer – E, Sgt J. Greenwood – WOp/AG, Sgt E. A. Dutton – WOp, F/S A. H. Looms – WOM/AG, Plt Off D. C. Rundle – N (crew). Passengers: AC L. Ballard, Surg Lt J. H. Wainwright, LMM A. Guy, ACMM V. Bardsey, Nurse E. J. A. Mehaffey, all M

Liberator shot down by *Oblt* Kurt Necesany, *St Kap* 14/KG 40

Liberator BZ731/D of 53 Sqn. SOS received 1205hrs. Flt Lt J. A. Dewhirst – P, Fg Off K. C. Hollison – 2P, Fg Off G. R. Rowland, Plt Off G. W. Snelling, Sgt J. E. Devine, F/S B. G. Kemp, F/S I. Chadwick, all M

Whitley shot down by *Oblt* Albrecht Bellstedt, 14/KG 40, *PlQ* 24W/1745, 1129hrs

Whitley LA880/R of 10 OTU. Fg Off G. C. Hamilton – P, Plt Off J. D. S. Goldring – P, Fg Off G. W. F. Button – N, Plt Off S. Lees – B, Sgt F. Mills – WOp, Sgt J. A. J. Jarman – AG, all M

Liberator damaged in combat with *Oblt* Kurt Necesany, *St Kap* 14/KG 40

Liberator FL959/N of 224 Sqn. Fg Off J. V. Gibson and crew uninj

21 Jul 43   Halifax shot down by *Hptm* Hans Morr, *St Kap* 15/KG 40

Halifax DG391/RR of 295 Sqn. Missing returning from Ras El Mar; reported being attacked by Ju 88s. Fg Off P. T. Muirhead DFC – P, F/S S. McCormick – N, Sgt N. R. Waite – E, Sgt E. Williams – WOp, Sgt R. J. Broad – AG; passengers Wg Cdr W. S. Barton DFC, Fg Off E. H. Ottway, Fg Off Taylor. All M

26 Jul 43   Wellington shot down by *Lt* Gerhard Blankenberg, 13/KG 40, 200km NW of Cap Ortegal, *PlQ* 24W/1745, 1120hrs (shared by *Uffz* Heinz Hommel; *Lt* Knud Gmelin involved)

Wellington HZ640 of 304 Sqn. Flt Lt S. J. Rolinski, Sgt R. Zagorowski, Flt Lt W. Jagiello, Sgt S. Zawilinski, Sgt S. Ehrlich, Fg Off J. Kulicki, all +. Took off 0555hrs?

27 Jul 43   Sunderland damaged in combat with V/KG 40

Sunderland DV969/E of 10 Sqn RAAF. Fg Off R. C. W. Humble and crew uninj

29 Jul 43   Beaufighter possibly damaged in combat with *Lt* Gerhard Blankenberg, 13/KG 40

Beaufighter LX819/WR-U of 248 Sqn crashed on landing at Predannack, 1615hrs. Fg Off G. K. Thompson and Sgt C. F. Barnes, both inj

31 Jul 43   Halifax damaged in combat with Ju 88s

Halifax T (B?) of 502 Sqn. Fg Off M. J. Davey and crew uninj

1 Aug 43   Catalina shot down by *Lt* Knud Gmelin, 13/KG 40, *Lt* Friedrich Maeder
             and *Lt* Lothar Wolff, 15/KG 40, 48.10N 12.00W (360km SW of Brest,
             PlQ 24W/2733), 1552hrs (shared by *Uffz* Heinz Hommel; ac of *Lt* Gmelin
             shot down)

             PBY-5 serial 08231/J named 'Aunt Minnie' of VP 63, USN. Shot down
             at 47.10N 12.00W, 1600hrs. Lt W. P. Tanner – Commander, Ensign R.
             J. Bedell – 2P, ACM3C D. C. Paterson – waist gunner, all rescued
             wounded by HMS *Bideford* 1440hrs 2 August 43 at 39.04N 09.08E. Lt
             (jg) B. E. Robertson – N, AP1c A. A. Rittel – bow gunner, ACMM(AA)
             W. H. Golder – Captain, AMM2c D. R. Carmack – 2nd mech, AMM3c
             R. B. Law – 3rd mech, ACRM(AA) R. C. Scott – 1st radioman, ARM2c
             W. O. Rude – 2nd radioman/waist gunner, all +

2 Aug 43   Hampden shot down by *Lt* Lothar Wolff, 15/KG 40, 0605-1133hrs
             (shared by *Uffz* Heinz Hommel and *Uffz* Herbert Klose)/*Lt* Max
             Wittmer, 14/KG 40, 0840hrs, *PlQ* 24W/1867 (shared by *Lt* Arthur
             Schroeder and *Lt* Friedrich Maeder, 13/KG 40)

             Hampden AT182 of 1404 (Met) Flt. Plt Off W. C. Liebermann – P, Sgt
             J. Cunningham – WOp, Sgt W. M. Crosbie – WOp, Plt Off A. A.
             Pottinger – N, all M

3 Aug 43   Sunderland damaged in hour-long combat with seven Ju 88s of V/KG
             40, *PlQ* 14W/9850, 1837hrs

             Sunderland DD852/J of 10 Sqn RAAF. Fg Off R. W. Gross – N, Sgt G. L.
             Fry – FIIE, Sgt R. F. Owen – FMEAG, F/S H. Pengilly – WOp/AG, all
             W; F/S H. A. Bird – AG, +. Fg Off B. A. Williams and rest of crew uninj

8 Aug 43   Sunderland damaged in combat with V/KG 40, 1245hrs (eight attacks)

             Sunderland DP177/F of 10 Sqn RAAF. Flt Lt N C Gerrard and crew uninj

             Liberator shot down by *Hptm* Horst Grahl, Stab V/KG 40, NW of Cap
             Ortegal, 1148hrs (27 attacks by eight aircraft)

             B-24D Liberator Q of 4th Sqn, 479th Anti-Submarine Gp. Shot down
             by German fighters between 1159 and 1225hrs. Capt R. L. Thomas Jr –
             P, 1/Lt G. E. Good – N, 2/Lt J. L. Garrick – bomb, F/O C. G. George –
             Co-pilot, T/Sgt D. E. Bowsman – Rad Op, S/Sgt C. J. Woodward – E,
             S/Sgt J. H. Perce – AG, T/Sgt D. J. Gray Jr – rad op, S/Sgt R. T. Dodd
             – Asst rad op, S/Sgt G. E. Henriot Jr – Asst E, all M

11 Aug 43   Mosquito shot down by *Lt* Gerhard Blankenberg, 15/KG 40

             Mosquito DZ375/L of 192 Sqn. Took off 1635hrs for operation over
             the Bay. Fg Off E. W. K. Salter and WO R. C. Besant DFM, both M

             Sunderland shot down by V/KG 40

             Sunderland DP177/F of 10 Sqn RAAF. Flt Lt N. C. Gerrard, Fg Off K.
             D. Smith, Fg Off I. W. Bowen, Plt Off J. I. Rowland, Sgt D. Bennington,
             Sgt W. E. Mathews, W/O F. Jones, W/O J. G. Webster, Sgt J. G. Dwyer,
             Sgt J. E. Challinor, Sgt J. R. Dallas, Plt Off R. J. Adams, all +

12 Aug 43   Liberator damaged by three Ju 88s of V/KG 40, 1528hrs

             Liberator BZ793/H of 53 Sqn. W/O C. C. McPherson and crew uninj

13 Aug 43   Sunderland shot down by *Lt* Artur Schroeder, 13/KG 40

Sunderland DV968/M of 461 Sqn. Radioed under attack by Ju 88s at 1449hrs. Fg Off W. J. Dowling, Fg Off D. T. Galt DFC, Fg Off J. C. Grainger, Fg Off K. M. Simpson DFC, F/S R. K. Turner, Sgt L. S. Watson, F/S E. A. Fuller DFM, W/O S. F. Miller, F/S A. Lane, W/O R. M. Goode DFM, F/S C. Longston, all +

Wellington shot down by *Lt* Dieter Meister, 13/KG 40

Wellington HZ638 of 304 Sqn. Took off 0936hrs. Plt Off S. Kielan, Sgt W. Pastwa, Flt Lt S. Widanka, Sgt L. Dangel, Sgt F. Gorka, Sgt K. Czarnecki, all M

15 Aug 43   Sunderland shot down by V/KG 40 and ditched off Scilly Islands

Sunderland JM685/X of 461 Sqn. Damaged in combat with Ju 88s at 1800hrs and force-landed off Hugh Town, Scilly Islands, 2040hrs. W/O I. Jones – W, F/S R. V. Woodhouse, both +. Flt Lt P. R. Davenport and rest of crew uninj

Wellington shot down by *Lt* Friedrich Maeder, 13/KG 40, 1532-2036hrs (shared by *Uffz* Heinz Hommel)

Wellington shot down by *Hptm* Hans Morr, *St Kap* 15/KG 40

Wellington MP760/Q of 612 Sqn. Took off 0846hrs. Plt Off K. Harrison – P, Plt Off R. A. Wilson – 2P, Sgt J. H. Greaves – WOp, Sgt A. W. Mark – WOp, Fg Off C. H. Phelps – N, Sgt D. B. Green – AG, all M

Wellington HZ351/T of 547 Sqn. Took off 1151hrs. Fg Off J. Whyte – P, Fg Off W. J. K. Dixon, Plt Off A. Fisher, F/S A. L. Bathurst, F/S L. G. Simpson, F/S H. E. Taylor, all +

Wellington MP565/C of 547 Sqn. Took off 1303hrs. Sgt D. P. Stephen – P, Sgt S. Steward – P, Fg Off L. Durbin – N, Fg Off R. D. S. Noble – WOp/AG, Sgt K. F. Dunford – WOp/AG, Sgt H. J. Oliver – WOp/AG, all M

Halifax shot down by *Oblt* Albrecht Bellstedt, 14/KG 40

Halifax HR745/S of 58 Sqn. Shot down by Ju 88s, 47.55N, 09.31W, 1548hrs. F/S I. S. Dunbar, F/S J. Trotter, F/S R. J. H. Baron, Sgt H. J. Shaw, F/S R. R. P. MacKenzie, F/S L. A. Davies, Sgt R. Major, Sgt S. E. Hillman, all +

16 Aug 43   Halifax shot down by *Hptm* Hans Morr, *St Kap* 15/KG 40, 100km WNW of Cap Ortegal, 1930hrs

Halifax HR746/M of 58 Sqn. Fg Off M. H. Jenkins – P, Fg Off H. M. Park, Plt Off P. Y. Williams, Sgt A. J. King, Sgt G. S. Holloway, Plt Off G. W. Webster, Sgt S. R. Johnston, Sgt W. G. Hargreaves, Sgt A. W. S. Bundy, all M

18 Aug 43   Sunderland shot down by *Hptm* Horst Grahl, Stab V/KG 40

Sunderland W3985/T of 10 Sqn RAAF. Flt Lt H. W. Skinner, Fg Off V. D. W. Collins, Fg Off W. N. Hill, Fg Off R. R. Swinson, Sgt A. Slater, Sgt W. P. Greatz, F/S R. A. Giles, F/S K. M. Meldrum, Sgt A. R. Aldridge, F/S H. E. Burbridge, Sgt N. H. Orford, all +

Liberator shot down by *Hptm* Hans Morr, 15/KG 40, 1742hrs

B-24D Liberator coded 'G' of 19th Sqn, 479th Anti-Submarine Gp. Shot down by German fighters 45.09N 11.23W, 1742hrs. 1/Lt S. M. Grider – Capt, 2/Lt C. H. Moore – P, T/Sgt F. G. Antosz – Eng, T/Sgt G. E. Peeples – rad op, S/Sgt H. E. Bischoff – AG, Sgt L. Rosenberg – Asst rad op, all rescued 23 August 43. 2/Lt E. A. Kelton – N, 2/Lt P. Levine – bomb, S/Sgt J. K. Daniels – Asst eng, S/Sgt H. E. La Plante – radar op, all M

Wellington shot down by *Oblt* Hermann Horstmann, *St Kap* 13/KG 40

Wellington HZ407/K of 547 Sqn. F/S J. Clark, Plt Off L. G. Springer, Sgt C. R. Byers, Sgt G. Hastell, Sgt H. J. Graham, Sgt G. Smith, all M

Liberator damaged by V/KG 40

B-24D Liberator of 19th Sqn, 479th Anti-Submarine Gp. Damaged in combat with Ju 88s, 45.45N 09.42W, 1825hrs. Lt. A L. Leal and crew uninj

22 Aug 43   Wellington shot down by *Oblt* Kurt Necesany, *St Kap* 14/KG 40, 130km W of Cap Ortegal (shared by *Lt* Lothar Wolff)

Wellington HZ576 of 304 Sqn. Fg Off B. Porebski, Sgt K. Gawlik, Fg Off B. Matuszewski, Sgt W. Walkiewicz, Sgt S. Szcepaniak, F/S T. Wojnilowicz, all +

23 Aug 43   Liberator damaged by *Lt* Ulrich Hanshen, 15/KG 40 (Ju 88 also shot down)

B-24D Liberator of 4th Sqn, 479th Anti-Submarine Gp. Attacked by Ju 88s, 46.53N 09.18W, 0813hrs. Three crew W; 1/Lt K. H. Dustin and remainder uninj

24 Aug 43   Halifax shot down by *Oblt* Hermann Horstmann, *St Kap* 13/KG 40

Halifax DT636 of 58 Sqn. Attacked by fourteen Ju 88s, crashed in Bay of Biscay and sank immediately, 1315hrs. Flt Lt G. A. Sawtell – P, F/S L. C. Matthews – WOp, Sgt J. W. Bailey – WOp, Sgt B. E. Mitchell – WOp, Sgt W. A. Tennant – WOp, F/S A. C. Wilder – E, F/S T. R. Urquart – N, Fg Off J. M. Clarke, all M

27 Aug 43   Liberator shot down by *Hptm* Hans Morr, *St Kap* 15/KG 40, near Cap Finisterre

Liberator 42-40767 of 389th BG. Reported missing Bay of Biscay. Lt D. C. Lighter – P, Lt D. Reinard – P, Lt S. Williams – N, T/Sgt C. Speece, S/Sgt F. Poitras – AG, and passengers Sgt H. S. Haft, M/Sgt C. Cronberg, T/Sgt E. Keller, all M; Sgt C. R. Woolfe and Sgt M. Weems +

30 Aug 43   Sunderland shot down by *Uffz* Heinz Hommel, 13/KG 40, 120km NW of Cap Ortegal, *PlQ* 14W/0647, 1217hrs (shared by *Oblt* Dieter Meister and *Uffz* Juergen Heicke)

Sunderland JM707 of 461 Sqn. Shot down in Bay of Biscay, 1106hrs. Fg Off C. R. Croft – Capt, Plt Off J. A. Tamsett – P, F/S R. G. Harris – P, F/S W. Stewart – FMEAG, Sgt H. J. Ferrett – FMEAG, Fg Off G. J. Bushell – O, W/O J. Gamble – WOpAG, F/S W. Yeomans – WAG, F/S G. Ritchie – WAG, F/S R. J. Hunter – WAG, F/S H. Smedley – WOM, all M

Liberator damaged in combat with V/KG 40

Liberator BZ948/M of 311 Sqn damaged in combat 1100hrs. Sgt A. Sipek – WOp, +; Plt Off J. Stach, F/S B. Heza, Fg Off Dolezal, F/S A. Martis, F/S E. Reich, Sgt F. Benedikt, all uninj

2 Sep 43   Liberator shot down by *Oblt* Kurt Necesany, *St Kap* 14/KG 40 (see also 3 Sep 43)

Liberator FL938/P of 224 Sqn. Shot down by Ju 88s, 1630hrs. Fg Off G. H. Wharram, Plt Off W. R. Collins, Fg Off J. C. Miller, Sgt E. A. Moloney, Sgt D. H. Bareham, all +; Sgt R. J. Foss, Plt Off J. R. Wilcox, Plt Off D. M. Johnstone, Sgt W. W. Dilks picked up by HMS *Wildgoose*, 6 Sep 43

Liberator FL959/G of 224 Sqn. Fg Off J. V. Gibson, Plt Off K. T. Every, Plt Off V. Lower, Fg Off H. R. Tierney, Sgt A. A. Thompson, Fg Off P. P. R. Mackintosh, W/O W. J. Volasivitch, Sgt H. T. French, all +; Sgt K. Graves safe

PB4Y-1 Liberator serial 32033 of VB103. Lt K. W. Wickstrom – P, Ens C. K. Martin, AP1C L. R. Perry, AMM1C N. M. De La Rue, ARM2C W. B. Wadsworth, AOM2C R. J. Olsen, AMM3C W. B. Marshburn, S2C J. N. Rubin, ARM3C M, Steinberg, all M

3 Sep 43   Liberator shot down by *Lt* Knud Gmelin, 13/KG 40

No RAF loss (see 2 Sep 43)

4 Sep 43   Liberator shot down in combat with 13/KG 40; *Lt* Gerhard Blankenberg also shot down

PB4Y-1 Liberator serial 32022 coded 'G' of VB103. Shot down by Ju 88s and ditched 75 miles NW of Finisterre, 1723hrs. Lt (jg) J. H. Alexander – P, Lt P. B. Kinney – 2P, Ens D. L. Barnett – Bow gunner, AOM3C C. Pytel – Bow gunner, ACMM R. S. Hoffmann – Top turret, ACRM J. T. Guthrie – Waist gunner, S1C H. J. Lasseigne – Waist gunner, S2C J. P. Dowdy – Tail gunner, ARM2C T. E. Tennant, all rescued with various minor injuries/wounds by Spanish trawler near Corcubion, Spain, 6 Sep 43

8 Sep 43   Liberator shot down by *Lt* Lothar Wolff, 13/KG 40, 240km W of Brest

B-24D Liberator 42-40790/B of 4th Sqn, 479th Anti-Submarine Gp. Shot down by enemy fighters 48.00N 10.54W, 1647hrs. 1/Lt E. I. Finneburgh – P, 1/Lt N. J. Evenson – bomb, T/Sgt T. L. Sutton – rad op, S/Sgt W. H. Hulen – radar op, S/Sgt J. H. W. Roux – Asst rad op, S/Sgt L. Helton – E, all +; F/O J. E. Schneider – co-pilot, 1/Lt A. J. Leone – N, T/Sgt L. A. Smith – Asst E, S/Sgt L. A. Footh – AG, all rescued

11 Sep 43   Mosquito shot down by V/KG 40, 380sms W of Brest

Mosquito DZ749 of 307 Sqn. Returned damaged from combat with Ju 88 of V/KG 40. W/O L. Szemplinski – P and F/S F. Tilman – N, uninj

16 Sep 43   Sunderland probably shot down by six Ju 88s of 14/KG 40 (*Lt* Willi Gutermann involved)

Sunderland EW578/E of 461 Sqn. Ditched after combat with Ju 88s c1537hrs at 45.42N 11.00W. Sgt P. Bamber – AG, W; Flt Lt D. Marrow – P, Fg Off P. T. Jensen – RG, Fg Off I. Peatty, Sgt J. T. Eshelby – E, Sgt A. N. Pearce – AG, Plt Off W. Done, Plt Off P. C. Leigh, F/S C. Sidney, Sgt P. R. Criddle, all uninj and rescued next day

18 Sep 43   Horsa shot down by *Oblt* Dieter Meister, 13/KG 40, 45.50N 10. 50W, 340km WSW of Cap Finisterre, 1207hrs (shared by *Oblt* Hermann Horstmann, *Lt* Knud Gmelin and *Uffz* Heinz Hommel)

Horsa HS102, towed by Halifax DG396/QQ of 295 Sqn (Fg Off A. G. Norman). Lt J. R. Prout, Sgt P. B. Hill, Sgt H. Flynn, all rescued

21 Sep 43   Sunderland shot down by 14/KG 40

Sunderland DV969/E of 10 Sqn RAAF. Fg Off A. G. Jennison – Capt, Fg Off A. N. Buckland – P, Plt Off A. W. Gunston – P, Fg Off A. L. Coomes – N, Sgt J. T. Law – E, Sgt S. C. E. Leech – FIIE, F/S N. D. K. Swinton – AG, F/S L. E. Waddington – AG, Sgt J. D. T. Daley – AG, F/S D. Harris – AG, Sgt C. S. Cameron – AG, all M

25 Sep 43   Mosquito and Beaufighter shot down by *Ofw* Kurt Gaebler, 15/KG 40

Mosquito HJ658 of 307 Sqn. F/S L. J. Lowndes and F/S I. Cotton, both M

Beaufighter A of 235 Sqn. Tail shredded by cannon fire and lost hydraulic system. Belly-landed at base 1911hrs. Plt Off L. D. Oakley – P, Plt Off J. Eaton – N, both uninj

4 Oct 43   Liberator shot down by *Oblt* Kurt Necesany, *St Kap* 14/KG 40

Liberator BZ753/S of 53 Sqn. SOS received 1034hrs, seen by a 224 Sqn ac to have been shot down. Flt Lt J. Rintoul – P, Fg Off D. B. Stewart – P, Sgt A. Fieldhouse – N, Fg Off C. W. Foster – WOp/AG, F/S D. W. McInnes – WOp/AG, F/S F. F. Mercer – WOp/AG, F/S W. F. Garrod – WOp/AG, F/S W. A. Dearman – WOp, Flt Lt E. M. C. Guest – P, all M

7 Oct 43   Beaufighter shot down in combat with V/KG 40

Beaufighter JM118/Q of 143 Sqn. Shot down in combat, 46.32N 10.24W, 208 miles NW of Cap Ortegal, 1525hrs. F/S R. Cole and Sgt H. Moorehouse, both M

Liberators damaged in combat with V/KG 40

Liberator BZ787/E of 311 Sqn. Plt Off J. Stach and crew uninj

Liberator BZ779/J of 311 Sqn. Sgt A. Matijsek – WOp, F/S F. Ververka – RG, both W; F/S J. Kuhn and rest of crew uninj

B-24D coded 'P' of 2nd Sqn, 480th Anti-Submarine Gp. Capt G. L. Mosier – P and crew uninj

10 Nov 43   Sunderland shot down by *Oblt* Albrecht Bellstedt, *St Kap* 2/ZG 1, NW of Cap Ortegal, *PlQ* 14W/8413, 1800hrs

Sunderland EK572/V of 228 Sqn. Fg Off A. V. W. Franklin – P, F/S J. S. Jarvis – P, Sgt V. W. Moss – P, Sgt R. McCormick – WOMEAG, Sgt F. Lawrence – AG, Sgt D. J. MaCaree – AG, Sgt J. F. Phizacklea – WOp/AG, Sgt A. E. Nattress – E, Sgt A, W, Aitkin – ACHGD, all M; Fg Off W, E, Merrifield – N, Sgt A, Wells – FM, Sgt A. B. Boocock, all +. Last contact 1755hrs; crashed off Estaca De Bares, Spain. Six bodies recovered but only three identified and buried at Puerto De Barquero Cemetery, Manon, Coruna, Spain

17 Nov 43   Sunderland shot down by *Uffz* Fritz Haenel, 3/ZG 1, *PlQ* 14W/0615, 1430hrs (shared by *Lt* Ulrich Hanshen)

Sunderland DV993 of 10 Sqn RAAF. Fg Off R. C. Behrendt – Capt, Fg Off A. G. Hartwig – P, Fg Off C. Furzer – P, Fg Off A. F. Davis – N, Sgt K. Coghill – E, Sgt H. E. Knights – FIIA, W/O H. J. Hicks – AG, Sgt J. T. R. Jones – WOp, Sgt A. T. Brooking – AG, F/S C. H. S. Leggo – AG, Sgt P. Stanton – AG, all M

19 Nov 43   Wellington shot down by *Lt* Lothar Wolff, 2/ZG 1, NW of Cap Ortegal

Wellington shot down by *Lt* Willi Gutermann, 2/ZG 1, NW of Cap Ortegal

(two kills: *PlQ* 24W/1634, 1105hrs, and *PlQ* 24W/2648, 1120hrs)

Wellington LN704 of 15 OTU. Took off from Portreath 0745hrs for Rabat. Fg Off C. R. Leitch – P, Sgt M. J. Martin – P, Sgt J. M. Carruthers – passenger, Sgt R. N. DeL. Hogge – AG, Sgt W. R. Silcocks – AG, Sgt H. A. Wright – WOp, Sgt A. I. Hosie – E, Sgt P. Ringrose, Fg Off P. V. Wilson, all M

Wellington HZ129 of 15 OTU. Took off from Portreath 0737hrs. F/S R. H. Matherson – P, Sgt P. J. Deveney – WOp, F/S J. R. Forbes – AG, Sgt L. S. Harris – AG, F/S J. A. McC. Murray – AG, Sgt E. A. Robinson – N, all M. Passengers Sgt L. T. Smith and Sgt F. J. Wooldridge, both M

29 Nov 43   Sunderland shot down by *Uffz* Franz Frank, 1/ZG 1, *PlQ* 24W/2834, 1410hrs (shared by *Uffz* Heinz Hommel, *Lt* Knud Gmelin and *Oblt* Hermann Horstmann)

Sunderland JM676 of 461 Sqn. Fg Off D. S. P. Howe – Capt, Plt Off G. Y. Temple – P, Fg Off J. J. Dupont DFM – P, Fg Off G. W. B. Bye – N, F/S L. White – E, F/S J. H. Royal – WOp, F/S L. G. Studman – WOp, F/S W. K. Moritz – WOpAG, Fg Off K. V. Hore – AG, Fg Off E. R. Critcher – WOpAG, Sgt R. Jeffreys – FMEAG, Fg Off J. H. Poulton – WOp, all M

30 Nov 43   Sunderland badly damaged in combat with 6 Ju 88s of 2/ZG 1, *PlQ* 14W/0818, 1410hrs (*Uffz* Fischer shot down)

Sunderland DD865/L of 10 Sqn. Returned badly damaged. Flt Lt C. C. Clerk – P, Sgt L. T. Lang – Arm, F/S F. C. Callander – AG, all W, remainder of crew unhurt

1 Dec 43   Mosquito shot down by *Ogefr* Heinrich Roensch, BF, 2/ZG 1, *PlQ*
            14W/0863, 1205hrs

            Mosquito shot down by *Lt* Oxfort (?), 7/ZG 1, *PlQ* 14W/0863, 1200hrs

            Mosquito HJ656 of 157 Sqn shot down at 47.13N 08.00W, 1155hrs.
            F/S W. A. Robertson and F/S G. H. Spanton, both M

            Beaufighter shot down by I/ZG 1, *PlQ* 14W/0842, 1510hrs. 235 Sqn
            reported combat with Ju 88s at this time; no losses

12 Dec 43   Two Beaufighters shot down by *Lt* Knud Gmelin and *Oblt* Hermann
            Horstmann, 1/ZG 1, *PlQ* 14W/0818, 1409hrs (three Ju 88s shot down)

            Beaufighter JM132/T of 143 Sqn. Fg Off M. Bentley and Sgt A. C. L.
            Phillips, both M, c1412hrs

            Beaufighter JM158/A of 143 Sqn. Flt Lt S. A. Tucker and Fg Off R. J.
            Scott, both M, 1412hrs

5 Jan 44   B-17 shot down by *Ofw* Kurt Gaebler, 3/ZG 1, *PlQ* 14W/2686
            (Hourtin), 1107hrs

            Possibly B-17 G 42-31164 named 'Lucky Lady' of 337 BS/96 BG.
            Shot down by German fighters and crash-landed near small lake W of
            Bordeaux, post-1040hrs. 2/Lt R. A. Stakes – P, 2/Lt W. M. Foley –
            co-pilot, 2/Lt L. E. Grauerholtz – N, T/Sgt E. R. Aldridge – E, T/Sgt
            H. G. Rudd – rad op, S/Sgt H. H. Rocha – waist G, all E; S/Sgt C. J.
            Robinson – waist G, +; S/Sgt P. J. Farmer-Ball – G and S/Sgt R. M.
            Cox, both POW

7 Jan 44   Mosquito shot down in combat with *Fw* Johann Puetz, 7/ZG 1 (Ju 88
            shot down in combat)

            Mosquito HJ660 of 157 Sqn. Ditched after combat at 47.08N 07.30W,
            1632hrs. Fg Off P. E. Huckin and F/S R. H. Graham rescued six days later

1 Feb 44   Beaufighter shot down in combat with *Lt* Robert Baumann, 7/ZG 1,
            Mediterranean (also claimed by *Lt* Ulrich Hanshen, Stab III/ZG 1?)

            Beaufighter NE466/F of 39 Sqn. F/S F. A. Cooper – P and Sgt A. V.
            Bridle, both rescued uninj

14 Feb 44   Liberator probably shot down in combat with *Oblt* Kurt Necesany, Stab
            I/ZG 1 (German pilot shot down)

            PB4Y-1 Liberator number 32191 coded C of VB103. Badly damaged
            in combat with what they thought were Ju 188s at 48.00N 09.36W,
            1634hrs, and ditched at 50.35N 06.10 W, 170 miles SW of Bishops
            Rock, 1800hrs. ARM2c T. E. Ryan and ARM2c R. C. Erdmann, both
            M; AOM2c B. Faubion, +; Lt (jg) K. L. Wright – P, Lt (jg) L. M.
            Petersen, Ens R. W. Lacey, AMM1C W. E. Middleton, AMM2C R. C.
            McDaniel, AMM3C R. M. Greene, ACOM (AA) R. A. Zabcik,
            AOM2C C. F. Lilley Jr, all rescued

15 Feb 44   Sunderland damaged in combat with 16 Ju 88s of 2/ZG 1

            Sunderland EK574/Q of 10 Sqn RAAF. Damaged in combat 90 miles
            SW of Bishops Rock, 0915hrs, returned to Mountbatten. F/S G. S.
            Mills – RG, +; Flt Lt McCulloch and rest of crew uninj

26 Feb 44   Halifax shot down by *Uffz* Fritz Gilfert, 3/ZG 1, *PlQ* 15W/2845, 1045hrs

PB4Y-1 Liberator number 63929 coded 'R' of VB105. Shot down by enemy aircraft, 49.48N 10.34W, 1053hrs. Lt R. L. North – P, Lt J. E. Goodrich, Ens V. D'Harlingue Jr, AMM1c H. L. Counts, ARM1c W. F. Brown, AMM2c F. B. Malounek Jr, ARM2c F. J. Waldron Jr, AOM3c L. R. Merritt, AMM2c J. R. Van Benschoten, AMM3c W. W. Pendleton, ARM3c W. Pawlyk, all M

8 Mar 44   Beaufighter shot down by 2/ZG 1 (*Lt* Willi Gutermann involved) during escort sortie for KG 26

Beaufighter V8872 of 153 Sqn. Shot down 35 miles NW of Algiers, 1900hrs. F/S A. A. Applegate and F/S J. C. W. Marshall, both M

23 Mar 44   Sunderland shot down by *Hptm* Guenther Moltrecht, *St Kap* 1/ZG 1, *PlQ* 14W/0511, 1358hrs (*Uffz* Heinz Hommel, *Uffz* Rolf Dickel and six others involved)

Sunderland ML740/F of 461 Sqn. Shot down on anti-submarine patrol 1330hrs, survivors rescued by HMS *Saladin*. Plt Off J. H. Smith – P, Plt Off O. L. Howard – P, F/S R. A. Smythe – WOp, F/S D. R. Molan – WOp, F/S N. A. Royal – WOpAG, all M; Fg Off F. H. Bunce – P, F/S K. G. Angus – WOp, F/S R. N. Thompson – WOpAG, all inj; F/S F. A. Reid – WAG, Sgt F. Reed – Eng, Sgt D. W. Juke – FE, Fg Off M. G. J. Fuller – O, all rescued; F/S R. N. Thompson – WOpAG, rescued inj

Sunderland DV989 of 461 Sqn. Damaged in combat with Ju 88s. Fg Off H. M. Godsall and crew uninj

31 Mar 44   B-24 shot down by *Oblt* Dieter Meister, 1/ZG 1, *PlQ* 15W/0055, 1436hrs

PB4Y-1 Liberator number 63948 of VB110. Shot down by Ju 88s at 49.38N 10.16W, 1335hrs. Lt H. Barton – P, Lt (jg) .R .J Schuetz, Ens C. J. Parker, Ens P. W. Bash, ACMM W. C. Ketchem, AMM2c R. P. Krebbs, ARM2c E. V. J. Timberman, ARM3c A. P. Olliver, ARM3c E. H. McLean, AOM2c D. C. Gamble, AOM2c R. W. Mellette, AMM3c W. F. Smith, all M

B-24 shot down by I/ZG 1, *PlQ* 15W/1046, 1507hrs

PB4Y-1 Liberator number 63940/L/B-11 of VB110. Shot down by Ju 88s, 49.46N 08.59W, 1407hrs. Lt (jg) O. R. Moore – P, Lt (jg) G. A. Rapp, Ens R. M. Krueger, AMM1c S. R. Clayton, AMM2c W. A. Bozrich, AMM3c H. O. Prather, S2c G. P. Enfinger, AOM2c J. R. Stewart Jr, ARM1c W. N. Swanson, ARM2c P. I. Jordan, all M

11 Apr 44   Two Mosquitoes shot down near Lorient by *Lt* Knud Gmelin, 1/ZG 1, 0936 and 0940hrs; one Mosquito shot down by *Uffz* Gerhard Zimmermann (BF to *Lt* Gmelin), *PlQ* 14W/3880, 0937hrs

Mosquito (unconfirmed) shot down near Lorient by *Uffz* Josef Horvath, 1/ZG 1, c0935hrs (Ju 88 shot down and pilot +)

Mosquito LR345/WR-W of 248 Sqn. Shot down 0935hrs. Wg Cdr O. J. M. Barron DFC and Bar/Fg Off R. T. Woodcraft, both M

Mosquito LR349/WR-Y of 248 Sqn. Shot down 0935hrs. Flt Lt K. Liversidge and Sgt L. E. Newens, both POW

Mosquito MM505 of 151 Sqn. Ditched 47.00N 02.00W after combat, 0945hrs. Plt Off H. K. Kemp, +; F/S J. R. Maidment, M

Mosquito LR363/WR-T of 248 Sqn. Crash-landed at Portreath after combat. Flt Lt S. G. Nunn and Fg Off J. M. Carlin, both uninj

Mosquito shot down by *Uffz* Fritz Gilfert, 3/ZG 1, *PlQ* 14W/3874, 1538hrs

Mosquito shot down by *Uffz* Fritz Sprang, 3/ZG 1, *PlQ* 14W/3874, 1538hrs

Mosquito shot down by *Uffz* Ernst von der Schmidt, 1/ZG 1, *PlQ* 14W/3874, 1538hrs

Mosquito shot down by *Oblt* Albrecht Bellstedt, 2/ZG 1, *PlQ* 14W/3715, 1538hrs

Mosquito MM475 of 151 Sqn. Shot down 1530hrs. W/O W. G. Penman and Sgt E. C. C. Stevenson, both M

Mosquito MM438 of 151 Sqn. Badly damaged in combat and written off on return to base. F/S J. Playford and W/O G. D. Kelsey, both uninj

2 May 44   Halifax shot down by *Lt* Artur Ewert, 9(NJ)/ZG 1, Toulouse, 0150hrs
No recorded RAF loss

4 May 44   Stirling shot down by *Lt* Artur Ewert, 9(NJ)/ZG 1, CE6, 0058hrs
No recorded RAF loss

11 May 44   Beaufighter shot down by *Lt* Ulrich Hanshen, Stab III/ZG 1
Possibly Beaufighter LX882/A of 272 Sqn. Took of 1805hrs and shot down off Veghaia (E of Minorca) during anti-aircraft patrol. F/S R. Rowell – P, F/S R. Satchell – N, both M

27 May 44   Enemy aircraft shot down by *Hptm* Fritz Kunkel, *St Kap* 9(NJ)/ZG 1
No recorded RAF loss

Total confirmed air combat victories

Sunderland	17 (+1 possible)
Wellington	17
Liberator/B-24/PB4Y-1	16
Whitley	15
Mosquito	10
Beaufighter	9 (+1 possible)
Halifax	7
B-17/Fortress	3 (+1 possible)
P-39	2
Hampden	2
Hudson	3
Lancaster	1
DC-3	1
P-38	1
Boston	1
Blenheim	1
Catalina/PB5Y	1
Horsa	1
Unknown:	1
Total:	**109 (+3 possible)**

Appendix E

Aircraft losses for III and V *Kampfgeschwader* 40 and I and III *Zerstörergeschwader* 1, July 1942-July 1944

20 Jul 42   Ju 88 C-6, 360015, F8+KD, III/KG 40

Lt Karl Stoeffler – F, *Ofw* August Moeller – BO, both +; *Ofw* August Werner – BF, rescued W

Shot down by Wellington HX423/15 OTU (F/S Smallwood) and crashed 20nm off Sisargas Islands, Spain. *Ofw* Werner and body of *Ofw* Moeller picked up by fishing boat *San Antonio de Padua* and landed at La Coruna

22 Jul 42   Ju 88 C-6, 360017, III/KG 40/Zerst Kdo/KG 6

Hptm Carlhanns Weymar – F, *Uffz* Ludwig Rodert – BF, *Gefr* Siegfried Wetzel – BS, all +

Collided with FW 200 C-4, Wk Nr 0136, CE+IA of 9/KG 40 (*Fw* Alfred Praschl) and crashed 17km SW of Mérignac

20 Aug 42   Ju 88 C-6, 360018, 3E+AY, Z/Kü.Fl.Gr 106, but on the strength of IV/KG 40

Oblt Adolf Runge – P, *Ogefr* Franz Mueller – BO, *Uffz* Fritz Streng – BF, all +

Shot down in combat with Lancaster of 61 Sqn (Plt Off J. E. Madsen) and crashed in sea off Caion, Spain

1 Sep 42   Ju 88 C-6, 360209, V/KG 40

Crash-landed at Mérignac after suffering engine failure due to combat damage probably with Sunderland of 461 Sqn (Fg Off R. H. H. Hosband); 30% damage

2 Sep 42   Ju 88 C-6, 360020, V/KG 40

Ofw Hans Mlodoch – F, *Ofw* Anton Homm-BF, *Ofw* Gerhard Pohl – BS, all +

Crashed and burned at Mérignac

8 Sep 42   Ju 88 C-6, 360025, F8+GX, 13/KG 40

Lt Wolfgang Graf von Hoensbroech – F, *Ogefr* Artur Walter – BS, *Gefr* Ulrich Orte – BF, all M

Shot down by Beaufighters of 235 Sqn (Sqn Ldr H. Thompson and Plt Off Ward in LA-T, and Plt Off E. D. Neal and Plt Off Cameron-Rose in LA-W), *PlQ* 14W/7811, 1100hrs

9 Sep 42   Ju 88 C-6, 360022, F8+KX, 13/KG 40

Hptm Paul Heide (*St Kap*) – F, *Ogefr* Rudi Wiencke – BF, *Fw* Karl
Gruendler – BS, all M

Probably shot down in combat with Whitley Z9209 of 77 Sqn

16 Sep 42   Ju 88 C-6 (undamaged), 13/KG 40

Hptm Georg Esch (*St Kap*) – F, *Fw* Kurt Doss – W

Probably involved in combat with Wellington HF836/E of 304 Sqn (Fg
Off M. Targowski) at 1615hrs, which was attacked by six Ju 88s, or
Beaufighter Y of 235 Sqn (Sgt J. Warburton and Sgt Sillitoe), which
damaged a Ju 88 275km SW of Brest, 1027hrs (Beaufighter damaged)

17 Sep 42   Ju 88 C-6, 360024, 13/KG 40

Fw Henny Passier – F and *Uffz* Ottmar Grimmer – BF, rescued W; *Uffz*
Emmerich Grass – BS, +

Shot down by Beaufighters of 235 Sqn at 1820hrs (Sgt G. E.
Woodcock and Sgt W. J. Ginger in LA-P and Flt Lt R. R. Casparius
and F/S F. Davies in LA-H)

24 Sep 42   Ju 88 C-6, 360201, F8+GX, 13/KG 40

Uffz Ernst Harms – F, *Gefr* Christian Henke – BF, *Gefr* Karl-Heinz
Schramm – BS, all M

Probably shot down by Beaufighters of 235 Sqn (Flt Lt R. R. Casparius
and F/S F. Davies in EL339/LA-O and Fg Off G. H. Carson and Sgt D.
Armstrong in LA-P), area known as 4807, 1035hrs. Possibly claimed
by Wellington H/304 Sqn (Sgt J. Bakanacz), 46.50N 07.32W, 1545hrs.
Reported lost in *PlQ* 14W/7800

27 Sep 42   Ju 88 C-6 (undamaged)

Gefr Georg Jung – BS, W

Damaged in combat, *PlQ* 15W/4060, probably with Beaufighters of
248 Sqn (Plt Off J. Maurice and F/S C. C. Corder in EL304/WR-C and
Sgt J. Hammond and W/O H. McColl in EL362/WR-X), 1722hrs

5 Oct 42   Ju 88 C-6, 360189, 13/KG 40

Uffz Johann Kaltenbrunner – F, *Uffz* Heinz Schultz – BF, *Uffz* Johannes
Stellmayer – BS, all +

Crashed at Lorient due to pilot error

8 Oct 42   Ju 88 C-6, 360211, F8+CX, 13/KG 40

Fw Helmut Wagner – F, *Uffz* Wilhelm Schadow – BF, *Ogefr* Gerhard
Eistert – BS, all M

Probably shot down in combat with Beaufighters of 248 Sqn (Fg Off R.
G. Stringer and Sgt S. Hunter in WR-X, Sgt J. Duncan and Sgt T. R.
Weaver in WR-C, and Sgt W. G. Woodcock and Sgt Colman in WR-
D), 1506hrs

9 Oct 42   Ju 88 C-6, 360161, V/KG 40

Crash-landed at Lorient due to pilot error; 20% damage

16 Oct 42   Ju 88 C-6, 13/KG 40

Lt Dieter Meister and crew uninj

Possibly damaged in combat with Wellington R1413 of 304 Sqn (Fg
Off M. Targowski), *PlQ* 14W/0924, 1638hrs (Wellington shot down)

1 Nov 42   Ju 88 C-6, 360165, F8+LX, 13/KG 40

Lt Walter Berger – F, *Uffz* Werner Nohe – BF, *Uffz* Fritz Eppendahl –
BS, all M

Ju 88 C-6, 360049, F8+MY, 14/KG 40

Lt Hermann Flothmann – F, *Uffz* Wilhelm Goganzer – BS, both +

Shot down into Bay of Biscay, probably by Beaufighters of 235 Sqn
(Fg Off P. C. Schaefer and F/S Lawton in T5269/LA-H, Plt Off G. R.
Leahy and F/S A. D. Ross in LA-A, and Sgt A. J. Keeling and Sgt J.
Crook in LA-B)

3 Nov 42   Ju 88 C-6, 360059, Stab V/KG 40

Hptm Gerd Korthals (*Gr Kdr*) – F, *Ofw* Franz Fritz – BF, *Uffz* Heinz
Winteler – BF, all +

Suffered mechanical failure and crashed at Lorient

5 Nov 42   Ju 88 C-6, 360240, 14/KG 40

Uffz Paul Sause – BF-W (pilot *Lt* Artur Thies?)

Flipped over on landing at Mérignac

Ju 88 C-6, 360051, V/KG 40

Landing accident at Bordeaux; 30% damage

18 Nov 42   Ju 88 C-6, (360076?), F8+KX, 13/KG 40

Uffz Heinz Hommel – F and crew uninj

Returned with three holes in wing following combat with 13 B-24Ds of
93rd BG near Lorient

26 Nov 42   Ju 88 C-6, 360026

Lt Arno von Heinburg – F, *Gefr* Manfred Gesenberg – BO, *Ogefr* Kurt
Schwarz – BF, all +

Engine failure and crashed at Quimper

29 Nov 42   Ju 88 C-6, 360233, V/KG 40

Ofw Wilhelm Knapp – F, *Fw* Franz Bergs – BS, *Fw* Erich Liebig – BF,
all W

Crash-landed at Lorient due to damage received in combat probably
with Beaufighters of 248 Sqn (Flt Lt A. R. De L. Inniss and F/S J.
Phillips in WR-B, F/S J. Hammond and W/O H. McColl in WR-Y);
55% damage

23 Dec 42   Ju 88 C-6, 360077, 15/KG 40

Lt Robert Baumann – F, *Uffz* Herbert Jugnischke – BF, both W; *Ogefr*
Walter Boldt – BO, d 3 Jan 43

Slewed off runway on take-off at Lorient and hit bank; 95% damage

Ju 88 C-6, 360062, V/KG 40

Crash-landed at Mérignac due to pilot error; 25% damage

Ju 88 C-6, 360011, V/KG 40

Ran out of fuel and crash-landed at Lacanau; 80% damage

Ju 88 C-6, 360082, V/KG 40

Became lost and ran out of fuel. Crash-landed at Langon but written off

30 Dec 42   Ju 88 C-6, 360097, 15/KG 40

Uffz Heinz Lengemann – BO, +; *Lt* Guenter Serke – F and *Ogefr* Heinz Schulze – BF, both inj

Suffered engine failure and crashed at Mérignac

Ju 88 C-6, 360075, F8+BG, Stab V/KG 40

Hptm Helmut Dargel (Gr Kdr) – F, *Uffz* Wolfgang Zunker – BF, *Uffz* Georg Richter – BO, all M

Shot down in combat with Airacobras, 350km SW of Lorient (*PlQ* 14W/8759), 1138hrs

3 Jan 43   Ju 88C-6, V/KG 40

Ogefr Kurt Muehlbauer – F, *Gefr* Willi Blam – BO, both W

Wounds resulted from combat S of Lorient, possibly with B-17s of First Bombardment Wing

29 Jan 43   Ju 88 C-6, 360073, F8+IU, V/KG 40

Ofw Johannes Kriedel – F, *Ogefr* Friedrich Hein – BO, *Uffz* Felix Winkelmann – BF, all M

Ju 88 C-6, 360072, F8+HZ, 15/KG 40

Uffz Paul Paschoff – F, *Ogefr* Alfred Bilger – BO, *Ogefr* Norbert Bernhard – BF, all M

Shot down by Beaufighters of 248 Sqn (Flt Lt A. R. DeL. Inniss and F/S J. Phillips in WR-B, Sgt J. McLeod and Sgt L. T. Inglis in WR-L, Fg Off P. A. S. Payne and Plt Off J. E. Langley in WR-D, Sgt D. A. Catrane and Sgt R. J. Fordham in WR-K), W of Ushant, 1240hrs. 1/Lt W. S. Johnson of 1st Sqn, 480th Anti Submarine Gp, reported combat with two Ju 88s, 1329-1332hrs

30 Jan 43   Ju 88 C-6, 360098, F8+KY, 14/KG 40

Ofw Georg Heuer – F, *Ogefr* Walter Hofrichter – BO, *Uffz* Fritz Weber – BF, all +

Ju 88 C-6, 360012, F8+HY, 14/KG 40

Hptm Hans-William Reicke (*St Kap*) – F, *Ogefr* Manfred Schweigert – BO, *Fw* Walter Barthelmes – BF, all +

Shot down by Beaufighters of 248 Sqn (Fg Off E. W. Cunningham and Plt Off J. G. Fawden in EL321/WR-M, F/S J. Duncan and F/S T. R. Weaver in WR-F, Sgt J, Bell and Sgt A. W. Parnell in JL447/WR-G), *PlQ* 14W/0783, 1131hrs. Aircraft of Fg Off Cunningham and Sgt Bell also lost, one of whom collided with *Hptm* Reicke

5 Feb 43   Ju 88 C-6, 360115, V/KG 40

Undercarriage damaged while taxiing at Mérignac; 20% damage

9 Feb 43   Ju 88 C-6, 360068, F8+BZ, 15/KG 40

Oblt Franz Isslinger – F, *Fw* Otto Wagner – BF, *Uffz* Franz Weber – BO, all M

Ju 88 C-6, 360069, F8+FZ, 15/KG 40

Ofw Heinrich Dettmer – F, *Ogefr* Albert Sundermann – BO, *Uffz* Willy Berchtold – BF, all M

Reported to have been shot down in combat with Sunderland; probably shot down by Beaufighters of 248 Sqn (Sqn Ldr D. L. Cartridge DFC and Flt Lt M. O. Osborne in WR-G, Flt Lt G. H. Melville-Jackson and F/S A. Umbers in WR-F, Plt Off J. C. White and Plt Off R. C. Arthur in WR-H), 1501hrs

22 Feb 43   Ju 88 C-6, 360225, F8+FY, 14/KG 40

Fw Wilhelm Andrians – F, *Uffz* Willibald Groell – BO, *Uffz* Richard Rankl – BF, all M

Believed to have suffered engine failure and force-landed in sea

23 Feb 43   Ju 88 C-6, 360088, V/KG 40

Crash-landed at Mérignac due to engine failure; 30% damage

27 Feb 43   Ju 88 A-4, 6669, V/KG 40

Uffz Karl Schlatter – F, *Uffz* Anton Kotek – BF, *Ogefr* Willi Kallenbacht – BO, all +

Crashed and burned at Lorient

22 Mar 43   Ju 88 C-6, 360052, F8+BY, 14/KG 40

Lt Artur Thies – F, *Fw* Paul Sause – BF, *Uffz* Werner Hoffmann – B, all M

Ju 88 C-6, 360352, F8+HY, 14/KG 40

Uffz Werner Steurich – F, *Uffz* Karl Bass – BF, *Ogefr* Alfred Hoessel – BS, all M

Both shot down at 0922-35hrs, 45.00N 03-04.00W, by Mosquitoes of 264 Sqn (Flt Lt W. G. Gibb and Plt Off K. F. Mills in DD727 (share), Fg Off R. M. Muir and Fg Off F. Mountain in DD737 (share), W/O D. McKenzie and Plt Off J. M. Simpson)

23 Mar 43   Ju 88 C-6, 360065, 15/KG 40

Lt Friedrich Apel – F, *Uffz* Otto Neustadt – BO, *Ofw* Wilhelm Simon – BF, all +

Dived into the sea during combat with a Liberator of 511 Sqn (Flt Lt G. T. R. Francis). Note: Beaufighters of 404 Sqn (Flt Lt A. A. Delahaye and Sgt C. A. Smith in V8214/G, Fg Off R. A. Schoales and Plt Off A. D. Powell in V8203/H, Fg Off J. H. Armour and Plt Off J. Seward in T3430/K, F/S K. S. Miller and Sgt J. Young in T3155/N, F/S V. F. McCallam and Sgt R. R. Carter in V8205/R, and F/S H. R. Browne and Sgt R. H. Dickey in V8131/T) claimed a Ju 88 damaged, 47.09N 08.00W, SW of Ushant, 1538hrs

24 Mar 43   Ju 88 C-6, 360116, F8+LB, 13/KG 40

Hptm Georg Esch (*St Kap*) – F, *Uffz* Karl-Friedrich Winkelmann – BO, *Ofw* Fritz Mayerhofer – BF, all +

Hit sea during air combat practice while searching for *U-665* in *PlQ* 14W/9427. Crew managed to get into dinghy but their bodies were later washed ashore and buried at La Coruna, Spain

Ju 88 C-6, 360364, F8+HY, 14/KG 40

Gefr Florian Stabentheiner – BO and *Fw* Max Taberthofer – BF, both +

Force-landed at La Albericia airfield, Santander, Spain (*PlQ* 24W/1512) after combat with Halifax BB277/H of 58 Sqn (Fg Off R. A. H. Ayles). Halifax also shot down

18 Apr 43   Ju 88 C-6, 360080, V/KG 40

Lt Günther Hass – F, M

Suffered engine failure and ditched; rest of crew safe.

9 May 43   Ju 88 C-6, 360385, V/KG 40

Lt Heinz Weide – F, *Ogefr* Wolfgang Petzold – BO, *Uffz* Rudolf Semmelmann – BF, all +

Crashed on take-off at Lorient and caught fire

15 May 43   Ju 88 C-6, 360067, F8+CZ, 15/KG 40

Lt Hans Neumann – F, *Uffz* Phillipp Benz – BO, *Uffz* Wilhelm Meyer – BF, all M

Reported to have been shot down by a Sunderland, probably Sunderland DD837 of 228 Sqn (Flt Lt G. A. Church), *PlQ* 14W/0721

17 May 43   Ju 88 C-6, 360423, F8+CG, 15/KG 40

Lt Werner Hensgen – F, *Uffz* Rudolf Seifert – BO, *Uffz* Karl Baumann – BF, all M

Reported to have been shot down by a Sunderland, probably Sunderland W4004 of 10 Sqn RAAF (Flt Lt M. K. Kenzie), *PlQ* 14W/0621.

Ju 88 C-6, 360350, V/KG 40

Ogefr Rudolf Lindner – BO, W

Flipped over at Mérignac; 90% damage

20 May 43   Ju 88 C-6, 360076, F8+KX, 13/KG 40

Lt Hans Vieback – F, *Fw* Heinrich Gottwald – BO, *Uffz* Josef Kuhlmann – BF, all +

Shot down by Beaufighters of 235 Sqn (Sqn Ldr A. F. Binks and Fg Off G. P. Marsden in LA-B, and Plt Off H. S. Vandewater and F/S A. D. McLachlan in LA-G), 48.06N 07.59W, 1410hrs

5 Jun 43   Ju 88 C-6, 360131, V/KG 40

Uffz Helmuth Schneidewind – F, *Ogefr* Paul Boseker – BF, *Ogefr* Hermann Bueckinger – BM, all +

Crashed near Bordeaux due to pilot error

11 Jun 43   Ju 88 C-6, 360288, F8+HZ, 15/KG 40

Fw Fritz Hiebsch – F, *Uffz* Peter Hofmann – BO, *Uffz* Erwin Seidel –
BF, all +

Reported to have been shot down by Mosquitoes, *PlQ* 14W/9625. Shot
down by Mosquito of 25 Sqn (detached to 264 Sqn) flown by Flt Lt J.
Singleton and Fg Off W. G. Haslam, 45.45N 07.45W, 1620hrs (Plt Off
J. W. Newell of 456 Sqn also claimed two Ju 88s damaged, 1617hrs,
Fg Off J. E. Wootton of 25 Sqn a Ju 88 damaged)

12 Jun 43   Ju 88 C-6, 360096, V/KG 40

Damaged undercarriage on landing at Mérignac; 30% damage

19 Jun 43   Ju 88 C-6, 750259, F8+LY, 14/KG 40

Lt Willi Gutermann – F, *Uffz* Rolf Stumpf – BO, *Uffz* Hermann Klein –
BF, rescued W

Shot down by Sqn Ldr H. G. Bodien and Fg Off R. W. Sampson of 151
Sqn, *PlQ* 14W/8578 (43.50N, 07.50W), 1900hrs. Crew rescued by
fishing boat *Maria Carmen*
7nm from Cape Burela, 1100hrs 21 Jun 43, and landed at Gijon

20 Jun 43   Ju 88 C-6, 360113, F8+AX, 13/KG 40

Uffz Waldemar Derr – F, *Ogefr* Josef Mathaei – BO, *Uffz* Werner
Wachs – BF, all M

Reported to have been shot down, *PlQ* 14W/8414; no reported RAF
losses. Aircraft possibly shot down 19 Jun 43 by Mosquitoes of 151 Sqn

1 Jul 43   Ju 88 C-6, 360383, F8+PX, 13/KG 40

Probably *Oblt* Hermann Horstmann (*St Kap*) – P and crew, uninj

Force-landed at La Albericia airfield, Santander, Spain, due to oil leak
in port engine, 1515hrs. *Oblt* Horstmann force-landed in Spain about
this time and was later repatriated. Fg Off R. J. Merrifield of 53 Sqn
reported that one Ju 88 that 'attacked him' landed in Spain and another
had possibly ditched

5 Jul 43   Ju 88 C-6, 360349, V/KG 40

Damaged undercarriage due to pilot error; 25% damage

8 Jul 43   Ju 88 C-6, 15/KG 40

Lt Lothar Wolff – F, *Uffz* Hans Melzer – BO, both W

Ju 88 C-6, V/KG 40

Uffz Karl Lenz – BO, W

Ju 88 C-6, V/KG 40

Uffz Otto Trutt – BO, W

All aircraft slightly damaged in combat with Liberator BZ716/B of 53
Sqn (Fg Off J. F. Handasyde), 46.08N 08.50W, 1640hrs

12 Jul 43   Ju 88 C-6, 360078, F8+NZ, 15/KG 40

Uffz Georg Frassek – F, *Ogefr* Heinz Dock – BO, *Uffz* Helmut Heinze
– BF, all POW

After combat with Whitley BD681/N of 10 OTU (Sgt C. T. Rudman),
shot down in sea W of Cap Finisterre, 1600hrs. Whitley also shot down

19 Jul 43   Ju 88 C-6, 750285, V/KG 40

Damaged undercarriage while taxiing; 15% damage

24 Jul 43   Ju 88 C-6, 360019, V/KG 40

Uffz Guenther Koenig – F, *Fw* Albert Richter – BF, *Gefr* Karl Reinl – BS, all inj

Crash-landed near Cognac due to engine failure; 75% damage

26 Jul 43   Ju 88 C-6, 750346, V/KG 40

Engine caught fire on patrol, ditched and crew rescued, uninj

29 Jul 43   Ju 88 C-6, 360391, V/KG 40

Crashed at Mérignac after patrol; 30% damage. Possibly involved in combat with Fg Off G. K. Thompson and Sgt C. F. Barnes flying Beaufighter WR-U of 248 Sqn (which crashed on return to base)

1 Aug 43   Ju 88 C-6, 360118, F8+IX, 13/KG 40

Lt Knud Gmelin – F, *Uffz* Hans Becker, *Uffz* Gerhard Zimmermann, uninj

Shot down in combat with PBY5 of VP 63 (Lt W. P. Tanner). PBY5 also shot down. Ditched *PlQ* 14W/9751, 1707hrs; crew rescued by 1 *Seenotstaffel*, 2020hrs

8 Aug 43   Ju 88 C-6, 360367, 14/KG 40

Lt Max Wittmer-Eigenbrodt – F, *Uffz* Hugo Frank – BF, *Uffz* Georg Kurschatke – BO, all +

Shot down, *PlQ* 24W/1512, possibly by B-24D Liberator Q of 4th Sqn, 479th Anti-Submarine Gp (Capt R. L. Thomas) – Liberator also shot down – or B-24D Liberator K of 19th Sqn, 479th Anti-Submarine Gp (Capt Owen), 45.30N 09.20W, 1310hrs

23 Aug 43   Ju 88 C-6, 360399, 15/KG 40

Lt Ulrich Hanshen – F, *Uffz* Josef Vojacek – BF, *Ofw* Otto Bonn – BO, all rescued inj

Shot down in combat with B-24D Liberator V of 4th Sqn, 479th Anti Submarine Gp (1/Lt K. H. Dustin), 46.53N 09.18W, 0817hrs (0935hrs German time)

30 Aug 43   Ju 88 C-6, 750399, F8+FX, 13/KG 40

Uffz Ernst Itzigehl – F, *Uffz* Ulrich Lentz – BO, *Gefr* Heinz Hobusch – BF, all M

Probably shot down by Liberator BZ948/M of 311 Sqn (Plt Off J. Stach), 45.48N 09.32W, 1100hrs, or possibly by Sunderland JM707 of 461 Sqn (Fg Off C. R. Croft), *PlQ* 14W/0647, 1217hrs (Sunderland also shot down)

31 Aug 43   Ju 88 C-6, 360432, F8+PY, 14/KG 40

Lt Horst Muller – F, *Uffz* Karl Heinz Nicolai – BO, *Fw* Paul Luebbers – BF, all M

Missing (no Allied claims, so probably crashed as result of mechanical failure)

3 Sep 43   Ju 88 C-6, 360070, V/KG 40

Crash-landed at Mérignac due to pilot error and burned out

4 Sep 43   Ju 88 C-6, 360382, 13/KG 40

Lt Gerhard Blankenberg – F, *Ofw* Bernhard Henrichs – BO, *Uffz* Otto Wawris – BF, all M

Shot down in combat with PB4Y-1 Liberator of VB103 (Lt (jg) J. H. Alexander); PB4Y-1 also shot down

7 Sep 43   Ju 88 C-6, 360095, F8+BZ, 15/KG 40

Uffz Heinz Ludwig – F, +; *Ogefr* Hans Bersch – BF, *Gefr* Herbert Drumm – BO, both M

Possibly shot down by B-24 Liberator P of 4th Sqn, 479th Anti-Submarine Gp (Lt Young), which damaged a Ju 88, 45.01N 11.08W, 1630hrs

11 Sep 43   Ju 88 C-6, 750333

Uffz Franz Huber – F, *Uffz* Georg Neininger – BO, *Ogefr* Rudolf Goehler – BF, all M

Shot down in combat with Mosquitoes of 307 Sqn (Sqn Ldr M. Lewandowski and Fg Off J. Mika in HJ656, and W/O L. Szemplinski and F/S F. Tilman in DZ749; latter aircraft damaged in combat)

21 Sep 43   Ju 88 C-6, 750433, 13/KG 40

Uffz Juergen Heicke – F, *Uffz* Hans Richter – BO, *Gefr* Walter Warnemuende – BF, all M

Probably shot down by Mosquitoes of 456 Sqn (Flt Lt G. Panitz and Fg Off R. S. Williams in HJ818, and Fg Off C. S. Samson and Plt Off A. M. Abbey in HJ816), 47.00N 09.00W, 1708hrs. (Fg Off J. W. Newell also claimed a Ju 88 damaged and Plt Off G. F. Gatenby a Ju 88 probable)

23 Sep 43   V/KG 40 suffered the following damage (including Ju 88 C-6 F8+CN of 14/KG 40, ac of *Lt* Herbert Hintze) during an air attack on Lorient:

Ju 88 C-6: Wk Nrn 360381, 750419 and 750417 – 100%; 750426 – 85%; 360100 – 75%; 750428, 750690 and 750445 – 65%; 750599 – 55%; 360394 – 50%; 750335 – 30%; 750360 – 20%; 750441, 360115 and 360361 – 10%

Bu 131: Wk Nr 6170 – 10%

Fi 156: Wk Nr 1373 – 10%

25 Sep 43   Ju 88 C-6, 360395, F8+FZ, 15/KG 40

Stfw Kurt Linden – F, *Uffz* Walter Thimm – BO, *Uffz* Wilhelm Bueckle – BF, all M

Ju 88 C-6, 750412, F8+NY, 14/KG 40

Lt Erhard Kromer – F, *Uffz* Alfred Mueller, *Uffz* Rudolf Ludwig, all +

Shot down by Mosquitoes of 307 Sqn (W/O F. Jankowiak and F/S J. Karais in HJ652, Sqn Ldr J. Damsz and Flt Lt I. Szponarowicz in HX859, and W/O L. Steinke and Plt Off S. Sadowski in DD724), *PIQ* 14W/0639. (Plt Off L. D. Oakley, Fg Off B. L. Hammond and F/S Shaw from 235 Sqn each damaged a Ju 88.) Some records state that *Lt* Kromer was shot down on 26 Sep 43 but there are no Allied claims

7 Oct 43   Ju 88 C-6, 750392, 14/KG 40

Lt Hermann Mueller – F, *Uffz* Karl Kohal – BO, *Gefr* Wilhelm Gah – BF, all M

Ju 88 C-6,750015, F8+GY, 14/KG 40

Lt Helmut Schulli – F, *Fw* Karl Wenz – BO, *Uffz* Bernhard Kothmann – BF, all M

Ju 88 C-6,750434, 14/KG 40

Oblt Gustav Christner – F, *Fw* Edmund Leubner – BF, *Uffz* Alfred Knefel – BO, all +

Ju 88 C-6, 750374, 14/KG 40

Uffz Hans Schulzky – F, W

Belly-landed at Lorient; 20% damage

First two aircraft shot down in *PlQ* 24W/1622; third shot down in *PlQ* 24W/1951. First two probably shot down by Beaufighters of 143 Sqn (Sqn Ldr E. Dickman-Wilkes and Fg Off N. E. Muckle in JM279/Y, and Fg Off G. F. Browne and F/S G. T. Flower in JM158/A), 46.32N 10.24W, 1518hrs. Remaining aircraft probably shot down by Liberator BZ779/J of 311 Sqn (F/S J. Kuhn). Capt G. L. Mosier in B-24D coded 'P' of 2nd Sqn, 480th Anti-Submarine Gp, also claimed Ju 88 damaged

Becomes I/ZG 1 13 Oct 43

22 Oct 43   Ju 88 C-6, 360392, Stab/ZG 1

Undercarriage damaged at Lorient; 15% damage

23 Oct 43   Ju 88 C-6, 360358, 3/ZG 1

Crew uninj

Suffered engine failure near Cap du Raz, *PlQ* 24W/1726, 1530hrs, and ditched off coast at Ile de Seine, 1658hrs; crew rescued by fishing boat

3 Nov 43   Ju 88 C-6, 750904, 2/ZG 1

Lt Hans Schulz – F, *Ogefr* Konstantin Uhde – B, both +; *Ogefr* Roland Duerr – BF, W

Crashed at Horton near Mérignac during training flight

20 Nov 43   Ju 88 C-6, 360403, 2N+GL, 3/ZG 1

Oblt Hans Schuster (*St Kap*) – F, *Ofw* Alois Olszowi – BF, *Uffz* Heinrich Bartling – B, all +

Shot down, *PlQ*/14W/8415 (5-10km N of Cap Ortegal), 1442hrs, in combat with four Beaufighters and four Mosquitoes. Flt Lt J. C. Newbery and Fg Off D. Alcock in Beaufighter WR-P of 248 Sqn, and Flt Lt G. C. L. Dyke and W/O C. R. Aindow of 157 Sqn, each claimed a Ju 88 probably destroyed. Further three Ju 88s damaged by Wg Cdr J. A. Mackie, Flt Lt G. C. L. Dyke, Fg Off Clifton of 157 Sqn, 1353-1410hrs, 8 miles N of Estaca Point, as well as Fg Off H. J. Thomas in Beaufighter LA-A of 235 Sqn, 1431hrs off Cape Ortegal, and Fg Off A. C. Driver in Beaufighter LA-G of 235 Sqn at 1432hrs off Cape Ortegal

23 Nov 43   Ju 88 C-6, 360404, I/ZG 1

Fw Otto Lusser – F, *Ogefr* Klaus Mueller – B, *Ogefr* Heinz Bart – BF, all +

Collided with below and crashed 10km NW of Lorient

Ju 88 C-6, 750707, I/ZG 1

Ofw Erich Bindzus – F, *Uffz* Werner Geissler – BO, *Fw* Karl Wegmann – BF, all +

Collided with above and crashed 10km NW of Lorient

30 Nov 43   Ju 88 C-6, 750413, 2N+BD, 2/ZG1

Uffz Hermann Fischer – F, *Ogefr* Karl Speckin – BF, *Gefr* Rudolf Martin – BS, all M

Shot down in combat with Sunderland L of 10 Sqn, RAAF (Flt Lt Clerk), 46.18N 09.05W, 1411hrs/*PlQ* 24W/1816, 1455hrs

1 Dec 43   Ju 88 C-6, 750592, 2N+SL, 3/ZG 1

Uffz Anton Meierl – F, *Fw* Herbert Nepomucky – B, *Uffz* Hans-Ulrich Gruntz – BF, all M

Ju 88 C-6, 750377, 2N+MD, 2/ZG 1

Ogefr Max Vetter – F, *Gefr* Wilfried Landhoff – BF, *Uffz* Helmut Rauer – BS, all M

Ju 88 C-6, 750957, 2N+SD, 2/ZG 1

Lt Gerhard Neumann – F, *Ogefr* Ernst Feuerberg – BF, *Uffz* Wilhelm Meinz – BS, all M

Shot down, *PlQ* 14W/0863-0861, 1150-1215hrs. Bounced by Mosquitoes of 157 Sqn (Flt Lt G. C. L. Dyke and W/O C. R. Aindow (two kills), and Fg Off B. M. Whitlock and Fg Off M. B. Hull (one kill)), 47.25N, 09.00W, 1155hrs (another Mosquito was shot down in this combat). *Uffz* Meierl and crew spotted in dinghy, 1450hrs

Ju 88 C-6, 750418 (?), 2/ZG 1

Fw Walter Stohl – F, *Uffz* Rudolf Hadatscheck – BF, *Uffz* Hermann Pflueger – BS, all +

Shot down in combat with four-engined bombers and crashed at Pesch/Eifel

12 Dec 43   Ju 88 C-6, 750437, 2N+PC, 1/ZG 1

Oblt Hermann Horstmann (*St Kap*) – F, *Fw* Rudolf Korczowy – BO; *Fw* Georg Kunz – BF, all M

Ju 88 C-6, 750830, 2N+KC, 1/ZG 1

Lt Friedrich Maeder – F, *Ogefr* Herbert Baumert – BO, *Uffz* Werner Ess – BF, all M

Ju 88 C-6, 750820, 2N+DC, 1/ZG 1

Uffz Franz Frank – F, *Gefr* Werner Goebler – BF, *Uffz* Adolf Wirth – BO, all M

Shot down in combat with Beaufighters of 143 Sqn (Wg Cdr E. H. McHardy and Sgt R. Morgan in JM163/G, and F/S F. G. Newport and Sgt J. M. Slater in JM136/P), *PlQ* 14W/0818, 47.30 N 10.00W, 1412hrs (two other Beaufighters were lost)

22 Dec 43   Ju 88 C-6, 750591, 7/ZG 1

Damaged while taxiing at Lorient; 35% damage

7 Jan 44   Junkers Ju 88 C-6, 750388, 7/ZG 1

Fw Johann Puetz – F, *Uffz* Kurt Utlaut – BF, *Uffz* Josef Bittner – B, all M

Shot down by Fg Off P. E. Huckin and F/S R. H. Graham of 157 Sqn, 46.22N 07.00W (300km SW of Brest), 1625hrs. (Mosquito damaged in combat and forced to ditch, crew rescued later)

29 Jan 44   Ju 88 R-2, 2N+FH, 1/ZG 1

Fw Herbert Klose – F, *Uffz* August Blume – BF, both uninj; *Uffz* Rolf Johenneken –B, inj

Landing accident at Lorient after combat mission, 1930hrs; 85% damage

1 Feb 44   Ju 88 C-6, 360124, 2N+PL (2N+PK?), 7/ZG 1

Lt Robert Baumann – F, POW; *Uffz* Herbert Jugnischke – BF, M; *Fw* Willi Held – BO, +

Shot down off North African coast during escort mission for I and III/KG 26 by F/S F. A. Cooper and Sgt A. V. Bridle in Beaufighter NE412/F of 39 Sqn (Beaufighter also shot down)

Ju 88 C-6, 360079, 2N+UR, 7/ZG 1

Uffz Helfried Schlegl – F, *Uffz* Hermann Hegemann – BF, *Gefr* Franz Mroz – BS, all +

Shot down, *PlQ* 03E/2960, during escort mission for I and III/KG 26 by one of the following: F/S W. J. Pryce and F/S P. W. Farndon in Beaufighter NE466/A of 39 Sqn – Ju 88 destroyed; Fg Off W. D. Cox and F/S N. C. Baker in Beaufighter LX789/B of 39 Sqn – Ju 88 damaged; Fg Off H. S. Boardman and F/S J. R. Mordan in Beaufighter V8844 of 153 Sqn – two Ju 88s destroyed

14 Feb 44   Ju 88 C-6, 750967, Stab I/ZG 1

Oblt Kurt Necesany (*Gr Ia*) – F, *Fw* Lothar Clemens – BF, *Fw* Werner Rueger – BO, all M

Believed shot down in combat with PB4Y-1 Liberator C/VB103 (Lt (jg) K. L. Wright), 48.00N 10.00W (*PlQ* 14W/8911), 1734hrs. Liberator later ditched due to damage

26 Feb 44   Ju 88 C-6, 750941, 2N+PL, 3/ZG 1

Fw Heinz Baldeweg – F, uninj; *Ogefr* Georg Blach – BF, *Fw* Wilhelm Buxbaum – BO, both M

Missing from operational flight, *PlQ* 25W/2048, possibly shot down in combat with PB4Y-1 Liberator of VB103 (Lt R. L. North), 100 miles W of Fastnet Rock (49.48N, 10.34W). PB4Y-1 also shot down

7 Mar 44   Ju 88 C-6, 750814, 3/ZG 1

Fw Heinz Doehler – F, *Uffz* Ernst Bongers – BF, *Uffz* Friedrich Gargulak – BO, all +

Crashed during night training flight, 6km S of Toulouse

8 Mar 44   Ju 88 C-6, 750893, 2/ZG 1

Fw Wilhelm Zimmer – F, *Uffz* Nikolaus Winter – BF, *Uffz* Artur Sieger
– BO, all M

Shot down by RAF fighters, *PlQ* 3E/2887, during escort mission for
III/KG 26 and II/KG 100

Ju 88 C-6, 750469, 1/ZG 1

Oblt Edgar Podzimek – F, *Uffz* Paul Mohwinkel – BF, *Uffz* Hans
Becker – BO, all M

Shot down by RAF fighters, *PlQ* 3E/3228, during escort mission for
III/KG 26 and II/KG 100

Ju 88 C-6, 750709, 2/ZG 1

Uffz Gerd Rauschke – F, *Uffz* Heinrich Roensch – BF, *Uffz* Otto
Hillenbrand – BS, all + (buried Istres)

Shot down by Beaufighters during escort sortie for III/KG 26 and
II/KG 100, *PlQ* 3E/2800. Possibly collided with crane in Marseille
harbour.

Following claims for Ju 88s were made by Beaufighters of 153 Sqn:
F/S G. H. Foster and F/S R. Turner in ND172 – Ju 88 probable, Ju 88
damaged; W/O A. C. Beattie and F/S J. Dickinson in KV931 – Ju 88
destroyed; Fg Off W. McAdam and W/O Saunders – Ju 88 destroyed

10 Mar 44   Ju 88 C-6, 750965, 2N+AA, Stab/ZG 1

Obstlt Lothar von Janson (*Gesch Komm*) – F, *Uffz* Heinz Scholdei –
BO, *Uffz* Hans Schwarzrock – BF, all M

Shot down, *PlQ* 14W/3522, probably by Mosquitoes of 157 Sqn (Flt Lt
R. J. Smyth and Sgt G. Lang, and Lt F. H. Sandiford RNVR and Lt L.
F. Thompson RNVR), 45.00N 03.40W, 1712hrs

Ju 88 C-6, 7/ZG 1

Fw Karl Bauer – F, *Fw* Josef Mrechen – BF, *Uffz* Karl-Heinz Tomke –
BO, all +

Shot down, *PlQ* 14W/5412, probably by Mosquitoes of 248 Sqn (F/S
W. Tonge and F/S R. Rigby in LR349/WR-Y, and Flt Lt L. T.
Cobbledick and Fg Off W. R. M. Belcher in HJ828/WR-J, who claimed
three destroyed, one damaged), N of Cap Penas, 0924hrs

13 Mar 44   Ju 88 C-6, 360411, 3/ZG 1

Uffz Herbert Altenhöner – F, *Uffz* Helmut Kommar – BF, *Uffz* Helmut
Staas – BO, all +

Crashed 11km SE of Mont de Marsan during night flying practice

Ju 88 C-6, 750955, 3/ZG 1

Ogefr Heinz Gehre – F, *Uffz* Eberhard Moelder – BF, *Gefr* Hermann
Budde – BO, all inj

Crashed 15km E of Mont de Marsan during night flying practice

23 Mar 44   Ju 88 C-6, 750719, 2/ZG 1

Uffz Rolf Leonhardt – F, *Uffz* Erich Haas – BF, *Uffz* Karl-Heinz Ewert
– BO, all +

Crashed 28km ENE of Vannes during non-combat flight

5 Apr 44   Ju 88 C-6, 750411, 2N+FK, 2/ZG 1

Uffz Hans Reichelmann – F, *Ogefr* Hermann Weissbrod – BF, *Gefr* Edwin Hess – BO, all inj

Taxied into bomb crater after landing at Vannes after combat mission and rolled over

11 Apr 44   FW 44, 1564, 9/ZG 1

Lt Klaus Uhsemann – F, *Ogefr* Heinrich Barnasch – ground crew, both +

Crashed at Saintes, 5km NW of Saujon, during non-combat flight; died 12 Apr 44

Ju 88 R-2, 751043, 1/ZG 1

Hptm Guenther Moltrecht (*St Kap*) – F, +; *Uffz* Hans Groetzinger – BO, *Uffz* Guenther Dietermann – BF, both M

Seen to dive into sea during combat, c0935hrs

Ju 88 C-6, 750891, 2/ZG 1

Lt Helmut Messerschmitt – F, *Uffz* Hans Schuessler – BF, *Uffz* Rolf Stumpf – BO, all M

Ju 88 C-6, 750404, 2/ZG 1

Uffz Hans Reichelmann – F, *Ofw* Willi Boldt – BO, *Ogefr* Hermann Weissbrod – BF, all M

Ju 88 R-2, 750953, 1/ZG 1

Uffz Hermann Forell – F, *Ogefr* Wilhelm Beyer – BF, *Uffz* Hubert Kuhnert – BO, all +

Ju 88 R-2, 751046, 1/ZG 1

Uffz Josef Horvath – F, +; *Gefr* Hans Namhoff – BF, *Uffz* Werner Herrmann – BF, both W

Shot down by Mosquitoes, 0935hrs. Ditched and survivors rescued c1500hrs and landed at La Baule

Ju 88 C-6, 750105, 2/ZG 1

Uffz Gerhard Fritz – F, +; *Uffz* Paul Ullmann – BF, W; *Uffz* Jörg Zink – BF, uninj

Shot down by Mosquitoes and crashed in Loire Estuary, *PlQ* 14W/3880

Ju 88 C-6, 750961, 3/ZG 1

Uffz Fritz Sprang – F, *Uffz* Alfons Hiesinger – BF, both W; *Uffz* Wilhelm Lengfeld – BO, M

Shot down, *PlQ* 14W/3874

Ju 88 C-6, 2N+DL, 1/ZG 1

Uffz Ernst von den Schmidt – F, *Uffz* Rolf Johenneken – BO, both uninj

Damaged in combat and returned to Lorient on one engine, 1622hrs; BF not known

11 Apr 44   All shot down in one of the following combats:

Off St Nazaire, 0937hrs:

151 Sqn   Wg Cdr G. H. Goodman and Fg Off W. F. E. Thomas in MM448 – one destroyed

Fg Off C. J. Turner and Fg Off M. C. Partridge in MM494 – one destroyed

Flt Lt J. H. Etherton DFC and Flt Lt N. L. Gibbs DFM in MM479 – one damaged

Flt Lt D. S. Handley and Capt J. W. Bray USAAF in HK503 – one probable

F/S A. Heath and Plt Off J. B. Cottrill in MM468 – one damaged

One Mosquito shot down

248 Sqn   F/S W. W. Scott and F/S J. Blackburn in LR339/F – one probable

Fg Off G. N. E. Yeates and Fg Off T. C. Scott in LM346/Z – one destroyed

Two Mosquitoes shot down and one crashed on return

151 Sqn claimed the following kills, 1530hrs:

Sqn Ldr R. H. Harrison and Fg Off E. P. Horrey in MM446 – one destroyed, one damaged

F/S J. Playford and W/O G. D. Kelsey in MM438 – two destroyed, one damaged

One Mosquito shot down, one written off on return

17 Apr 44   Ju 88 C-6, *Kdo Kunkel*

Gefr Hans Joeckel – F, *Gefr* Guenter Kessel – BF, *Ogefr* Franz Schwander – BW, all M

Crashed, *PlQ* 14W/4885, after engine failure

20 Apr 44   Ju 88 C-6, 750950, 3/ZG 1

Lt Josef Schwarz – F, *Uffz* Guenther Broemel – BF, *Uffz* Helmut Schulte – BO, all M

Ju 88 C-6, 750369, 7/ZG 1

Uffz Walter Kelle – F, *Uffz* Kurt Berns – BF, *Uffz* Stefan Goos – BO, all M

Ju 88 C-6. 360361, 7/ZG 1

Uffz Horst Besdziek – F, *Uffz* Erwin Buecken – BF, *Gefr* Gerhard Koerner – BO, all M

Ju 88 C-6, 750420, 7/ZG 1

Oblt Martin Reuter (*St Kap*) – F, *Uffz* Friedrich Blumenroether – BF, *Uffz* Heinz Mueller – BO, all M

All believed missing during escort sortie for II/KG 77, III/KG 26 and II/KG 100 over Mediterranean during attack on convoy 'Whoopee'; no recorded Allied claims

11 May 44   Ju 88 C-6, 8/ZG 1

Uffz Heinrich Lang – F, *Gefr* Hubert Licht – BO, *Ogefr* Werner Drewes – BF, all M

Shot down over Mediterranean during escort sortie for III/KG 26. Claims by Wg Cdr P. M. Dobree-Bell and Fg Off D. R. Ibbotson in Beaufighter HK398 of 256 Sqn – Ju 88 destroyed, 2114hrs; Fg Off J. M. Nicolson and Fg Off A. H. Ching in Beaufighter HK410 of 256 Sqn – Ju 88 destroyed, 2100hrs; Sqn Ldr D. R. West and Fg Off J. H. Smithes in Beaufighter HK192 of 256 Sqn – Ju 88 probable; Flt Lt A. H. Norris and Fg Off D. Sherriff in Beaufighter KW114 of 153 Sqn – Ju 88 destroyed, Ju 88 damaged, 2030-2310hrs; Fg Off H. C. Barr and Fg Off J. Barnett in Beaufighter KV969 of 153 Sqn – Ju 88 destroyed, Ju 88 damaged

18 May 44   Ju 88 C-6, 750998, 2N+HH, 1/ZG 1

Lt Graf Frhr Franz Felix von Sprinzenstein – F, *Uffz* Paul Ullmann – BO, both W

Crash-landed after combat mission at Salon due to engine failure

6 Jun 44   Ju 88 C-6, 750924, 2/ZG 1

Uffz Kurt Schwartz – F, *Fw* Wilhelm Starkert – BF, *Uffz* Karl Schmidt – BO, all M

Shot down N of Caen

Ju 88 C-6, 750942, 2/ZG 1

Uffz Walter Herrmann – F, *Gefr* Manfred Unger – BS, both M; *Gefr* Lothar Rams – BF, +

Shot down N of Caen

Ju 88 C-6, 2/ZG 1

Uffz Erich Keller – F, *Uffz* Othmar Kraml – BF, *Gefr* Fritz Sandermeier – BO, all W. Shot down by AA fire

Ju 88 C-6, 750597, 2/ZG 1

Ogefr Gerhard Weber – BS, +

Shot down in flames N of Caen

7 Jun 44   Ju 88 C-6, 750104, 2N+NK, 2/ZG 1

Fw Edmund Freiwald – F, *Uffz* Eugen Luttenberger – BS, both M; *Fw* Rudolf Gebicke – BF, POW

Shot down by AA fire between Caen and Bayeux, 0930hrs

Ju 88 C-6, 750441, 2N+CK, 2/ZG 1

Uffz Hans Roeder – F, *Gefr* Lothar Schirmacher – BO, both +; *Uffz* Heinrich Heymann – BF, POW

Shot down by AA fire and crashed near Caen, 1230hrs

Ju 88 G-1, 710411, 2N+BL, 3/ZG 1

Uffz Kurt Strobel – F, *Uffz* Walter Schneider – BF, *Gefr* Erich Dressler – BO, all M

Shot down N of Caen

7 Jun 44   Ju 88 C-6, 750899, Stab III/ZG 1

Oblt Ulrich Hanshen (Gr Adj) – F, *Ofw* Werner Herrmann – BF, *Ofw* Fritz Quapp – BO, all M

Shot down over Channel

Ju 88 C-6, 750699, 7/ZG 1

Fw Josef Hollerith – F, *Uffz* Johann Lechner – BF, *Ogefr* Helmut Rieger – BO, all +

Shot down near Falence

Ju 88 C-6, 360431, 7/ZG 1

Lt Kurt Loew – StFhr, *Fw* Gerhard Haberger – BO, both M; *Uffz* Heinrich Seifert – BF, returned safe

Shot down over Channel

Ju 88 C-6, 751102, 1/ZG 1

Uffz Guenther Theiss – F, *Ofw* Rudi Dobslaff – BO, both W; *Fw* Egon Purwin – BF, +

Damaged in combat with British fighters NW of Caen. BO and BF were from 3/ZG 1

Ju 88 C-6, 750374, 2/ZG 1

Ofw Dietrich Wolf – F, +

Suffered 90% damage during strafing attack NW of Caen. *Ofw* Wolf fatally wounded

Ju 52 3/M, 640750

Shot down by fighter off Cazaux while carrying ground crew from 7/ZG 1; 15 missing

Allied claims for Ju 88s on this day are considerable but the following could be considered:

126 Wg (401, 411 and 412 Sqns) took off 0817hrs and attacked twelve Ju 88s inland from 'Gold' beach, 0950hrs:

Wg Cdr G. C. Keefer – Ju 88 destroyed

Sqn Ldr L. M. Cameron, 401 Sqn – two Ju 88s destroyed

Flt Lt R. H. Cull, 401 Sqn – Ju 88 destroyed

Fg Off G. D. Billing – Ju 88 destroyed

Fg Off D. F. Husband, 401 Sqn – Ju 88 destroyed

Flt Lt G. B. Murray and Fg Off W. A. Bishop – Ju 88 destroyed

Flt Lt A. F. Halcrow, 411 Sqn – Ju 88 probable

Fg Off P. M. Charron, 412 Sqn – Ju 88 destroyed

Fg Off J. P. Laureys – Ju 88 damaged

Flt Lt H. L. Phillips – Ju 88 damaged

145 Wg (329, 340 and 341 Sqns) intercepted five Ju 88s N of Caen. Wg Cdr W. V. Crawford Crompton set the port engine of one on fire, which spiralled down to crash near Caen

9 Jun 44   Ju 88 R-2, 750897, 2N+AH, 1/ZG 1

Lt Knud Gmelin (*StFhr*) – F, +; *Uffz* Gerhard Zimmermann – BF, *Uffz* Wilhelm Dunker – BO, both W

Shot down by light flak near Caen and crashed at Epron, 0615hrs

Ju 88, Erg/ZG 1

Fw Fritz Haenel – F, *Uffz* Karl Obermeyer – BF, both +

Shot down by flak and crashed near Hermanville, 0530hrs

Ju 88 C-6, 750892, 2/ZG 1

Uffz Ludwig Dietler – BF, M

Landed N of Caen

Ju 88 R-2, 2N+NH, 1/ZG 1

Uffz Rolf Dickel – F, *Uffz* Rolf Johenneken – BO, *Uffz* Aegidius Berzborn – BF, all uninj

Hit barrage balloon during mission

10 Jun 44   Ju 88 C-6, 750335, 2N+CR, 7/ZG 1

Uffz Erich Engeln – F, *Uffz* Otto Sommer – BF, both +; *Flg* Hans Cox – BO, POW

Shot down by AA fire and crashed at Benouville, 0530hrs

Ju 88 C-6, 360316, 2N+GT, 9(NJ)/ZG 1

Uffz Xaver Schmiedberger – F, *Uffz* Heinz Masmeier – BF, *Gefr* Erwin Lamla – BO, all +

Shot down over Channel. Possibly claimed by Sqn Ldr A. S. Jepson of 409 Sqn, who shot down a Ju 88 30 miles N of Le Havre

28 Jun 44   Ju 88 C-6, 750898, 9(NJ)/ZG 1

Uffz Werner Migge – F, *Ogefr* Hans Joachim Koehler – BS, both +; *Ogefr* Horst Michael – BF, M

Crashed 2km E of Dancey near Chateaudun. Probably shot down by Flt Lt J. Howard-Williams and Fg Off F. Macrae of Fighter Interception Unit, who shot down a Ju 88 near 15 miles W of Chateaudun, 0220hrs

Total aircraft and personnel casualties

Lost in action	88
Lost in accidents	26
Lost in unknown circumstances	2
Interned in Spain	2
Lost on ground to Allied air attacks	3
Total:	**121**
Personnel	
Killed or missing in action	222
Killed in accidents	58
Prisoners of war	7
Wounded/injured	51

Appendix F

Miscellaneous inconclusive air combats

Date	Type attacked	Time	Reported by	Opponent
27 Sep 42	3 Spitfires		*Oblt* Necesany	
9 Nov 42	Liberator		"	B-24Ds of either 44th or 93rd BG
11 Nov 42	Whitley	1015hrs	"	Whitley 'L' of 502 Sqn (Plt Off Chalmers)

'No 502 Squadron Whitley "L", Captain Plt Off Chalmers, while flying below cloud base at 2,500 feet, sighted five Ju 88s at 2,000 feet half a mile distant, which altered course to intercept at 1015hrs on 11 November 1942. Enemy aircraft approached from astern and aircraft "L" made steep turn and climbed into cloud cover while front gunner got in a burst of 100 rounds at 300 yards range, estimating hits on one enemy aircraft. Whitley later sighted enemy aircraft through cloud on several occasions but contact was not resumed.' *HQ Coastal Command Intelligence Summary No 178*

Date	Type attacked	Time	Reported by	Opponent
11 Nov 42	Liberator		*Oblt* Necesany	B-24D of 330 BS, 93rd BG
"	Sunderland	1145hrs	"	Sunderland 'H' of 461 Sqn (Flt Lt Cooke)

'No 461 Squadron Sunderland "H", Captain Flt Lt Cooke, while flying at 1,500 feet sighted four Ju 88s near sea level at 1145hrs on 11 November 1942. One enemy aircraft closed to 400 yards firing short bursts of cannon. Sunderland dived to 400 feet, jettisoning depth charges, and gained cloud cover without sustaining either damage or casualties.' *HQ Coastal Command Intelligence Summary No 178*

Date	Type attacked	Time	Reported by	Opponent
18 Nov 42	13 Liberators	1200-1315hrs	*Uffz* Hommel	B-24Ds of 93rd BG
21 Nov 42	Liberator	1302-1804hrs	"	B-24D of 330th BS, 93rd BG (Maj R. D. Potts Jr)
22 Nov 42	Liberator	1157-1615hrs	"	B-24Ds of either 44th or 93rd BG
"	Wellington	1255hrs	"	Wellington X9745 S of 311 Sqn (FS Petrasek)
24 Nov 42	Sunderland	1400hrs	"	Sunderland Z of 10 Sqn (Fg Off Beeton)

'No 10 Squadron Sunderland "Z", Captain Fg Off Beeton, while flying at 2,500 feet sighted three Ju 88s 3 miles distant at 1,000 feet at 1400hrs on 24 November 1942. Sunderland climbed for cloud cover and enemy aircraft made several attacks but inflicted no damage. Sunderland replied with 200 rounds of machine gun fire but no hits were observed and enemy aircraft were eventually lost in cloud.' *HQ Coastal Command Intelligence Summary No 179*

29 Nov 42	5 Beaufighters	1157-1412hrs	*Uffz* Hommel	
"	Wellington	"	"	
5 Dec 42	"	1500hrs	"	Wellington C of 311 Sqn (Sgt Soukup)

'No 311 Squadron Wellington "C", Captain Sgt Soukup, while flying at 2,000 feet sighted six Ju 88s in loose formation at sea level at 1500hrs on 5 December 1942, Bay of Biscay. Aircraft made for cloud cover, which was approximately 15 miles distant, but before reaching it the leading enemy aircraft broke away from formation, made a steep climbing turn and opened fire at 800 yards range. Rear gunner of "S" replied and a second Ju 88 then approached to attack, but "S" entered cloud, and although both enemy aircraft were seen again after approximately 5 minutes they both finally disappeared. No hits were scored on enemy aircraft and no damage was sustained by "S".' *HQ Coastal Command Intelligence Summary No 179*

10 Apr 43	Sunderland	1130-1738hrs	*Uffz* Hommel	
17 Apr 43	8 Beaufighters		*Oblt* Necesany	
28 Apr 43	Halifax, Whitley and 8 Beaufighters	0912hrs	*Uffz* Hommel	Halifax F of 58 Sqn (Fg Off Griffiths)

'Halifax "F" on anti-submarine patrol at 2,000 feet sighted four Ju 88s 45 degrees to starboard at 1,500 feet 1 mile distant, with three other Ju 88s about 600 to 800 yards astern of the first formation and about 600 feet above them. "F" jettisoned depth charges and climbed to 3,000 feet for what cloud cover there was. The Ju 88s positioned, two on each beam, two slightly ahead and one below. Enemy aircraft then attacked repeatedly throughout prolonged engagement but only one at a time from all quarters except dead astern. Attacks with exception of three were not pressed home. These three were: 1. during attack on port bow in which enemy aircraft flew into crossfire of front and mid-upper gunners (both of whom claim hit) and broke off astern with brown-black smoke from starboard engine and was not seen again. 2. from starboard – port bow tracer was seen to hit round engine. Aircraft not seen again. 3. high on port quarter, came within 100 yards and peeled away to starboard. Rear gunner claims hits and enemy aircraft last seen with black smoke from port engine. Captain of "F" made diving turns to meet each attack, and aircraft gained partial cloud cover in thin cloud. At 0955 hours, when last attack was made, only four enemy aircraft were in contact with "F". Three then broke away, one shadowed for a further 2 miles. Crew sustained no injury and aircraft undamaged.' *HQ Coastal Command Intelligence Summary No 200*

13 May 43	Sunderland	1300-1720hrs	*Lt* Hanshen	
14 Jun 43	B-17	1745-2305hrs	*Lt* Hanshen	
26 Jul 43	Liberator	1200hrs	*Uffz* Hommel	B-24D L of 19th Sqn, 479th ASG (Lt Grider)

'Liberator "L" on anti-submarine patrol sighted nine Ju 88s and immediately took evasive action into cloud with the enemy aircraft in pursuit. During the next 11 minutes, several of the enemy aircraft attempted individual attacks to which the Liberator replied whenever possible. Combat was broken off when "L" entered thick bank of cloud. No damage was sustained.' *HQ Coastal Command Intelligence Summary No 213*

31 Jul 43	Sunderland	1130-1625hrs	*Uffz* Ernst	
1 Aug 43	Beaufighter	13301826hrs	*Uffz* Hommel	
2 Aug 43	Hampden	1426hrs	*Uffz* Ernst	Hampden T of 415 Sqn (Plt Off Savage)

'Hampden "T" on anti-submarine patrol sighted five Ju 88s in loose formation. Pilot climbed for thick cloud. Enemy aircraft commenced climbing quarter attack, opening fire with cannon and machine gun at 500 yards and pressing home attack to some 2/300 yards. Some enemy aircraft then commenced beam attacks; "T" gunners replied with accurate fire to all attacks and pilot took violent evasive action. "T" gained cloud at 1435hrs after more than twelve attacks. Aircraft sustained considerable damage but no casualties.' *HQ Coastal Command Intelligence Summary No 214*

| 17 Aug 43 | Halifax | 1510-1720hrs | *Uffz* Ernst | B-24D of 479th ASG? |
| 21 Aug 43 | Halifax | 1750hrs | *Oblt* Necesany | Halifax L of 58 Sqn (Fg Off Hartley) |

'Halifax "L" on anti-submarine patrol sighted a Ju 88 followed by six others dead ahead. Enemy aircraft passed "L" at 1,000 yards. Halifax fired three shorts bursts at one enemy aircraft, which swerved away. Enemy aircraft then attacked "L" from various directions for over 30 minutes while our aircraft dodged in and out of cloud cover. During combat, "L" fired about 3,000 rounds at enemy aircraft. Our aircraft sustained no damage.' *HQ Coastal Command Intelligence Summary No 216*

| 21 Aug 43 | Sunderland | 1731hrs | *Oblt* Necesany | Sunderland X of 228 Sqn (Flt Lt Fitzearle) |

'Sunderland "X" on anti-submarine patrol sighted six Ju 88s at 600 feet, 1,200 yards on starboard beam. "X" jettisoned depth charges and sought cloud cover. Three enemy aircraft manoeuvred to attack from port and three from starboard. As "X" entered cloud, one of the three enemy aircraft to starboard commenced firing at 800 yards, registering no hits. As "X" traversed clear patches before entering large bank of cloud, enemy aircraft were observed singly and fired three short bursts from ranges of 800-1,000 yards. "X" then entered cloud and contact was lost. Our aircraft sustained no damage.' *Coastal Command Intelligence Summary No 216*

| 21 Aug 43 | Wellington | 1743hrs | *Oblt* Necesany | Wellington Y of 547 Sqn (FS R. Cherry) |

'Wellington "Y" on anti-submarine patrol sighted eight Ju 88s and climbed for cloud cover. "Y", while passing through gaps in cloud, fired 50 rounds at 300 yards at one enemy aircraft seen on port beam; no hits were observed and no return fire was experienced. Owing to cloud, it was impossible to say whether the enemy aircraft were flying in formation or not. It was estimated that none of the remaining seven aircraft approached nearer than 1,000 yards.' *Coastal Command Intelligence Summary No 216*

| 26 Aug 43 | 3 Liberators | | *Oblt* Necesany | Either K of 19th Sqn, 479th ASG or E of 53 Sqn (WO McPherson) |

'An "OA" was sent when eight Ju 88s were sighted at sea level below aircraft. These aircraft did not attack, however.' *53 Sqn Operations Record Book*

| 9 Sep 43 | Liberator & Wellington | 0930hrs | *Uffz* Ernst | Liberator A of 224 Sqn (Fg Off Batchelor) |

'Liberator "A" on anti-submarine patrol emerged from cloud and sighted six Ju 88s, which made more than eight attacks on "A". One enemy aircraft caught in crossfire from our aircraft dived away, emitting black smoke and at least momentarily out of control. "A" then reached a small patch of cloud, which it left at 0935hrs, and at 1015hrs the six enemy aircraft were again sighted astern. However, only two attacked, and after some minutes "A" again reached cloud cover and the combat ended. "A" did not sustain a single hit.' *Coastal Command Intelligence Summary No 219*

| 15 Sep 43 | Halifax | 1546hrs | *Fw* Hommel | B-24D of 22nd Sqn, 479th ASG (Lt Staple) |
| 16 Sep 43 | Liberator | 1516hrs | *Lt* Gutermann | PB4Y-1 B of VB-103 (Lt Kemper) |

'Liberator "B" on anti-submarine patrol encountered five Ju 88s, two of which attacked from astern and were not seen again. Three more Ju 88s were then seen to starboard, only one of which came in to attack. "B" meanwhile had been climbing for cloud, which was safely reached. About 2 minutes after the first attack, "B" sustained very slight damage and no casualties.' *HQ Coastal Command Intelligence Summary No 220*

| 18 Sep 43 | Liberator | 1355hrs | *Uffz* Ernst | B-24D K of 22nd Sqn, 479th ASG (Lt Van Zyl) |

'Liberator "K" on anti-submarine patrol sighted eight Ju 88s, which attacked our aircraft. The leading enemy aircraft's first burst caused damage to rudder controls, fuselage and top turret. "K" took evasive action by climbing for cloud cover. Enemy aircraft continued to attack but caused no further damage. "K" replied at 600 yards and one enemy aircraft was last seen smoking heavily and diving downwards and crew also claim another enemy aircraft probably damaged. Hits were seen on a third, which was smoking as if slightly damaged, and a fourth enemy aircraft was also hit and was seen to be smoking as our aircraft reached cloud cover.' *HQ Coastal Command Intelligence Summary No 220*

| 18 Sep 43 | Liberator | 1025hrs | *Fw* Hommel | PB4Y-1 32039 B of VB-103 (Lt Krause) |

'Liberator "B" on anti-submarine patrol sighted eight Ju 88s in line astern. The first two enemy aircraft dived to attack, opening fire at long range, to which our aircraft replied with front guns estimating possible hits. By this time a further three Ju 88s had arrived making a total of eight and during the next 15 minutes a general melee ensued in which the rear gunner of "B" with a good burst scored hits and saw black smoke and a spurt of flame from starboard engine of one of the enemy aircraft, which commenced to dive. No further results were seen although two more of the enemy aircraft were seen smoking, and towards the end took no further part in the action. Our aircraft sustained no damage or casualties.' *HQ Coastal Command Intelligence Summary No 220*

Note: B-24D P of 2nd Sqn, 480th ASG (Maj L. E. Jarnagin – P, 1/Lt Dyke, 1/Lt Frick, 2/Lt Jensen, S/Sgt A. R. Miller, S/Sgt Cole, S/Sgt Wallen, T/Sgt Holtsclaw, S/Sgt Russell, T/Sgt Lindsey) was lost in combat with enemy aircraft.

18 Sep 43	Sunderland		*Fw* Hommel	
21 Sep 43	3 Mosquitoes	1708hrs	"	456 Sqn
23 Sep 43	Mosquito	0732-1233hrs	*Lt* Gutermann	
23 Oct 43	Liberator	1315-1400hrs	*Oblt* Necesany	Liberator D of 311 Sqn (Plt Off Stach)

'Liberator "D" on anti-submarine patrol was attacked by seven Ju 88s, and in a combat lasting 45 minutes "D" shot down one Ju 88 and damaged another. Our aircraft sustained neither casualties or damage.' *HQ Coastal Command Intelligence Summary No 226*

3 Nov 43	Liberator	1320hrs	*Lt* Hanshen	
5 Nov 43	Wellington	1045hrs	*Lt* Gutermann	
7 Nov 43	Liberator	1036hrs	*Einzelmeldung*	PB4Y-1 M of VB-110 (Lt Cdr J. R. Reedy)

'Six Ju 88s took off between 0906 and 0909hrs for a *Freie Jagd* south-west of Ireland. At 1037hrs a Liberator was spotted 3km distant in *PlQ* 24W/1984, course 210 degrees. Disappeared into cloud.' *Luftflotte 3 Einzelmeldung Nr 104, 7 Nov 43*

| 9 Nov 43 | Sunderland | 1425hrs | *Einzelmeldung* | Sunderland S of 461 Sqn (Fg Off Dobson) |

'Sunderland "S" on anti-submarine patrol sighted six Ju 88s; two enemy attacked from port beam and two from port quarter. Combat lasted 28 minutes during which time one of the enemy aircraft was severely damaged. "S" suffered only slight damage.' *HQ Coastal Command Intelligence Summary No 228*

| 11 Nov 43 | Liberator | 1255hrs | *Einzelmeldung* | PB4Y-1 K of VB-110 (Lt J. O. Buchanan) |

'Liberator "K" on anti-submarine patrol was attacked by eight Ju 88s and in an inconclusive combat it is believed that "K" scored hits on two of the aircraft but no damage to these was apparent. "K" suffered neither casualties nor damage.' *HQ Coastal Command Intelligence Summary No 228*

| 17 Nov 43 | Liberator | 1039hrs | *Einzelmeldung* |
| " | " | 1123hrs | " |

'Four Ju 88s took off 0917-0918hrs for a *Freie Jagd* between 48 and 49 deg N, 13 deg W. At 1039hrs in *PlQ* 14W/9975 one Liberator at 2,600m altitude, course 60 deg. After eight attacks, disappeared into cloud. Hits observed on wing and fuselage. 1123hrs, in *PlQ* 24W/1812, one Liberator at 2,500m altitude, course 50 deg. Speed 350km/h. After ten attacks, hits in wing and port engine, black smoke from port engine. Aircraft lost in cloud. First aircraft grey/white camouflage, the second dark green. The first had no turret, the second had a turret. Both had British markings.' *Luftflotte 3 Einzelmeldung Nr 24, 18 Nov 43*

| 19 Nov 43 | Sunderland | 1130hrs | *Lt* Gutermann | Sunderland W of 228 Sqn (Fg Off Finucane) |

'Sunderland "W" while on anti-submarine patrol was attacked by four Ju 88s and claims to have damaged three of them; one enemy was seen with smoke coming from the port engine. "W" suffered neither casualties nor damage.' *HQ Coastal Command Intelligence Summary No 229*

| 1 Dec 43 | Sunderland | 1135hrs | *Einzelmeldung* | Sunderland L of 228 Sqn (Flt Lt Grimshaw) |

'Eight Ju 88s took off at 1000-1005hrs for a fighter sweep in *PlQ* 14W/0860 and to look for the Ju 88 lost on 30 November 1943. At 1135hrs a Sunderland was spotted in *PlQ* 14W/0865, altitude 900m, course 120 deg, speed 250km/h. Seven attacks before escaping into a rain shower.' *Luftflotte 3 Einzelmeldung Nr 11, 2 Dec 43*

| 20 Dec 43 | Liberator | 1424hrs | *Uffz* Ernst | PB4Y-1 P of VB-105 (Lt Welsh) |

'Liberator "P" on anti-submarine patrol was attacked by eight Ju 88s. In the ensuing combat, one enemy aircraft was probably seriously damaged. Our aircraft sustained neither casualties nor damage.' *HQ Coastal Command Intelligence Summary No 234*

| 29 Dec 43 | Catalina | 1515hrs | *Einzelmeldung* | Probably VP-63 |

'Two Ju 88s took off at 1239hrs on an escort for *Marine Gruppe West* between *PlQ* 14W/7433 and 6418. At 1515hrs, in *PlQ* 14W/7443, a combat was fought with a

Catalina. Hit in the fuselage before it disappeared into cloud.' *Luftflotte 3 Einzelmeldung Nr 21, 30 Dec 43*

5 Jan 43	B-17	0812–1320hrs	*Lt* Gutermann	(8th AF)
8 Jan 44	4 Mosquitoes	1620hrs	"	157 Sqn
13 Feb 44	4 Mustangs	1625–1848hrs	*Fw* Hommel	
"	Liberator	1350-1852	*Lt* Hanshen	
23 Mar 44	Sunderland		*Fw* Hommel	Sunderland of 461 Sqn (Fg Off Godsall)
25 Mar 44	B-17 (damaged)		0649-1102hrs	"
31 Mar 44	B-17 and 4 Liberators	1500hrs	*Oblt* Gutermann	PB4Y-1 D of VB-103 (Lt (jg) B. S. Higginbotham)

'Liberator "D" while on anti-submarine patrol sighted two Ju 88s. As a result of combat that followed, one enemy aircraft is claimed as damaged; our aircraft suffered no damage.' *HQ Coastal Command Intelligence Summary No 248*

20 Apr 44	3 Spitfires & Beaufighter	1810-2300hrs		(Mediterranean)
10 May 44	Beaufighters	1352-1514hrs	*Uffz* Johenneken	"
11 May 44	5 Beaufighters	2100hrs	*Fw* Hommel	153 and 256 Sqns, Mediterranean
12 May 44	Marauder and Beaufighter	1318-1804hrs	"	(Mediterranean)
13 May 44	Marauder	0635-0930hrs	*Uffz* Johenneken	(Mediterranean)
1 Jun 44	Lancaster	0005-0330hrs	*Uffz* Ernst	(Attack on Saumur?)
2 Jun 44	Lancaster	0027-0217hrs	"	"
6 Jun 44	Mosquitoes	0835-1102hrs	*Uffz* Johenneken	248 Sqn?
9 Jun 44	Liberator	0027-0302hrs	*Uffz* Ernst	

Appendix G

Translation of operational instructions for
Fliegerführer Atlantik

The following was translated from a captured document and explains the operational rationale of *Fliegerführer Atlantik* towards the end of 1943.

Fliegerführer Atlantik

I.   Operational instructions from CinC Luftwaffe

Strategy against enemy shipping in the Atlantic in co-operation with CinC U-Boats and Naval Group West.

Safeguarding arrival and departure of German naval forces (both surface and submarine) against enemy attacks. Operations against enemy supply shipping in the event of enemy landings.

II.   General principles

1. Concentration of all appropriate forces in the right place at the right time in accordance with the operational demands of CinC U-Boats and the requirements of *Fliegerführer Atlantik*'s own operations.

2. Most economical operational use of reconnaissance forces until the commencement of operations by CinC U-Boats or *Fliegerführer Atlantik*. For this purpose, full advantage to be taken of technical and weather conditions.

3. Flights into areas where controlled by enemy day or night fighters are operating are to be avoided. Wherever possible, operations of *Fliegerführer Atlantik* are to be confined to areas where there is no enemy twin-engined fighter defence.

III. Reconnaissance

1. Reconnaissance to be carried out mainly with ship-locating radar. Reconnaissance by sectors at 1,000 metres altitude. Operations not to be dependent on visibility.

2. The situation over the Atlantic will dictate the areas in which aircraft with strong defensive armament are to be used. Area of operations to be widened by exploitation of weather conditions.

3. Navigational accuracy of aircraft position up to distances of 2,000km with a margin of error or +/- 10-20km.

4. *Convoy reconnaissance*. In areas requested by CinC U-Boats or laid down by *Fliegerführer Atlantik*. Generally, reconnaissance of area to be covered should start in the morning. On the days when operations

are planned by CinC U-Boats or *Fliegerführer Atlantik*, reconnaissance should be repeated in late afternoon with a view to shadowing.

    a. In the case of submarines, reconnaissance to continue into the night.

    b. In the case of bomber formations, reconnaissance to continue until time of attack and observation of results.

    5. *Reconnaissance for Naval Group West.* Reconnaissance of sea area used by our own blockade runners, auxiliary cruisers and prize vessels arriving and leaving.

Intentions

    a. To safeguard against enemy surface vessels.

    b. Prompt recognition of ships arriving and lead them to cover. Operations to be carried out over a wide area and to the limit of range.

    6. Reconnaissance to safeguard against enemy landing attempts on the Atlantic coast of France. Operations to be carried out in late afternoon. They are to cover the sea area through which the enemy can pass during the hours of darkness.

    7. *Armed Reconnaissance.* Armed reconnaissance against single enemy ships off the Spanish-Portuguese coast by flights of two or three long-range bombers. Action only to be taken if movement is confirmed by intelligence from secret sources. Attack at dusk or on a clear night.

IV.   Shadowing with ship-locating radar possible by day or night

    1. *For CinC U-Boats*

Commence at dusk. DF signals. Use of flares for marking location of convoy. Shadowing aircraft to keep as near as possible to convoy. Shadowing to be carried on as far on into the night as possible.

    2. *For Bomber Formations*

    a. Loose shadowing by daylight with shadowing aircraft being relieved. *Schwan* buoys to be dropped [water-borne VHF beacon – Author]

    b. As combat shadowing aircraft about one hour before bombers attack. Shadowing aircraft to be between bomber formation and target. DF signals, flares to be dropped should necessity arise.

V.   Operations

    1. At present in use: He 177 with *Kehl* glider bomb control and FW 200 with *Kehl* or *Lofte* bomb sight. Both types of equipment can only be used in slight, high or medium high cloud. Since convoys frequently make use of bad weather conditions as cover, it is

recommended that the He 177 be fitted also with torpedoes.

2. Attacks can only hold out a promise of success when strong forces are used. Minimum strength one bomber *Gruppe*.

3. Attacks to be carried out during the evening, up to dusk, so that return flights can be carried out under cover of darkness.

4. When flying in cloudless weather, the bombers are to be escorted by twin-engined fighters to the extent of their range.

VI.   Use of twin-engined fighters

1. *Intentions:*

   a. To attack enemy anti-submarine aircraft.

   b. To protect own aircraft.

2. *Operations.* Twin-engined fighters to operate only when visibility is good and there is little cloud. Possible to operate as freelance fighter patrols, escort or covering force.

VII. Anti-submarine operations

To be carried out along own coast in areas not covered by submarine chasers:

1. As systematic search.

2. As aircraft standing by for action.

VIII. Action to be taken in the event of an enemy landing

1. So long as the base of *Fliegerführer Atlantik* is not directly threatened, increased reconnaissance in the Bay of Biscay and Atlantic and attacks against landing forces still at sea.

2. In the event of a landing in the area of *Fliegerführer Atlantik* then, according to the developments of the situation:

   a. Reconnoitre and attack the enemy landing fleet or

   b. Support the ground operations by attacking forces that have already landed.

3. In the event of the enemy capturing the bases of subordinate units, units will be withdrawn to prepared positions and will continue to operate as laid down in sub-para 2.

IX.   Signals

1. Complete wireless silence to be broken only by:

   a. Reports of enemy.

   b. Emergency reports.

2. Restriction to a minimum of ship-locating and aircraft-locating radar.

3. Exchange of messages with own naval forces by means of signal lamps only. VHF will be used only to warn ships of immediate danger.

Types of aircraft available to *Fliegerführer Atlantik*

I. **Reconnaissance aircraft**

1. **FW 200**

This is at present available in three different models:

a. Normal FW 200 with a radius of action of 1,500km.

b. FW 200 fitted with auxiliary fuselage tanks (known as long-range Condor) with a radius of action of 1,750km.

c. FW 200 fitted with auxiliary fuselage tanks and two exterior tanks (known as maximum-range Condor) with a radius of action of 2,200km.

Only the long-range and maximum-range Condor are suitable for the present operational commitments of *Fliegerführer Atlantik*. Use of the maximum-range Condor is limited due to the difficulties involved in taking off at night because of overloading and its use can only be recommended for major operations. In view of its inadequate armament and its lack of speed, the FW 200 cannot be used in areas covered by enemy twin-engined fighters. Recent encounters between the FW 200 and enemy twin-engined fighters when cloud cover has been insufficient have nearly always led to the destruction of the FW 200.

Further development of the FW 200 is not recommended since:

a. It has been exploited to the limit of its potentialities.

b. It is being replaced by the He 177.

2. **Ju 290**

The Ju 290 meets the present requirements as far as radius of action is concerned. Thanks to its good armament and even better proposed armament, it is also suitable for operations in areas covered by enemy twin-engined fighters. At the moment, the Ju 290 is the most suitable aircraft for Atlantic reconnaissance. Its use is at present restricted to certain areas and to certain seasons of the year due to the absence of de-icing equipment.

Recommendations for further improvements

a. Greater radius of action (experiments are being carried out to increase it to 4,000km)

b. Fitting of de-icing equipment.

c. Fitting of a special bomb rack for flares (proposed).

     d. Fitting of *Kehl* equipment for long-range operations (proposed for Ju 390).

3. **Ju 88 D-1 or A-4**

This aircraft does not come up to operational requirements either in range or speed. The Ju 88 D-1 has to be used by *Fliegerführer Atlantik* for sea reconnaissance in areas covered by British day and night fighters. Duties can only be carried out when weather conditions are particularly favourable.

Requests for suitable aircraft have been made to *General der Aufklärungsflieger* (CinC Reconnaissance Units).

4. **BV 222**

On account of its performance, the BV 222 has been called upon to carry out roughly the same duties as the Ju 290. Its operational potentialities are only restricted because of:

     a. Its insufficient armament and unprotected tanks.

     b. Its lack of speed.

Its tactical radius of action will be increased by 300km to 2,700km when in January 1944 delivery is taken of the new V-10 and V-11 sub-types fitted with diesel engines.

5. **BV 138**

In view of its lack of speed and small radius of action, this aircraft is only suitable for defensive reconnaissance along the French coast and on anti-submarine patrols. For these purposes, however, it is very suitable.

II.   **Bombers**

He 177

With a tactical radius of action of 1,500km, this aircraft cannot, by any means, be used in all the sea areas covered by *Fliegerführer Atlantik*'s reconnaissance. Its use is thus limited to the Western Atlantic and north-west Biscay. The performance of the He 177 makes it suitable for use with *Kehl* and as a torpedo bomber. The He 177 is well armed and has no cause, particularly in formation flights, to fear any type of enemy aircraft operating over the Atlantic.

Recommendations for further development

     a. Radius of action to be increased to that of reconnaissance aircraft while retaining the same bomb capacity.

     b. To be adapted for a quick change-over from *Kehl* to torpedo bomber (according to weather conditions).

   c. Increase in speed to cope with the expected appearance of faster
       enemy twin-engined fighters and as a countermeasure to anti-
       aircraft defence.

III.   Fighters

1. **Ju 88**

   The twin-engined fighter formations are made up of Ju 88 C-6
   aircraft, sub-types R-2, H-2 to G-1.

   The armament of the H-2 and G-1 meets present-day requirements.
   The expected radius of both models of 1,600 to 1,800km is adequate
   for present needs but the ultimate objective must be to increase the
   range up to that of the long-range bomber.

   With regard to speed, the Ju 88 R-2, H-2 and G-1, which are fitted
   with BMW 801 engines, are superior in speed to most enemy
   aircraft used over the Atlantic with the exception of the Mosquito,
   which is now appearing in ever-increasing numbers.

2. **FW 190**

   In areas other than the normal operational zones of RAF fighters, the
   FW 190 is the most useful of the limited number of operational
   aircraft in use by *Fliegerführer Atlantik*. The most unsatisfactory
   aspect of all is that, in spite of new developments expected in the air
   situation over the Atlantic, the radius of action of the FW 190 (even
   with auxiliary tanks) is still too small. What is required is a fighter
   with at least the same armament as the FW 190 but a greater radius
   of action without auxiliary fuel tanks.

3. **Ar 196**

   In armament, radius of action and performance, this aircraft is
   obsolete. The Ar 196 can only be used for reconnaissance in coastal
   areas and for anti-submarine patrols and escort duties.

Notes

Chapter 1
[1] This was Arado Ar 196 A-3, *Werk Nummer* 0162 coded 6W+XN of 5/196. *Ofw* Anton Jox (F) and *Fw* Hermann Krüger (B) were both killed.
[2] F/S Matthews and crew were shot down by an AR 196 of 5/196 west of Brest on 6 September 1942 while flying a Whitley, serial Z9387.
[3] This was probably Wellington DV665, coded 'B', of 311 Sqn, which went missing over the Bay of Biscay about the time *Oblt* Stolle shot down his Wellington.
[4] The pilot was in fact Polish and had already successfully beaten off an attack by V/KG 40 exactly a month before. This time he and his crew were all killed.
[5] The American invasion of Tunisia.
[6] This was B-24D, serial 41-23712, which crashed on 29 October 1942 killing Capt William Williams and 10 crew.

Chapter 2
[1] This was probably helped by the move of 235 Squadron to RAF Leuchars in Scotland towards the end of January 1943.

Chapter 3
[1] The *Luftwaffe* records state that a Ju 88 was lost on 20 June; no Allied claims were made on this day for Ju 88s and, as the crash location matches that of *Lt* Gutermann's Ju 88, it is assumed that the date has been incorrectly recorded and the aircraft was in fact another victim of 151 Squadron.

Chapter 4
[1] This was not his regular aircraft and was usually flown by Lt Ralph Spears, who named it after his aunt.
[2] No German aircraft were lost in this encounter and there are no records of any Ju 88 being damaged.

Chapter 5
[1] This occurred on 7 August when the aircraft was flown by Fg Off J. F. Green and Plt Off G. B. Forrest. The combat with 8/JG 2 resulted in the loss of one Beaufighter and the deaths of Sqn Ldr Richard Winnicott and Fg Off Arthur Stocker.
[2] On 8 October 1943 II/ZG 1 lost ten fighters, and a further four suffered varying degrees of damage following combat with Spitfires of 66, 453 and 610 Squadrons. Two weeks later the *Gruppe* was withdrawn to Germany and not replaced.
[3] Lorient had been attacked by American bombers on 23 September and, in addition to losing a number of aircraft, the airfield became temporarily unusable.
[4] *Lt* Geyr was a pilot with I/KG 6 and was flying the Ju 188.
[5] Fg Off Blackwell managed to escape from his German captors the following day and eventually arrived back in England on 29 January 1944.

Chapter 6
[1] Although *Lt* Robert Baumann was responsible for setting the Beaufighter's engine on fire, credit for the kill was given to *Lt* Ulrich Hanshen.
[2] It was a Sunderland from 461 Squadron, which spotted the dinghies at 1020 hours.
[3] Two Liberators of 311 Squadron attacked later in the day, but both the *I 29* and its surface escort made it to Lorient next day unscathed.

[4] A sad postscript to the death of Fg Off Keith Kemp occurred two years after the war had ended. During the exhumation of a communal grave containing sixteen bodies washed ashore from the sinking of SS *Lancastria* in June 1940, an additional body was discovered. It was the body of an airman with pilot's wings, a pilot officer rank and a 'New Zealand' flash on the shoulders. It appeared that the body had been washed ashore and buried by the Germans without them informing anyone. Despite having no identification, it was later discovered that the body was that of Keith Kemp. The positive identification could be made when a half-sovereign was found in one of the pockets of the uniform – Keith's mother said he always carried one as a good luck charm.

Index

Places

Units and ships, Allied (units are RAF squadrons unless otherwise indicated)

Units, ships and submarines, German/Axis

The Luftwaffe's Blitz

Chris Goss

Due to the failure of the day campaign during what has become known as the Battle of Britain, on 7 September 1940, the Luftwaffe commenced bombing London and major cities, predominantly by night. The Blitz continued until 10 May 1941 with many towns and cities across the country being attacked and London being struck 57 nights in succession.

By the end of May 1941, over 43,000 civilians, half of them in London, had been killed by bombing and more than a million houses destroyed or damaged in London alone. The Blitz failed to break the morale of the British people and any thoughts of a German invasion were eventually cancelled with German attention being transferred to the Soviet Union. Accordingly, the intensity of the attacks against mainland Britain lessened considerably.

Much has been written about the Blitz from a British perspective but here we see the story from the viewpoint of the German aircrew involved, many of whom were shot down and taken prisoner. Using over 30 first hand Luftwaffe accounts and previously unpublished photos, *The Luftwaffe's Blitz* details their assault against the United Kingdom in 1941. Integrated with accounts from the aircrew of the RAF's embryonic night fighter force as they fought against the Luftwaffe night after night in difficult and often primitive circumstances, this book provides a new perspective on the Blitz from the attacker's point of view.

208 pages, soft cover
Over 120 photographs
9 780859 791571 £10.95

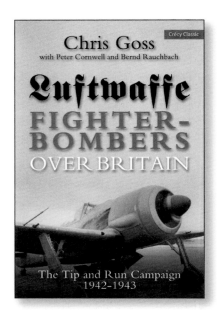

Luftwaffe Fighter-Bombers over Britain
The Tip and Run Campaign
1942-1943
Chris Goss

As the Battle of Britain came to a close, the *Luftwaffe* began arming its single-engined fighters with bombs, using them in preference to twin-engined bombers against many daylight targets. Two units were designated for these *Jagdbomber* (literally fighter-bomber) attacks – 10/JG 2 and 10/JG 26. Their targets included shipping and coastal installations, railways, gas holders and selected military and civilian objectives. The detrimental effect on British morale caused by these 'Tip and Run' attacks was great.

How could the British military combat the raids effectively? How could the local populations cope? Questions were asked in Parliament but no effective answer supplied. The locals lived in fear. Where and when would the next attack occur? *Luftwaffe Fighter-Bombers over Britain* analyses the campaign from March 1942 – June 1943 using contemporary records and first-hand accounts from both the German and British sides and highlighting, amongst others, unopposed attacks on London, Bexhill, Eastbourne, Hastings, Yeovil, Salisbury, the Isle of Wight, Great Yarmouth, Torquay and Bournemouth. Tactics are considered from both attacker and defender viewpoints, their successes and their failures.

Incorporating almost 300 previously unpublished photographs, and packed with detailed
research, *Luftwaffe Fighter-Bombers over Britain* tackles a previously little known aspect of the World War II air war and will appeal to those experiencing the raids, those with an interest in local history, the military researcher and aviation historian.

344 pages, soft cover
Over 250 photographs
9 780859 791762 £10.95

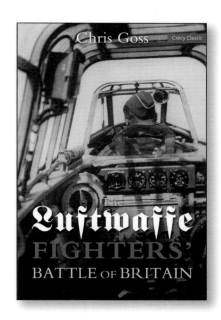

The Luftwaffe Fighters' Battle of Britain and **The Luftwaffe Bombers' Battle of Britain**
The inside Story July – October 1940
Chris Goss

The story of how the outnumbered RAF fought and defeated the superior Luftwaffe in the Battle of Britain will always be a source of fascination. However, accounts of summer 1940 have tended to centre on the British defenders, both in the air and on the ground, whilst the story of the losing German side has remained largely untold.

In 1939 the Luftwaffe was opposed to an RAF which was disorganised and inferior in both technology and number. Using first-hand accounts from Luftwaffe pilots, bestselling author Chris Goss explains how those same German aircrew felt just months later when they flew against a tenacious enemy with nothing to lose.

The Luftwaffe Fighters' Battle of Britain and *The Luftwaffe Bombers' Battle of Britain* provide a new insight into the experiences of the German fighter and bomber crews from the attacker's viewpoint.

The Luftwaffe Fighters' Battle of Britain
208 pages, soft cover
234mm x 156mm
Over 140 photographs
9 780859 791519 £10.95

The Luftwaffe Bombers' Battle of Britain
208 pages, cased
246mm x 189mm
Over 140 photographs
9 780947 554828 £19.95

Albert Ball VC
Chaz Bowyer
Fascinating story of the Royal
Flying Corps' first celebrity
ace with 44 kills.
280pp soft cover
Over 75 b&w photographs
9 780947 554897 £10.95

**Enemy Coast Ahead
– Uncensored**
Leader of the Dambusters
Wing Commander Guy
Gibson VC DSO DFC
One of the outstanding
accounts of WWII seen
through the eyes of one of its
most respected and
controversial personalities.
288 pages, soft cover
b&w photographs and
illustrations throughout
9 780859 791182 £10.95

Fist from the Sky
Peter C Smith
The story of Captain
Takashige Egusa the Imperial
Japanese Navy's most
illustrious dive-bomber pilot
272 pages, soft cover
Over 75 B+W photographs
9 780859 79122 9 £10.95

Janusz Zurakowski
Legend in the Skies
Bill Zuk and Janusz
Zurakowski
A rare combination of skilled
engineer, painstaking test pilot
and unparalleled display pilot.
336 pages, soft cover
Over 75 b&w photographs
9 780859 79128 1 £10.95

In the Skies of Nomonhan
Japan versus Russia –
September 1939
Dimitar Nedialkov
A new perspective on this
interesting and largely
unknown pre World War II
encounter.
160 pages, soft cover
Over 50 b&w photographs and
20 colour profiles
9 780859 79152 6 £10.95

Pure Luck
Alan Bramson
An authorised biography of
aviation pioneer Sir Thomas
Sopwith, 1888-1989
Foreword by HRH The Prince
of Wales
288 pages, soft cover
Over 90 b&w photographs
9 780859 791069 £10.95

Thud Ridge
Jack Broughton
F-105 Thunderchief missions
over the hostile skies of North
Vietnam
288 pages, soft cover
79 photographs plus maps and
plans
9 780859 791168 £10.95

Sigh for a Merlin
Testing the Spitfire
Alex Henshaw
The enthralling account of
Alex Henshaw's life as a test
pilot with the Spitfire.
240 pages, soft cover
b&w photographs throughout
9 780947 554835 £10.95

Spitfire
A Test Pilot's Story
Jeffrey Quill
The autobiography of an
exceptional test pilot and RAF
and Fleet Air Arm fighter
pilot.
336 pages, soft cover
b&w photographs throughout
9 780947 554729 £10.95

Stormbird
Hermann Buchner
Autobiography of one of the
Luftwaffe's highest scoring
Me262 aces.
272 pages, soft cover
140 b&w photographs and 16
page colour section
9 780859 791404 £10.95

We Landed By Moonlight
Hugh Verity
Secret RAF Landings in
France 1940-1944
256 pages, soft cover
b&w photographs throughout
9 780947 554750 £10.95

Winged Warfare
William Avery ('Billy')
Bishop VC, DSO MC
A unique autobiographical and
contemporary account of one
of the highest scoring fighter
aces of World War I.
224 pages, soft cover
integrated b&w photographs
9 780947 554903 £10.95

Order online at **www.crecy.co.uk** or telephone +44 (0) 161 499 0024
Crécy Publishing 1a Ringway Trading Est, Shadowmoss Rd, Manchester, M22 5LH
enquiries@crecy.co.uk